WED. 10 to 11   MAKE UP

Logic and Contemporary Rhetoric

The Use of Reason in Everyday Life

Third
Edition

Doc. Holiday

1st test 99%
2nd test 90%

QUIZ - 88%
quiz   100%
quiz   84%

Howard Kahane

University of Maryland,
Baltimore County

Wadsworth Publishing Company
Belmont, California
A division of Wadsworth, Inc.

For Bonny sweet Robin . . .

Ignorance is preferable to error; and he is less remote from the truth who believes nothing, than he who believes what is wrong.

—Thomas Jefferson

It ain't so much the things we don't know that get us in trouble. It's the things we know that ain't so.

—Artemus Ward

Philosophy editor: Kenneth King

Editing and production supervision: Brian and Suzanne Williams

Copyediting: Winn Kalmon

Composition: Graphic Typesetting Service

© *1980 by Wadsworth, Inc.*

© *1976, 1971 by Wadsworth Publishing Company, Inc. All rights reserved.*

Printed in the United States of America

1 2 3 4 5 6 7 8 9 10—84 83 82 81 80

Library of Congress Cataloging in Publication Data

Kahane, Howard, 1928-
    Logic and contemporary rhetoric.

    Bibliography: p.
    Includes index.
    1. Fallacies (Logic) 2. Reasoning. 3. Judgment (Logic) I. Title.
BC175.K25 1980   160   80-11529
ISBN 0-534-00850-X

Contents

Preface

*We have met the enemy and
he is us.*

—Walt Kelly's "Pogo"

*Eternal vigilance is the
price of liberty.*

—Wendell Phillips

The purpose of this third edition is the same as for the other two: to help students improve their ability to reason about everyday political and social issues, and thus to help raise the level of political discussion in America. It differs from other texts in the same way as previous editions, by concentrating on everyday issues and problems and by drawing its examples and exercises almost exclusively from actual everyday political rhetoric, as it occurs in newspapers, on television, etc., rather than using the traditional, canned, or made up examples which fill other texts. (It also differs in assembling a broader range of material—see below.)

This third edition is superior to the previous editions in many minor and several major respects (it has changes on every page):

1. Hundreds of new examples replace older, dated ones.

2. A whole new chapter, Chapter One, on good reasoning, has been introduced to balance the concentration on fallacies, and as an aid in distinguishing good (cogent) from bad (fallacious) reasoning and argument.

3. Several new exercise sets have been introduced, and every set retained from previous editions has been updated.

4. The chapter on language (Chapter Six) has been updated by including the basis of the McGraw-Hill guidelines (concerning the replacement of sexually offensive language), which have been adopted by most publishers.

5. The chapter on managing the news (Chapter Nine) has been completely restructured so as to more clearly make its points about how and why the news is slanted as it is.

This book divides into five parts:

1. Chapter One concerns good reasoning and in a sense provides an overview of the rest of the book.

2. Chapters Two through Five deal with fallacious reasoning, concentrating on how to avoid fallacies by becoming familiar with the more frequently encountered types (illustrated by live specimens).

3. Chapter Six concerns language itself, because (as shown in the chapter) an understanding of the ways language can be employed to manipulate is important to good reasoning.

4. Chapter Seven provides some hints for analyzing extended passages and some practice in doing so.

5. And Chapters Eight, Nine, and Ten discuss our three main sources of information: advertising (singling out political advertising for extra scrutiny); the media (television, newspapers, radio, magazines); and public school textbooks (in the order considered, not *necessarily* in the order of their importance as information sources).

This book is unique in bringing together all of these apparently diverse elements, and unique among books on logic or fallacy in dealing with information sources. Inclusion of the material on information sources stems from ideas discussed in Chapter One concerning the importance of acquiring an accurate stock of background information, especially an accurate *world view* or broad picture of how the world operates; acquiring good background information, a good world view, requires the ability to evaluate available information sources, which, in the case of social or political information, means primarily learning how best to use the media, advertising, and textbooks.

In addition to the thanks still owed to those cited in previous editions, I would like to thank the publisher's readers for this edition: Frank Fair, Sam Houston State University; Dana Flint, Temple University; J. Thomas Howald, Franklin University; Thomas Payette, Henry Ford Community College; John Presley, Central Virginia Community College; and Dwight Van de Vate, Jr., The University of Tennessee, Knoxville. I would also like to thank Robert Cogan, Edinboro State College; Joan Straumanis, Denison University; Nelson Pole, Cleveland State University; Lee Creer, Central Connecticut State College; Alan Hausman, Ohio State University; Brenda Bland, University of Maryland, Baltimore (and several of her aides); and in particular professors B. R. Kahane, Anne Brudno, T. J. Wilkinson, Jr., Rachel Mullins, and Miana Brucar.

Good thinking requires being able to put two and two together to get four.

Chapter One

Good Reasoning

For every credibility gap, there is a gullibility fill.
—[Richard] Clopton's Law

If you don't think for yourself, others will think for you—to their advantage.
—Harold Gordon

If the thing believed is incredible, it also is incredible that the incredible should have been so believed.
—St. Augustine, *The City of God*

There is much truth to the old saying that life is just one damn problem after another. That's why problem solving is life's chief occupation. **Reasoning** is the essential ingredient in problem solving. When confronted with a problem, we reason from what we already know or believe to new beliefs useful for solving that problem. The trick, of course, is to reason *well*. It isn't easy, and it isn't automatic.

1. Arguments, Premises, Conclusions

Reasoning can be cast into the form of arguments. An **argument** is just one or more sentences or propositions (spoken, written, or just thought of), called **premises** of the argument, offered in support of another sentence or proposition, called the **conclusion** of the argument.

In logic textbooks, arguments, premises, and conclusions usually are neatly labeled so that there is no doubt which statements in an argument are offered in support of others—a sentence labeled "premise" clearly is intended to support one labeled "conclusion." Real life is another story.

In everyday life, few of us bother to label our remarks, perhaps because few of us bother very often to distinguish one argument from another in our own minds, much less separate premises from conclusions. But we do often give clues. Such words as "because," "since," and "for" usually indicate that what follows is a premise. And words like "therefore," "hence," "consequently," "so," and "it follows that" usually signal a conclusion. (Similarly, expressions like "It has been observed that . . . ," "In support of this . . . ," and "The relevant data . . ." generally introduce premises, while expressions like "The result is . . . ," "The point of all this is . . . ," and "The implication is . . ." usually signal conclusions.) Here is a simple example:

Since the Cambodians have illegally detained a U.S. vessel, *it follows that* the President of the United States has the duty to obtain its release by any means necessary, *because* the President has the duty to defend all U.S. property and the lives of all U.S. citizens.

Put into textbook form, the argument reads:

1. The President of the United States has the duty to defend all U.S. lives and property.
2. The Cambodians have illegally detained a U.S. vessel.
3. The President of the United States has the duty to obtain its release by any necessary means.[1]

Life is too short and talk too plentiful for us to bother separating out arguments, premises, and conclusions all the time. But it is a good idea to learn how to do so and to develop the habit of doing so when discussing or thinking about important subjects. It's surprising how much of what we hear or read consists mainly of unsupported conclusions, and it's even more surprising how persuasive such argument-less rhetoric can be. Yet an unsupported statement should never convince us of anything we don't already know or believe.

2. *Fallacious and Cogent Reasoning*

Reasoning—and the arguments into which reasoning is cast—is either **cogent** (good) or **fallacious** (bad). The focus of this book is on fallacious reasoning, because the rhetoric we all are exposed to in daily life (for instance, on television and in newspapers, magazines, and textbooks) so frequently invites fallacious reasoning that protection from this blight is essential.

However, we can't get the knack of avoiding fallacious reasoning without knowing roughly what cogent reasoning is like. (Of course, we want to know what good reasoning is like anyway for its own sake.) So let's take a very quick look at the basics of cogent reasoning.

3. *Criteria for Cogent Reasoning*

To reason **cogently,** three criteria must be satisfied: (1) we must start with acceptable, or **warranted,** premises; (2) we must include all available relevant information;[2] and (3) our reasoning must be **valid,** which means roughly that

---

[1] The symbol "∴" is used to signal that a conclusion follows.

[2] This is an extremely stringent requirement that in real life is beyond the ability of most of us most of the time. The point is to come as close as possible to satisfying it, bearing in mind the seriousness of the problems to be solved and the cost (in time and effort) of obtaining or recalling relevant information. (One of the marks of genius is the ability to recognize that information is relevant to a topic when the rest of us aren't likely to notice.)

it must have correct form or structure. (The second criterion is important primarily with respect to what is called inductive reasoning.)

We get warranted premises for an argument from the conclusions of other valid arguments and from reports of observations. And we learn what is relevant to a given argument by appeal to broad theories whose main points are conclusions of still other valid arguments. So validity is a key ingredient of cogent reasoning.[3]

4. *Two Basic Kinds of Valid Argument*

There are two basic kinds of valid argument: **deductive** and **inductive.** The essential property of a **valid deductive argument** is this: *If its premises are true, then its conclusion must be true also.* To put it another way, if the premises of a valid deductive argument are true, then its conclusion *cannot be false.*

On the other hand, the premises of a **valid inductive argument** provide good but not conclusive grounds for the acceptance of its conclusion. The truth of the premises of a valid inductive argument does not guarantee the truth of its conclusion, although it does make the conclusion *probable.* (That's why the expression "probability argument" often is used instead of "inductive argument.")

Here is an example of a valid inductive argument:

Premise: 1. So far, very few presidents of U.S. colleges and universities have been brilliant intellectuals.

Conclusion: 2. Probably very few future presidents of U.S. colleges and universities will be brilliant intellectuals.

There may be a few readers who will want to deny the truth of the premise of this argument. But even they will have to admit that *if* they were to accept it as true (on good grounds), then it would be reasonable to accept the argument's conclusion also. And yet, the conclusion may turn out to be false, even if its premise is true, since it is conceivable that boards of overseers, regents, and state legislators will start selecting more intellectual college presidents.

Contrast the above inductive argument with the following valid deductive argument:

Premise: 1. Every U.S. president has lied to us.
2. Dwight D. Eisenhower was a U.S. president.

Conclusion: 3. Dwight D. Eisenhower lied to us.

---

[3] For a more detailed account of valid reasoning, see the author's *Logic and Philosophy*, 3d ed. (Belmont, Calif.: Wadsworth, 1978).

Assuming for the moment that the first premise is true (we all know that the second premise is true), it is inconceivable that the conclusion be false. It would be inconsistent (contradictory) to believe both premises yet deny the conclusion. For in saying the two premises we have implicitly said the conclusion.

We have here the fundamental difference between deductive and inductive reasoning: The conclusion of a valid deductive argument is just as certain as its premises while the conclusion of a valid inductive argument is less certain that its premises. Inductive conclusions have that extra element of doubt (however slight), because they make claims not already made by their premises. In contrast, the conclusion of a valid deductive argument is no more doubtful than its premises, because its conclusion is already contained in its premises (although often only implicitly).

A Misconception About Deduction and Induction

There is a widespread but erroneous idea about the difference between deductive and inductive validity. This is the idea that in valid deductive reasoning we go from the general to the particular, while in valid inductive reasoning we move from the particular to the general. But there is nothing to this idea. For instance, the valid deductive argument

  1. All Republican politicians are to the right of Teddy Kennedy.
∴ 2. All who are not to the right of Teddy Kennedy are not Republican politicians.

moves from the general to the equally general. And the valid inductive argument

  1. Richard Nixon made promises in 1960 and 1968 he didn't intend to keep.
∴ 2. Richard Nixon made promises in 1972 he didn't intend to keep.

moves from the particular to the equally particular. And the valid inductive argument

  1. So far, all Democratic candidates have been to the left of Gerald Ford.
∴ 2. The next Democratic candidate to run for office will be to the left of Gerald Ford.[4]

moves from the general to the particular, not the other way around.

So there isn't any truth to this old idea about the difference between deductive and inductive reasoning.

---

[4]Of course the premise of this argument is false. But the argument still is valid. For *if* its premise were true, then that would be good reason to accept the conclusion.

A Few Intuitively Valid Deductive Forms

Different arguments may have the same **form,** or **structure.** Here are two such arguments:

(1) 1. If the president doesn't act forcefully, he'll lose points in the polls.
    2. He won't act forcefully.
∴ 3. He'll lose points in the polls.
(2) 1. If Russian hawks get their backfire bomber, our hawks will have to be given something.
    2. The Russian hawks will get their backfire bomber.
∴ 3. Our hawks will have to be thrown a bone. (That is, our hawks will have to be given something.)

And here is the form or structure they share:

    1. If [some sentence] then [a second sentence].
    2. [The first sentence].
∴ 3. [The second sentence].

Or, using *A* and *B* to stand for the two sentences:

    1. If *A* then *B*.
    2. *A*.
∴ 3. *B*.

(This form is traditionally called **Modus Ponens.**)
Now, here are a few more of the commonly used and intuitively valid deductive forms:

    1. If *A* then *B*.
    2. Not *B*.
∴ 3. Not *A*.

(This form is called **Modus Tollens.**)

Example: 1. If blacks are genetically less intelligent than whites, then mixed racial blacks should have higher average test scores than pure blacks.
    2. They don't have average scores higher than pure blacks.[5]
∴ 3. Blacks aren't genetically less intelligent than whites.

Now here is an argument form called **distinctive syllogism:**

    1. *A* or *B*.
    2. Not *A*.
    3. *B*.

---

[5] See the box on pages 20–21.

Example: 1. Either it is our African policy to support majority rule or else our policy is anti-white.
2. It can't be that our policy is to support majority rule.
∴ 3. Our African policy must be anti-white. (See Chapter 7, where this argument is used in the analysis of a political column.)

And here is the valid argument form called **hypothetical syllogism.**

1. If *A* then *B*.
2. If *B* then *C*.
∴ 3. If *A* then *C*.

1. If the industrial countries get tough with OPEC, oil will become cheap and plentiful.
2. If oil becomes cheap and plentiful, then the energy problem will be solved.
∴ 3. If the industrial countries get tough with OPEC, then we can forget about the energy crisis (the problem will be solved).

These are examples of valid deductive forms taken from what is called **sentential logic** or the **logic of truth functions.** Here are two from what is called **predicate** or **quantifier logic:**[6]

1. All *F* are *G*.
2. This is an *F*.
3. This is a *G*.

Example: 1. All politicians are liars.
2. Ted Kennedy is a politician.
3. Ted Kennedy is a liar.

Beetle Bailey cartoon reprinted by permission of King Features Syndicate.

Humorous use of disjunction syllogism. *Gen. Halftrack's reasoning is this: Either the box is too small or we're not running this camp right. It's false that we're not running this camp right—that is, we* are *running it right. So the box is too small—build a bigger one. Halftrack omits as understood the premise that the camp is not being run wrong, just as we often do in daily life.*

---

[6] See the author's *Logic and Philosophy* for more on this distinction.

1. All *F* are *G*.
2. All *G* are *H*.
∴ 3. All *F* are *H*.

Example:

1. All hetero males without women resort to masturbation.
2. Those who masturbate eventually go crazy.
3. Hetero males who don't have women eventually go crazy.

We also can construct longer arguments by stringing together shorter ones. Here is an example, with its structure exhibited at the left:

1. If *A* then *B*.	1. If Dave Kingman hits his potential, he'll hit 65 home runs.
2. If *B* then *C*.	2. If he does (hit 65), the Cubs will take it all (win the World Series).
∴ 3. If *A* then *C*.	∴ 3. If Kingman hits his potential, the Cubs will take the World Series.
4. If *C* then *D*.	4. If the Cubs win, they're the best team.
5. Not *D*.	5. Unfortunately, they don't have the best team.
∴ 6. Not *C*.	∴ 6. They won't win the big one.
7. If not *C* then *E*.	7. If they don't win, all their players will be unhappy.
6. Not *C*.	6. They won't win the series.
∴ 8. *E*.	∴ 8. Their players are going to be unhappy.
8. All *F* are *G*.[7]	8.[7] All Cubs players are going to be unhappy.
9. This thing is an *F*.	9. Dave Kingman plays for the Cubs.
∴ 10. This thing is a *G*.	∴ 10. Kingman will be unhappy.

While everyday reasoning is so loose that it is often difficult, if not impossible, to separate it into distinct parts comprising arguments, still these simple forms are in fact frequently used in daily life (usually implicitly). They're rarely the inspired crucial ones only geniuses think of (those tend to be inductive), but they do come in handy for the pedestrian steps in reasoning which, when put together into longer arguments (usually with inductive steps), lead to significant everyday conclusions.

---

[7] Rephrased to exhibit its internal structure.

5.   *Inductive Reasoning*

The key steps in most everyday reasoning are inductive, not deductive. So let's concentrate on inductive reasoning, bearing in mind that inductive logic has not been figured out as well as deductive logic, and is therefore much more controversial.

The basic idea behind valid induction is that of *pattern*, or *resemblance*. We want our conception of the future, our idea about what this or that will be like, to fit a pattern we glean from what this or that was like in the past. We should expect the pattern of the future to match the pattern of the past. (The problem, of course, is to find patterns that fit what we have experienced of the past.)

Induction by Enumeration

Induction by enumeration is the simplest kind of inductive inference, and, according to some, is the foundation for all the rest. In the simplest form, we infer from the fact that all *A*'s observed so far are *B*'s to the conclusion that all *A*'s whatsoever are *B*'s. For instance, a study of 100 members of Congress which revealed that all 100 support the FBI in its effort to reduce crime would count as good evidence for the inductive conclusion that *all* members of Congress support the FBI in this effort. Similarly, a check of, say, fifteen secondary school civics texts from major publishing houses indicating that they all falsify the extent of the difference between American ideals and actual practice would be good evidence that all such texts stray from the truth in this way.

Obviously, some inductions of this kind are better than others. While there are several different theories about how to determine the *probability* attaching to the conclusion of a particular induction by enumeration, almost all agree on a few points.

①*Greater sample size yields greater probability*   The more instances in a sample, the greater the probability of a conclusion based on that sample. If our sample of civics texts had included 20 books instead of 15, and if we had checked 200 members of Congress instead of 100, then the conclusions drawn from these larger samples would be more probable. (The point is that more of the same sort of evidence doesn't change the conclusion of a valid inductive argument; it changes the degree of probability of that conclusion.)

② *More representative samples yield higher probabilities*   In addition to sheer size, the quality of a sample is important. We want a sample to be **representative** of the population it was drawn from. It won't do, for instance, to ignore the civics texts of a particular publisher if we have any reason to suspect that that company's texts might be better than the rest. Similarly, we don't want our sample of members of Congress to contain only Democrats, or only Republicans, because of the possibility that one party supports the FBI more than the other. In other words, we want to make sure that our sample is not *biased,* that it is as representative of the population as possible. The more representative a sample, the greater the probability of a conclusion drawn from it.

(3) *One definite counter-example refutes a theory*   One definite counter-example to an enumerative induction shoots it down. If we run across even one member of Congress who does not support the FBI in its war on crime, then our theory that all members of Congress do so is obviously false.

However, it's often hard to be sure that what looks like a counter-example really is. Suppose a woman taking a certain birth control pill becomes pregnant. Does this disprove the manufacturer's claim that the pill in question is 100 percent effective? Should it count as a genuine counter-example? Yes, if there is good evidence that the woman in question really did take her pills in the prescribed way and didn't, say, accidentally skip a day. Otherwise, no. The trouble is that in everyday life the needed evidence may be hard to come by. The moral is that it's risky to reject a theory or idea because of one or two counter-examples, unless we're very sure that at least one is the genuine article.

Higher-Level Induction

Inductions of a broader, more general, or higher level can be used to evaluate (correct or support) lower-level inductions. Suppose we find that every one of twenty men convicted of rape turns out to be an avid pornography fan. This is good low-level evidence that exposure to pornography is a cause of rape. One way to test this conclusion would be to look into the reading and viewing habits of more rapists—improving our low-level induction by increasing the size of our sample. But a better way would be to move to higher-level induction and try to determine *why* there might be (or might not be) a connection between rape and pornography.

If we find, say, that children in a psychological experiment play more violently after seeing violence on television, and discover that in their youth convicted criminals watched more violence on television than other kids and read more violent porno literature, then we might reason from this evidence to the higher-level conclusion that human beings in general tend to mirror what they see and read. And this in turn would be evidence for the lower-level theory that men exposed to violent porno literature will be more likely to engage in violent acts (like rape) than those not so exposed.

On the other hand, we might find that increased exposure to violence on television and in books leads to a decrease in violent behavior, supporting the idea that such exposure acts to "release" energy that otherwise might produce violent behavior. This would contradict the theory that exposure to violent sex in books and pictures leads to an increase in violent behavior like rape.

It may seem strange that evidence about the behavior of children exposed to TV violence could be more important in deciding whether there is a causal link between pornography and rape than checking up on the habits of more rapists. But the explanation is fairly simple. First, even if we find that, say, ten more rapists are pornography regulars, it still is possible that the connection between the two is through a third factor which causes both. In other words, the desire to rape and the need to read pornography may both be caused by something else, perhaps sexual problems of the parents of those prone to rape. By going to a higher-level theory to explain or correct lower-level results, we reduce the chance that an as yet undetected third factor causes the other two.

Second, if we can confirm a theory about the connection (or lack of connection) between rape and pornography by showing it to be a special case of a more general theory, then we make evidence relevant that would not be otherwise, thus greatly increasing the probability of our initial theory by increasing the instance variety of our sample (as well as its size).[8]

Reasoning by Analogy

In addition to induction by enumeration, high or low level, there also are several closely related forms of reasoning by **analogy.** In one version, we reason from the similarity of two things in several respects to their similarity in another. Thus, if we know that Smith and Jones have similar tastes in books, art, food, music, and TV programs and find out that Smith likes Buñuel movies, we're justified in concluding that Jones does so also.

In another version of reasoning by *analogy*, we reason from the fact that all items of a certain kind, *A*, checked up on so far, have some property, *B*, to the conclusion that some as yet unexamined *A* has the property B. We use this form of *analogy*, for instance, when we reason from evidence about 100 members of Congress improperly using franked mail to the conclusion that a certain other member is going to campaign via franked mail in the next election (and thus have an advantage over his challenger).

Reasoning by analogy is safer than induction by enumeration, since analogies have much weaker conclusions. We inferred above that one particular member of Congress would abuse his right to free official mail, which clearly is a weaker, and thus safer, prediction than that all members of Congress will abuse that privilege.

The strength of an analogy is judged in pretty much the same way as an induction by enumeration. For instance, the more tastes Smith and Jones share, the better our analogical conclusion that they share a liking for Buñuel

---

[8] This use of higher-level evidence to support or refute a lower-level conclusion is a familiar one in science. Physicists, for instance, used evidence about the tides and about objects falling toward the earth as evidence for Isaac Newton's very general law of universal gravitation. (Each observed case in which the tides or objects falling toward the earth conform to Newton's law constitutes an instance of the enumerative induction whose conclusion is Newton's law.) This law in turn implies Kepler's laws, which describe the orbits of planets around the sun as ellipses of a certain kind. So evidence about the motion of the tides and the velocity of objects falling toward the earth confirms Kepler's laws by confirming Newton's higher-level law of which Kepler's laws are a special case. (More precisely, Newton showed that Kepler's laws are very close approximations to the truth.) The relevance of childhood reading habits to adult rape is thus no more mysterious than the relevance of the tides to Kepler's laws about planetary motion.

flicks. And the more members of Congress we discover abusing their franking privileges, the better our analogical conclusion that a certain other member will do so in the next election.

Statistical Induction

Suppose we wish to investigate the acceptance of illegal campaign contributions from large corporations, instead of the misuse of franked mail. We would almost certainly find that some members of Congress never engage in such thievery. Checking on 100 randomly selected incumbents in Congress, we might find that only forty-seven have accepted illegal campaign contributions (so far as we can tell). We can't then conclude that all members of Congress accept illegal contributions, but we can conclude that about 47 percent of them do, based on the evidence that 47 percent of our sample did so. Such an inference is called a **statistical induction.**

It should be obvious that statistical induction is very much like induction by enumeration. In fact, some claim that induction by enumeration is just a special case of statistical induction in which the percentage of *A*'s that are *B*'s just happens to be 100 percent. (In other words, they interpret the "all" in the conclusion of an enumerative induction to mean "100 percent.") So it should be obvious that, just as in the case of induction by enumeration, the conclusion of a valid statistical induction becomes more probable as we increase sample size and instance variety—since it is then more likely that our sample will be representative of the population as a whole.

Causal Connections

When we reason in any of the ways described above, we usually are looking for explanations, or **causes.** For example, those who investigate the connection between pornography and rape would like to determine whether exposure to pornography *causes* men to rape. Observing a constant connection between exposure to pornography and rape, they may conclude that the one causes the other.

But sometimes we are not entitled to conclude that an observed constant connection indicates a causal connection, even if we believe that the connection will never be broken.

To take a famous example, before Newton some scientists believed that the earth would circle the sun forever, revolving on its axis every twenty-four hours. They thus believed in a constant connection, a one-to-one correlation, between occurrences of night and of day; that is, they believed that every time one occurred it would be followed by the other.

But they did not believe night *causes* day, nor day night. For they knew that *if* the earth stopped rotating on its axis (of course, they believed this would never be the case), then night would not follow day, nor day night. Thus, for them, night could not be the cause of day, nor day the cause of night.

By way of contrast, we assume that the constant connection between, say, putting sugar into coffee and the coffee tasting sweet *is* a causal connection, because (unlike the day/night case) we have no higher-level theories which show how this constant connection might be broken. In other words, we feel justified in assuming that the connection between sugar and sweet-tasting coffee is a causal connection because doing so does not conflict with higher-level (and thus better confirmed) inductive conclusions.

6. World Views

When evidence linked high White House officials to the Watergate burglary during the 1972 presidential campaign, a great many Americans dismissed it as just campaign rhetoric—it couldn't be true because President Nixon himself said it wasn't, and presidents of the United States don't lie to the American people about such matters. But other Americans responded differently, dismissing Nixon's denials as what one would expect from a politician running for office, even a president of the United States. Nixon's earlier denials that American forces had invaded Cambodia met with a similar mixed response.

Could it be true that officials of the American government, from the president on down, would lie about invading a foreign country? Yes, it could be true, and it was. Why then did so many Americans accept their government's denials, even in the face of clear-cut evidence to the contrary? Because of some of their basic beliefs about human nature and in particular about how the American system works. Given these beliefs, which formed part of what might be called their **world views,** it *was* unlikely that Nixon, Henry Kissinger, and other top officials would lie about such a serious matter; it *was* sensible to believe what their government—in particular their president—told them and to reject what otherwise would have been overwhelming evidence.

World views are crucial. Accurate world views help us to assess information accurately; inaccurate world views lead us into error. A world view is like a veil through which we perceive the world—a filter through which all new ideas or information must pass. Reasoning based on a grossly inaccurate world view yields grossly inaccurate conclusions (except when we're just plain lucky), no matter how good our reasoning may be otherwise.

This means that if we want to draw sensible conclusions, we must pay a good deal of attention to our world views (or, as they are also called, our *philosophies*), constantly checking them against newly acquired information, revising them when necessary so that our evidence and beliefs form as coherent a package as possible.

7. Self-Deception and Wishful Thinking

If life consists of one damn problem after another, and if world views are crucial to the solution of these problems, it might be supposed that intelligent people would constantly strive to have the most accurate world views possible. And, according to some world views, they do. But in fact (that is, according to the world view of the author of this book), this cannot be true. Allegedly reasonable human beings have always differed seriously in their world views, and thus in their particular beliefs, even when exposed to roughly the same evidence. Think, for instance, of their differing views on issues such as national defense, the "energy crisis," or whether Jimmy Carter would ever keep his promise to do something about unemployment. The same relevant evidence concerning, say, energy is available to all experts, yet their use of this information (including, sometimes, just ignoring it) varies greatly, largely because it fits differently into their different world views. When people differ on factual questions, some people—in fact lots of quite intelligent people—must be reasoning incorrectly or, more likely, be wedded to grossly inaccurate world views.

Cohodas's Observation: If it looks too good to be true, it is too good to be true.

—Howard Cohodas, quoted in *Washingtonian*, November 1979

But how could this be? The answer (according to the author's view of human nature—an important part of his world view) is **self-deception** or **wishful thinking.** It is a very human trait indeed to believe that which we want to believe and in particular to deny that which is too unpleasant. To take an extreme case, Jews in Nazi-controlled Europe during World War II overlooked all sorts of evidence about what was in store for them (extermination), and grasped at every straw in the wind favoring a less horrible fate (thereby making it more certain that they would in fact be exterminated). The point of facing reality is precisely to increase one's chances of enjoying a satisfying life.

But human beings deceive themselves about ordinary problems also. Take cigarette smoking. The evidence linking cigarette smoking to all sorts of fatal illnesses (lung cancer, heart diseases, emphysema) is overwhelming. Yet several tobacco company presidents have publicly denied the conclusiveness of this

Andy Capp by Reggie Smythe, © 1976 Daily Mirror Newspapers Ltd. Dist. Field Newspaper Syndicate.

evidence. They may be lying, but then again they may simply be deceiving themselves—it's hard to accept the idea that one's life is being spent selling a product that kills people. And legions of habitual cigarette smokers tell themselves they have to quit, or that they can quit any time they want to, while lighting up still another Marlboro or Winston. It takes a great deal of effort to reduce such self-deception, but that effort is very much worthwhile, given that the truths we conceal from ourselves so often return to haunt us (in the cigarette case, perhaps to kill us). Straight thinking, unlike wishful thinking, pays off by giving us better estimates of what life has to offer, of what we should seek or avoid, and of our strengths and weaknesses, thus giving us a better chance to succeed at whatever we want to do with our lives.

Silver Linings

Our rationalization of the month award goes to W. Clement Stone, the wealthy Chicago insurance executive who donated $201,000 to Richard Nixon's campaign in 1968 and $2 million more in 1972. Asked at his seat in the Illinois delegation at Kansas City if he had second thoughts about those contributions, he replied, "No, I'm not sorry. I'm glad I gave to Nixon. Watergate was good for the country. It allowed us to define standards of public morality."

Rationalization—*convincing oneself of (usually) plausible but untrue reasons for conduct —is an important component of self-deception. (The best way to fool others is to first fool ourselves.) This* New Times *item (17 September 1976) shows that even the rich and powerful need to forestall public embarrassment by rationalizing away foolish mistakes.*

---

8. Hints for Constructing Cogent World Views

World-view constructing should be an ongoing lifelong activity, an habitual response to the flood of information we all are exposed to. One way to become good at this activity is to develop rough-and-ready rules, or hints, to guide us. While rules that are useful to one person may not be so to another, the hints that follow have proved useful to the author of this text and to many students.

1. Check World Views for Consistency

To the extent that a world view is *internally inconsistent* (that is, one part contradicts another), or *inconsistent with our experiences* of the world, to that extent it must be incorrect. Truths do not contradict each other.

A world view that frequently leads us to beliefs contradicted by experience should be changed so as to accord more closely with reality—that, after all, is the point of world-view building. Failure to bring a world view into conformity with experience renders cogent reasoning less and less likely, and makes one's fate just that much more a matter of luck. So the first, and most important, hint for good world-view construction is to *habitually check one's world view for consistency with experience,* amending it when necessary to make it as consistent as possible.

This hint needs to be emphasized, because people find it hard to give up cherished or long-held beliefs. Beliefs about drugs are a good example. Medical evidence and everyday experience strongly indicate that the drugs in cigarettes (nicotine), hard liquor (alcohol), and coffee, tea, and cola drinks (caffeine), as well as several widely used prescription drugs (Valium, Quaaludes), are more habit forming than, say, marijuana or cocaine. Yet most Americans simply will not accept this, because it violates long-held and somehow psychologically more comfortable beliefs to the contrary.

A world view tends to be a hodgepodge of beliefs on different levels of generality—one reason it's so hard to root out inconsistencies. World views, at least for mere mortals, are thus unlike scientific theories, although a good world view will have lots of scientific theories in it. Science also contains theories on different levels of generality—physics, for example, certainly is more general than geography or geology. But a geological theory concerning, say, how valleys of a certain kind are formed over the ages is expected to be consistent with the rest of scientific theory. World views, on the other hand, rarely, if ever, are examined so carefully, although a few brave souls—true philosophers—do try.

2. *Evaluate Information Sources for Accuracy*

The crucial factor in formulating a reasonably accurate world view is the quality of information we are exposed to. As computer experts say, "Garbage in, garbage out." If we allow the usual (poor) information to just wash over us, using it uncritically in forming our basic beliefs as most people do, it is unlikely that our world views will be much better than those of most people—which means not very good at all.

So it is vital that we form an accurate theory concerning the quality of various sources of information, in particular the information obtained from professional "experts" (doctors, lawyers, teachers, elected officials), the media (television, radio, newspapers, magazines), friends and relatives, and textbooks (including this one). Under what conditions are these sources likely to give us the truth (in particular, give us information not colored by wishful thinking)? And, equally important, when are they likely to lie, or conceal the truth, and when tell it to us straight? The average person tends to believe what is said by those in positions of authority, and to digest whole what appears on television or in the newspaper. But some authorities and some media sources are better than others, because they are positioned better to know the truth, or because they are more highly motivated to tell the truth (or less highly motivated to conceal it). So hint number 2 for constructing a cogent world view is to *evaluate sources of information for their likely accuracy.* And the key to such evaluations is *past performance;* we should conclude by low-level induction that on the whole sources which proved more (or less) accurate in the past will prove to be so in the future.

3. *Construct Theories of Human Motivation*

Low-level induction by enumeration is a relatively slow process. But the factors that make a source of information reliable or unreliable often change swiftly. We thus sometimes need to use *higher-level induction* to correct lower-level conclusions. For example, higher-level theories about how human beings will respond to economic and other factors should have convinced us that the trend toward true investigative reporting started by the Woodward and Bernstein *Washington Post* Watergate exposés would prove too costly in time and political good will, and that reporters would tend to return to the same old ways of gathering the news (described in Chapter Nine).

The key to higher-level conclusions about news sources is a general theory of human motivation. Experts, friends, and those who run the media are just people, more or less like the rest of us. How much will what they tell us be motivated by personal goals or desires, such as economic gain? Almost all journalists are economically dependent on their jobs; to what extent is this likely to color their reporting of the news? Most television stations and newspapers are privately owned businesses that are expected to turn a profit for their owners; how is this likely to be reflected in the information they provide us? Most members of Congress almost without thinking fall into the exciting, seductive lifestyle of those at the center of power; will this usually lead to a strong desire for continual reelection, which in turn will influence campaign rhetoric? Information sources need to be evaluated in terms of human motivation for acquiring and telling the truth. We cannot assume, for instance, that members of Congress are "supposed" to tell the truth and therefore can be relied upon to do so, or that television stations "wouldn't be allowed" to mangle the news for private purposes.

The Official Rules by Paul Dixon (New York: Delacorte, 1978) is one of several books on the craze for a certain kind of saying, hard to characterize, that cleverly tells us interesting ideas about life. The most famous of these "rules" are Murphy's Law ("If anything can go wrong, it will"), the Peter Principle ("In every hierarchy, each employee tends to rise to his or her level of incompetence"), and Parkinson's Law of the Bureaucracy ("Work expands to fill the time available for its completion").

Most of these rules are literally false but contain a kernel of truth —sometimes a very large kernel, as in Allison's Precept (sometimes called the "Las Vegas Test" or the "Monte Carlo Test"): "The best simple-minded test of expertise in a particular area is an ability to win money in a series of bets on future occurrences in that area." Here are a few other gems, mostly from *The Official Rules*, relevant to topics discussed in this book:

Dogmatism: When we call others dogmatic, what we really object to is their holding dogmas that are different from our own.
—[Charles P.] Issawi's Law of Social Motion

In a medium in which a News Piece takes a minute and an "In-Depth" Piece takes two minutes, the Simple will drive out the Complex.
—[Frank] Mankiewicz's application of Gresham's Law (bad money drives out good) to television

Thirty seconds on the evening news is worth a front page headline in every newspaper in the world.
—[Edward] Guthman's Law of Media

If you want your name spelled wrong, die.
—[Al] Blanchard's Rule

The more ridiculous a belief system, the higher the probability of its success.
—Wayne R. Bartz *Key to Success*

There's something wrong if you're always right.
—Glasow's Law

Don't ask the barber whether you need a haircut.
—[Daniel S.] Greenberg's First Law of Expert Advice

People will accept your idea much more readily if you tell them Benjamin Franklin said it first.
—[David H.] Comins's Law

To every Ph.D. there is an equal and opposite Ph.D.
—B. Duggan [*The Official Rules* comments: "This law helps explain why it is so easy to find expert witnesses to totally contradict each other."]

Beware of and eschew pompous prolixity.
—Charles A. Beardsley (who was once president of the American Bar Association—he ought to know)

So hint number 3 for cogent world-view construction is to *develop and continually update general theories of human motivation,* in particular as they apply to the reliability of sources of information. Of course, induction is the main tool to use in doing this—the past is our only key to what reason can tell us about the future.[9]

4. Become Familiar with the Scientific View of the Universe

While no information is completely reliable, some kinds are more reliable than others. The safest kind, without question, if successful application is any guide, is information gained from the physical sciences (and, to an increasing extent, biology, now that the genetic code is being cracked).

One reason why these sciences are so accurate is that science is an organized, world-wide, ongoing activity, which builds and corrects from generation to generation. Another is that the method of science is just the rigorous, systematic application of cogent inductive reasoning from what has been observed of the world to expectations about future experiences that can be and are checked up on.[10] No one starting from scratch could hope to obtain in one lifetime anything remotely like the sophisticated and accurate conclusions of the physical sciences.

Scientific theories can get extremely complicated and technical, to the point that few nonscientists can thoroughly understand them. But the structure of good scientific reasoning usually is rather simple. Here is an example of simple, but good, scientific reasoning in psychology (Sandra Scarr and Richard A. Weinberg, Human Nature, *April 1978). While the tests referred to are not by themselves conclusive, they do provide some confirmation (and others much more) for their conclusions:*

The question that remains is: Given similar home environments, why does one child turn out to be brighter than another, and why is one determined by the age of four to become a musician while another sets his or her young sights on science? We know that improving the intellectual environment of children raises their average IQs; this happened to the adopted children in both the black and white studies.[11] But what accounts for the persistent differences between siblings, adopted or not?

---

[9] Since the social sciences have been making significant advances lately, we can simplify this task by tapping into relevant scientific theories concerning human motivation, even though this means sifting through conflicting theories (because social scientists have not yet settled on any single theoretical framework).

[10] A third reason is that the scientific community holds itself to very high standards of honesty —scientists rarely "cook" the results, perhaps because exposure is almost inevitable. Outright fraud, when discovered, becomes notorious—a good example being the Piltdown forgery. Compare that to the standards to which our illustrious public servants are required to adhere.

[11] Discussed elsewhere in the article. The two excerpts quoted here form just a small part of their very well-worked-out theory. From "Attitudes, Interests, and IQ" by Sandra Scarr and Richard A. Weinberg, *Human Nature*, April 1978, Copyright © 1978 by Human Nature, Inc. Used by permission of the publisher.

Our two studies show that in advantaged environments, differences between children are largely due to differences in genetic programming. We reached this conclusion by using two statistical methods. First we put all the factors that might have something to do with intelligence (such as qualities of the parents and the children's home life) into a long equation that told us the relative importance of each factor in predicting a child's IQ.

In the first set of equations, we tried father's education and occupation, mother's education, and family income as predictors of the differences in the children's IQs. These factors had a mild impact on differences in the biological children's scores, but hardly any impact on the adoptees' scores. When we added parental IQ, however, we got an enormous effect in predicting the biological children's scores—but parents' IQs had virtually no effect on the scores of the adoptees. The power of adding parental IQ to the equation must reflect the genetic contribution of the biological parents to their children's intelligence.

In contrast, the best predictor of IQ differences in adopted children was the education of their biological mothers (and, when we had the information, of their biological fathers). The education of the biological mothers was more closely related to IQ differences in their children than the same information about the adoptive parents—the adults with whom these children grew up. In both groups of adoptees, the black children and the white adolescents, the biological parents best accounted for the children's differences in IQ. . . .

Some people who believe in genetic differences between blacks and whites think that there is an easy way to prove their point: Blacks who have more European and less African ancestry should have higher IQs than blacks with less European and more African ancestry. Working with Andrew Pakstis, Solomon Katz, and William Barker, we tested this notion by giving several tests of intellectual skill to a sample of 350 blacks in the Philadelphia area. Instead of asking the participants directly what their heritage was, we could estimate each person's degree of African and European ancestry from blood samples, because Africans and Europeans differ in the average frequencies of certain types of blood groups and serum protein. If a person had a particular blood group or serum protein gene, the researchers could assign a probability that he got it from a European or African ancestor. The estimates were based on 12 genes. Though some error undoubtedly crept into the estimates, they were accurate enough, because they matched up with skin color and were similar for siblings.

The results were unequivocal. Blacks who had a large number of European ancestors did no better or worse on the tests than blacks of almost total African ancestry. These studies dispute the hypothesis that IQ differences between blacks and whites are in large part the result of genetic differences.

Grasping the general outline of the scientific picture of the universe and of the way we fit in it is doubly valuable. First, that picture can serve as the core onto which we can sketch increasingly sophisticated ideas as to how this or that works, so that new information can be systematically integrated with old. And second, it can help us to understand the vital issues of the day (for example, whether we're likely to run out of oil soon if present rates of consumption continue, the consequences of making abortion illegal, whether any "close encounters of the third kind" have actually occurred, the effectiveness of SALT treaties and negotiations, or the risks connected with nuclear power plants), and help us deal with life's day-to-day mundane problems (for instance, whether to take large doses of various vitamins, whether a particular "hair restorer" may actually work, how to choose the best painkiller for the money, how to safely siphon gasoline from one gas tank to another, or which breakfast foods are healthiest).

So a fourth hint for good world-view building is to *learn the basics of the scientific view of the world.* This means that world-view building is not something that can be done in a day, or even a few months. It is an ongoing lifetime activity with increasing benefits in terms of more accurate judgments—*provided* it is done carefully.

In the fight between you and the world, back the world.
—Franz Kafka

Natural laws have no pity
—Robert A. Heinlein, *Time Enough for Love: The Further Adventures of Lazarus Long*

Those who fail to remember the laws of science are condemned to rediscover some of the worst ones.
—Harold Gordon, in a takeoff on Santayana

---

9. Hints for Evaluating Particular Arguments

The point of constructing world views (aside from simple curiosity about how the world works) is to be better able to solve particular problems and deal with particular arguments. Waiting in line to buy gasoline is annoying; running out extremely disruptive. When service stations run out of gas, is that due to a genuine gasoline shortage? If so, what is the cause of the shortage? The government asks Americans to buy series E bonds; is the rate of inflation likely to be greater than the rate of interest on such bonds during the time they take to mature, so that investors in E bonds end up with less than they started?

Of course, world views don't answer questions like these all by themselves. We have to *reason* from our world views, coupled with particular facts, to sensible conclusions. While the general theory for evaluating the validity of particular reasons or arguments of this kind has been modestly well worked out, effective theories have not been discovered for *finding* sensible conclusions to consider or for bringing all relevant information to bear on a proposed solution. (One reason may be that, as remarked before, some people do better using one method, some another.) But again, a few rules or hints may prove useful.

① *Look for and Evaluate Presuppositions*

In the first place, we should try to *figure out and evaluate the unspoken presuppositions of an argument*. Life is short—no one spells out everything. Does a particular argument rest on a presupposition you don't share? If so, no matter how valid that argument may be, it would be a mistake to accept its conclusion.

This sounds obvious, but it takes practice to become good at it. Consider the argument that the quality of life in the United States must have improved considerably between 1960 and 1970, because productivity increased by about 40 percent during that period. The unspoken presupposition of this argument is that increased productivity results in increased quality of life, or (put another way) that increases in goods and services result in increases in human satisfaction. Lots of people, including some economics experts, seem not to have noticed that this presupposition needs to be added to the argument as a premise if the argument is to be valid (or perhaps they haven't bothered testing to see whether it stands up to experience).

Well, does the premise that increased productivity results in increased quality of life square with your experience, with your world view? If yes, then (neglecting questions of wealth distribution) you should accept the conclusion that the quality of life in the U.S. improved a great deal from 1960 to 1970. But if no, then this conclusion has to be rejected.[12] (In fact, there are all sorts of reasons for supposing that increased productivity does not necessarily lead to increased quality of life. For example, the private automobile has taken a great deal of the increase in U.S. productivity since World War II, in part because we have neglected short-distance public transportation while the average distance from home to work has increased. Enduring rush hour traffic jams alone in one's private auto takes a great deal more material wealth than does walking to work or taking a commuter train or bus, but is it more satisfying?)

② *Test Premises Against World View*

Obviously, it isn't only implicit premises (presuppositions) of an argument that need to be looked into. Explicit (stated) premises also need to be evaluated. In particular, we need to *test the premises of arguments for consistency with our world view*.

---

[12] This doesn't mean its negation, that the quality of life has not improved, should be accepted. It means that this argument should not convince us either way.

③ *Read Between the Lines*

A person who has a reasonably accurate world view often can get more information from a statement or argument than is expressly contained in it. Doing this is called "reading between the lines" and often is the essential ingredient in assessing political rhetoric as well as (interestingly) advertisements.

Take the Delta Airlines ad, "No other airline beats Delta's low fares to Miami, Ft. Lauderdale." Reading between the lines of this ad, we should conclude that Delta Airlines does *not* fly to Miami/Ft. Lauderdale for a lower price than competing airlines, because if they did their ad would make that stronger claim ("Delta flies to Miami for less money than any other airline.") rather than the weaker one that no one flies there for less. The point is that we should expect an advertiser to make the strongest price claim possible, and conclude that a less strong claim is made because stronger ones are false.[13]

At certain moments, as we have seen, athletes have feelings of floating and weightlessness. Sometimes, in fact, they even have out-of-body experiences. Now we would like to consider the possibility that the athlete is literally able to suspend himself in midair. In the earlier chapters we discussed the athletes' subjective feelings that they were floating or outside themselves. But is there an objective reality involved, something that can be verified by others? We think that there is. We have collected many statements by sportswriters, coaches, and other observers that attest to the fact that some athletes actually can, for brief moments, remain suspended in the air. Basketball players and dancers, especially, seem to demonstrate this amazing ability.

—*Human Behavior*, March 1979

This writer's world view tells him that if better evidence could have been obtained to prove this kind of levitation it would have been—first, because really proving it exists would have created a sensation, and second, because it would have been so easy to get (motion pictures would show it). Since they didn't get this proof, it's reasonable to suppose they couldn't, because, as the basic laws of physics suggest, no one can suspend himself in midair, even for an instant.

---

[13] Reading between the lines is the linguistic version of "sizing up" a person. A good poker player, for instance, looks for telltale signs of bluffing in personal mannerisms, since some players systematically signal a bluff by increased chatter or nervousness, while others do so by feigning unconcern. Similarly, an intelligent voter sizing up a political candidate looks for nonverbal as well as verbal signs of his or her true intent once in office.

Reading between the lines often requires great sophistication or subtlety, but sometimes it just requires adding or subtracting a few figures. Here is a quote from *Inquiry* magazine (15 October 1979) illustrating this:

> . . . Consider the state of agriculture between the Civil War and World War I, a period of immense growth in the American economy. Agriculture shared in that growth: The number of farms tripled, the number of acres of farmland doubled, and net farm income increased more than fourfold. Despite this growth, two stark figures stand out. Farm population decreased from 60 percent to 35 percent of the national total population, and agriculture's share of the national income dropped from 31 percent to 22 percent. In other words, agriculture did not keep pace with the rest of the economy.

Interesting figures. But by doing a little calculating, we can come up with two more interesting statistics. First, while lots of farmers must have gone broke, those that remained seem to have improved their financial position compared to nonfarm workers. And second, surprisingly, the average farm, contrary to what one might think, seems to have decreased in size during the period in question (figure out why).

. . . There is a technical reason why the intelligentsia in the Soviet Union consume more books than their Western colleagues. Where a Western scholar or writer can refer to just one source book, a Russian must often gather the same information bit by bit from various sources. Information about the history of religion is gleaned from quotes in antireligious brochures, the opinions of modern philosophers from Marxist articles condemning bourgeois or revisionist philosophy, and so on. For many years, for example, the only reference book on modern music was Shneerson's *Music Serving the Reactionaries,* which branded Stravinsky, Messiaen, Menotti, and others as agents of imperialism. But at least there one could pick up the names, dates, names of compositions, and a few ideas about these composers.

—*New York Review of Books* article by Lev Lifshitz-Losev, 31 May 1979

Reading-between-the-lines pickings are slim in the Soviet Union, but vital.

(4) Bring Unstated but Relevant Information to Bear

One of the crucial differences between geniuses and the rest of us is that a genius is able to bring information to bear on an issue which the rest of us tend not to recall or not to realize is relevant. Of course, only a few of us can be geniuses, but we can try to get into the habit of searching our minds for relevant information.

Take the question why American industry has just lost the competitive edge it enjoyed over other industrial nations since World War II. One answer often heard is that ever increasing energy costs, in particular high oil prices, have raised production costs of goods to levels which make American goods uncompetitive with foreign manufactured products. But if we think about it for a minute we should see that we know a fact which is not consistent with this explanation, so that it cannot be correct. The fact is simply that other industrial nations also have a problem with high energy costs (chiefly high oil prices), so that lower energy costs cannot be their advantage. We cannot expect others to give us information which would destroy their positions; we have to try to think of that information by ourselves. The hint this suggests is that we should always try to *bring all the relevant information we know to bear on an issue or argument*.

The problem is to become adept at thinking of relevant information. In the above example, quite typical, the trick was to *apply an alleged answer to similar cases*. If it works for them, then it is more likely that it works in the case in question. When we apply the high-energy-costs answer to the similar cases of other industrial nations, it doesn't work, which should tell us that perhaps it doesn't work in the case of the United States either.

One kind of information an author rarely provides is any bias or pressure that might have influenced his or her judgment. It's asking too much to expect to get such information, although on rare occasions we do get it. Take the question of animal overpopulation, starvation, and hunting. In a letter (*Harper's*, September 1978), Lewis Regenstein, executive vice-president of The Fund for Animals, suggests an interesting motive—perhaps wrong, as a reply suggested, but well worth looking into—for the oft-proposed defense of the "sport"[14] of deer hunting:

> Hunters consistently claim that deer herds must be "culled" to prevent overpopulation and starvation. . . . The main reason some areas temporarily end up with more deer than the habitat can support is that wildlife management officials deliberately try to create a "surplus" of deer— through stocking programs and manipulation of habitat—*in order to stimulate a demand for, and sell, a maximum number of hunting licenses, their main source of revenue* [italics added].

In evaluating certain kinds of information, it's important to check on who gets what or who benefits the most, because most of us are under a certain amount of pressure to make ends meet and therefore just might hold back information harmful to our financial interests.

---

[14] Notice how important it is what name we give a thing.

⑤ *Draw Undrawn Relevant Conclusions*

In late spring, 1979, a radio news program reported that while oil imports were down from a year earlier, demand was down slightly more. The announcer then quoted a Department of Energy explanation that oil companies (following a suggestion of President Carter's) were trying to build up reserves to avoid a fuel oil shortage the following winter. But there was a much better explanation available, so the DOE explanation should have been questioned. For it is precisely the oil companies, owners of increased stocks of oil, who benefit the most from the increased prices likely to result from a temporary shortage at the gas pump. The big oil corporations could have eliminated all shortages by pumping and refining more domestic oil. But our world views should tell us that corporations tend to act in the interests of their stockholders and (to a lesser extent) the interests of their high-level employees; in this case, the oil corporations had a strong motive for reducing the supply of gasoline (rather than, say, building up reserves by temporarily pumping more domestic oil)—namely, to drive up the price of gasoline so as to maximize profits. (But see some contrary views on the matter in Exercise 6 for Chapter Seven.)

The trick is to learn habitually to bring our world views and other relevant information to bear and then *draw relevant conclusions not drawn for us by others.* (Sometimes, all that is required is just to "add up" the information in an argument to reach a conclusion not reached by the arguer.)

⑥ *Consider the Strongest Version of an Argument*

In connection with the idea of bringing unstated but relevant information to bear on an argument, there is an additional rule to use when we're tempted to reject an argument, namely, to *be sure we have considered the strongest version of the argument* (the point of avoiding the "straw man" fallacy to be discussed in Chapter Four).

This is an important rule because all of us are tempted to reject conclusions we don't like much more quickly than those we do. (The corollary to this rule is that we should be doubly suspicious of the things we are eager to believe.)

⑦ *Don't Fall for Rhetoric Meant for the Converted*

One of the problems in evaluating information from news sources is that much news often is presented from a point of view we do not share. Most political magazines, for example, give us information within the context of articles which presuppose (in the case of many left-wing publications) that big business is the main villain in American society or (in the case of some right-wing publications) that labor unions and welfare government are the chief villains. Given the natural human tendency to want to hear what we already believe to be true rather than to investigate different points of view, readers tend to choose magazines and newspapers that reflect their own point of view, particularly with respect to political/social issues. A publication thus tends to reflect a particular world view shared by its readers but not often critically evaluated within its pages. So another hint for good reasoning about particular issues is to *try not to be persuaded by rhetoric meant for the already converted.*[15] (This is a special case of the rule not to be persuaded by rhetoric unless we already have reason to accept its presuppositions.)

⑧ *Avoid Thinking in Terms of Unverified Stereotypes*

A **stereotype** is a conventional, usually oversimplified or overblown, conception, view, or belief. Most stereotypes are accepted because of prejudice resulting from the desire to conform to group beliefs or the desire to draw quick and convenient conclusions even though lacking sufficient evidence.

Stereotypes concerning particular classes of people are especially dangerous. It is a stereotype that the French are great lovers, women more fickle than men, blacks beautiful (and very rhythmic), men emotionally tough guys, Indians good only when dead, Jews and Scots unusually frugal, and so on.

Since stereotypes are on the whole cultural in origin, thinking in terms of stereotypes is unlikely to be much better than the average in a culture, which means not be very good at all. A person who wants to think more subtly than the herd needs to pay attention to the hint to *avoid thinking in terms of stereotypes except where there is good evidence that a stereotype is accurate.*

⑨ *Break the Complicated into Simpler Parts*

One difficulty in trying to reason well is that problems often get very complicated and thus are hard to digest whole. So to make them easier to digest, try to *break complicated problems, ideas, or arguments into more easily grasped component parts.*

Again, take the vexing question whether there is an oil or gasoline shortage, a very large question indeed. Here is one way to divide this large question into smaller ones (a way that flows from the author's background beliefs about the issue plus his general world view—different background beliefs are likely to yield a different list):

1. What are the so-called "proven reserves" of oil, for the whole world and for the United States?

2. How much more recoverable oil—in addition to proven reserves—is there likely to be?

3. What is the current consumption of oil, in the whole world and in the United States?

4. Assuming sufficient supply, what is the most likely rate of increase in oil consumption, in the world and in the United States?

---

[15] There is also the charlatan's corollary: Don't fall for your own rhetoric.

5. What caused the several gasoline shortages, such as those in 1973 and 1979, according to: (1) the oil industry; (2) the U.S. government, and (3) critics of the oil industry or of government policy on the oil question?

6. Do the figures obtained in answering the fifth question jibe with those obtained in answering the first four?

7. What attempts have the relevant parties (the oil industry, the U.S. government, several state governments) made to avoid oil shortages, and how successful have they been?

8. What economically feasible alternative energy sources are there?

9. Who benefits the most from a failure to solve the problem?

Even if these are not the best possible questions to ask, answering them is certain to help us formulate better ones, and to understand better the energy issue as a whole.

In his Discourse on Method, *the philosopher and mathematician René Descartes laid down four rules that comprise his famous method of doubt:*

The first of these was to accept nothing as true which I did not clearly recognize to be so: that is to say, carefully to avoid precipitation and prejudice in judgments, and to accept in them nothing more than was presented to my mind so clearly and distinctly that I could have no occasion to doubt it.

The second was to divide up each of the difficulties which I examined into as many parts as possible, and as seemed requisite in order that it might be resolved in the best manner possible.

The third was to carry on my reflections in due order, commencing with objects that were the most simple and easy to understand, in order to rise little by little, or by degrees, to knowledge of the most complex, assuming an order, even if a fictitious one, among those which do not follow a natural sequence relative to one another.

The last was in all cases to make enumerations so complete and reviews so general that I should be certain of having omitted nothing.

To answer questions such as those just posed, considering that most of us are nonexperts, we must inevitably appeal to experts or to the media, at least to obtain facts and figures (for instance, on crude oil imports and domestic production). In doing so, we naturally want to be sure that our appeal to expert opinion is cogent, not fallacious. And that is why the fallacy called **appeal to authority** is discussed first, in the next chapter.

Summary of Chapter One

Reasoning is the essential ingredient in solving life's problems. Chapter One contains suggestions for good reasoning about these problems.

1. Reasoning can be cast into *arguments,* which consist in one or more *premises* supporting a *conclusion.* In real life (as opposed to in textbooks), rhetoric does not easily divide into arguments and does not have premises or conclusions neatly labeled. Still, clues are given: for example, the words "because," "since," and "for" usually signal premises, and "hence," "therefore," and "so" conclusions.

2. Reasoning is either *cogent* (good) or *fallacious* (bad).

3. Cogent reasoning has to satisfy three criteria; it must: (1) start with *warranted* premises; (2) use all relevant available information; and (3) be *valid.*

4. There are two basic kinds of valid reasoning: *deductive* and *inductive.* An argument is *deductively valid* provided that if its premises are true its conclusion must be true. An argument is *inductively valid* provided it furnishes good and, taken by itself, sufficient, even though not conclusive, evidence to support its conclusion. It isn't true that the difference between a valid deductive and valid inductive argument is that the former goes from the general to the particular while the latter goes from the particular to the general. Some of the most frequently used deductively valid argument forms are quite intuitive. For example, "If *A,* then *B,* and *A;* therefore *B—Modus Ponens.*

5. The key steps in most everyday reasoning are inductive, not deductive. The basic idea behind inductive reasoning is *pattern*—expecting unexamined cases to fit a pattern noticed in examined cases.

   The basic kind of induction is *low-level induction by enumeration,* in which we infer from the fact that all observed *A*'s are *B*'s to the conclusion that all *A*'s whatsoever are *B*'s. For example, assuming that since all members of Congress checked up on cheat, they all do.

   Here are a few hints for constructing and evaluating inductive inferences:

   a. Greater sample size yields greater probability.
   b. The more representative a sample (set of observations) is, the higher the probability of an induction based on it.
   c. One definite counter-example shoots down an induction. (But we have to make sure that it really is a counter-example.)
   d. We can check up on lower-level inductions by means of higher-level (more general) ones.
   e. *Analogical reasoning* is just like induction by enumeration, except that it yields a singular conclusion rather than a general one, and thus has a greater chance of being correct.

f. *Statistical inductions* are pretty much like other kinds, except that they infer from the fact that N percent of a sample has a certain property to the conclusion that N percent of the population has that property, rather than that all do.

g. One very important reason for using induction is to discover *causal connections*. In the absence of contrary evidence, we usually can conclude that an observed constant connection is a causal connection.

6. A person's basic beliefs about how the world and things in it work are called a *world view*. World views are vital because we use them in reasoning about practically all everyday problems of any import.

7. *Self-deception* is a serious impediment to good world-view construction, as well as to all other reasoning, one important species being rationalization.

8. There are several good hints for world-view constructing:
   a. We should check our world views for internal *consistency*, and for consistency with our experiences.
   b. We should evaluate information sources for accuracy. Some "experts" can't distinguish accurate information from a hole in the ground.
   c. We should construct theories of human motivation, in particular so as to better evaluate information sources.
   d. It is important to understand the basics of the scientific conception of the world, because science is just the systematic accumulation of inductively derived theories that are well supported by vast amounts of evidence.

9. There also are several hints for evaluating particular arguments:
   a. We should look for and evaluate the presuppositions of an argument, to make sure they fit with what we already know.
   b. We should do the same with respect to stated premises.
   c. We often can pick up useful information or ideas by *reading between the lines* of a passage.
   d. We should bring unstated but relevant information to bear on an issue. We can't expect others to tell us everything.
   e. We should draw undrawn relevant conclusions, again because we can't expect others to do this for us every time.
   f. We should consider the strongest versions of arguments so that we don't knock over "straw men."
   g. We should try not to fall for preaching to the converted.
   h. We should avoid thinking in terms of unverified stereotypes.
   i. We should get the knack of breaking complicated arguments or topics into their simpler parts, so that we can handle them more easily.

Truth Is Booty, Booty Is Truth

"There is already an inclination to trust the Veep-designate precisely because he is rich. 'When somebody is one of the wealthiest men in the world,' said Rep. John Rhodes of Arizona, the Republican leader in the house, 'he's got so much money there would be no point in cheating.' "

—*Newsweek*, 2 September 1974.

Does this Edward Sorel political cartoon (Village Voice, 17 September 1974) illustrate a fallacious appeal to the authority of (Nelson Rockefeller's) money?

Invalid Inference—I

We said in Chapter One that to reason cogently (correctly), we must (1) start with warranted premises; (2) include all relevant information at our disposal; and (3) reason validly. Fallacious reasoning is just reasoning that fails to satisfy one or more of these three criteria. It seems plausible, therefore, to divide fallacious arguments into three broad categories: (1) those that are fallacious because they contain unwarranted or questionable premises—let's call this category **questionable premise;** (2) those that are fallacious because they fail to use available relevant information—let's call this category **suppressed evidence;** and (3) those that are fallacious because they are invalid—let's call this category **invalid inference.**

Of course, we must remember that the fallacious arguments encountered in daily life tend to be vague and ambiguous, so that they can be classified in different ways depending on how we construe them. Take the following commercial:

> More people in America drink Budweiser than any other beer.

Taken literally, this isn't even an argument, much less a fallacious one. But it clearly implies that the listener should also drink Bud. So we can restate it to say:

> More people in America drink Budweiser than any other beer. (Premise)
> So you, too, should drink Budweiser. (Conclusion)

Stated this way, the argument is invalid, hence belongs in the fallacy category *invalid inference.* Yet we could just as well restate the commercial this way:

> More people in America drink Budweiser than any other beer. (Premise)
> The most popular beer is the best beer. (Premise)
> You should drink the best beer. (Premise)
> So you should drink Budweiser. (Conclusion)

Taken this way, the argument is valid but contains a questionable premise—that the most popular beer is the best beer. If we interpret the commercial this way, we cannot be guilty of *invalid reasoning,* but if we are persuaded by this argument, we are guilty of the fallacy of *questionable premise.*

Since most fallacious arguments can be classified in different ways, as the Budweiser example illustrates, there is no point in worrying too much about which fallacy label we apply to a particular fallacious argument. Fallacy categories are not constructed in heaven—they're just useful tools for spotting bad reasoning.

Let's now discuss several fairly standard fallacies that fall into the broad category of *invalid inference.* (Several others will be discussed in the next chapter.)

1.   Appeal to Authority

No one knows everything. So we often must consult experts before making decisions. But there are good and bad ways to do this; improper appeals to experts constitute the fallacy of **appeal to authority.** For instance, the fallacy of *appeal to authority* is committed by members of Congress who respond to Defense Department budget controversies by automatically accepting the opinions of Defense Department experts, because it is precisely those opinions that others challenge. In such a situation, we should expect our elected officials to examine the *evidence* of the military and others and draw their own conclusions.

Jones's Law of Authority: The importance of an authority figure in a field is inversely proportional to the amount that is known about the subject.
—Don Jones, quoted in the *Washingtonian,* November 1979.

It often is difficult to distinguish proper from improper appeals to authorities. How much can we trust authorities in a given field? Which sorts of things have experts figured out and which still remain essentially unknown? How can we spot the best experts in a given field? A well-thought-out world view should give us at least tentative answers to these questions. It also should provide us with rules of thumb for dealing with everyday problems that require us to consult expert opinion. Here are several such rules of thumb which conform to the world view of this writer and have proved useful to many others:

Authorities in One Field Aren't Necessarily Expert in Another

Famous athletes or movie stars who endorse all sorts of products in television commercials are a good example. There is no reason to suppose they know any more about beer or shaving cream than anyone else.

We Need to Become Experts on Controversial Topics

When experts disagree, the rest of us must become our own experts, turning to acknowledged experts for *evidence, reasons,* and *arguments,* but not for conclusions or opinions. This is especially true with respect to political matters because of the tremendous controversies they arouse. But it applies elsewhere too. The judge who merely accepts a psychologist's opinion concerning the sanity of an accused person ought instead to ask for the reasons that led the psychologist to this opinion. (After all, a different opinion could be obtained just by asking another psychologist.) Similarly, American presidents need to go into the complex details that lie behind the opinions of their economic advisors rather than confining themselves, as President Eisenhower is said to have done, to whatever could be typed onto one side of one page.

Some Experts Are More Trustworthy Than Others

Experts with an axe to grind are less trustworthy than just about anybody. It is to be expected, for instance, that corporation executives will testify to "facts" that place their corporations or products in a good light. Thus, we should expect that the executives of corporations that deal in products with harmful side effects (such as cigarettes, birth control pills, coffee, refined sugar, and nuclear power) will tend to deny or play down the unhealthy nature of their products and expect oil company bigwigs to deny that gasoline shortages result from attempts to control supply so as to drive up prices. (Can there be any doubt that the president of, say, Exxon would be fired if he publicly stated during a gasoline shortage that his company was holding off on refinery expansion in order to force increases in gasoline prices?)

> Since taking office, the thing that really shocks me is how little time a Congressman has to devote to any one issue. There's simply no way you can cram your way to knowledgeability on any one subject in three or four hours. We have so many issues to contend with that, with all our research facilities, the best we can do is pick up information in bits and snatches.
> —Representative James M. Shannon, Mass., quoted in *Parade* Magazine, 13 May 1979

Check the Past Records of Alleged Experts

Finally, anyone who has to appeal to an expert in a way which violates any of the above rules should at least *consult the past record of that authority.* Experts who have been right in the past are more likely to be right in the future than those who have been wrong. It is surprising how often even this rule of last resort is violated. Think of the many members of Congress who accepted expert military opinion that the war in Vietnam would end in 1969 or 1970, even after having heard pretty much the same military experts testify incorrectly so often about the end of that longest war in American history. Or think of President Carter's economic advisors, who remained in favor with the President even though their predictions for 1976–79 on inflation and unemployment proved to be way off the mark. If you have to rely on expert opinion, at least choose experts who have been relatively successful in the past.

Alleged experts on economic matters have notoriously poor track records, yet are still listened to as though they have a direct wire to the truth. Here are some predictions made in 1979 by government experts who were then in charge of American economic policy, starting with the big honcho himself, Jimmy Carter (assembled, surprisingly, by the National Enquirer, *July 1979):*

Predictions for 1979

	Date predicted	Inflation Rate predicted
Carter Administration spokesperson	Jan. 1978	5.5%
Congressional Budget Office head Alice Rivlin	July 1978	6.2-7.2%
President Carter	Oct. 1978	5.75%
Chief economic adviser Charles Schultze	Oct. 1978	6-6.5%
Federal Reserve Board Chairman G. William Miller	Nov. 1978	6.75-7.5%
Carter	Jan. 1979	7.5%
Miller	Jan. 1979	8%
Rivlin	Jan. 1979	7-9%
Treasury Secretary W. Michael Blumenthal	May 1979	8.5%
Miller	May 1979	8-8.5%
Wage and price director Barry P. Bosworth	May 1979	9%

The actual inflation rate in 1979 was about 13 percent (according to government figures released in early 1980). Were the "expert" predictions just pie in the sky for voter consumption?

Popularity

There are two important variations of the fallacy of *appeal to authority,* resulting from the fact that the "authority" need not be a single person or even a group of persons. The first variation is **popularity.**

Everyone knows how difficult it is to speak out in a group against the general sentiment of that group. The power of human cowardice, wedded to the desire to be on the winning side, is the basis for the fallacy of *popularity,* which is simply the human tendency to go along with the crowd, to believe what others believe. (Sometimes this is called the fallacy of **democracy,** or of **numbers.**) For many people, the crowd is the authority. For them, the fact that a view is generally accepted is sufficient to make that view respectable; the fact that a view is *not* generally accepted is sufficient to make it suspect.

Here is an argument that has these two assumptions as implicit premises.[1]

The freedom and flexibility afforded the broadcaster under the "fairness doctrine" to select in good faith the spokesmen for the *representative*[2] viewpoints seems the best means yet devised for insuring that the public is exposed to all *significant* points of view on important public issues.

In other words, only popular viewpoints are significant—an utterly foolish idea given the initial unpopularity of so many great ideas.

Here is Vice President Spiro Agnew and another example of the *popularity* variation of *appeal to authority.*[3]

Before I came down here, one [political pundit] told me that Southern voters wouldn't listen to Republicans. Southern voters won't support Republicans, and Southerners won't vote Republican. He told me he was *never* wrong. And then he drove off in his Edsel.

Since Edsels were a big sales flop, they obviously were the wrong car to buy. A humorous example, but human beings, especially in large groups, are manipulated by such trivia.

Now consider an example from the law. In the 1970 New Haven Black Panther trial, the jury first reported to the judge that they were deadlocked. The judge then read a part of an old Connecticut charge called the "Chip Smith charge," which is used to prod the minority on a jury to go along with the majority verdict. It asks the minority to reconsider in view of the verdict of the majority of jury members who "have heard the same evidence with the same attention and with equal desire to arrive at the truth and under sanction of the same oath."

---

[1] A remark by Leonard H. Goldenson of ABC, reported in a newspaper column by John S. Knight, 14 August 1970.

[2] Italics within quotes will sometimes be added for emphasis, as in this case.

[3] Mississippi Republican Dinner, Jackson, Mississippi, 20 October 1969.

The legitimacy of the Chip Smith charge rests on the assumption that the majority is more likely to be right than the minority. But if a juror is convinced by the Chip Smith charge that the majority view is correct "beyond a reasonable doubt" *because* it is the majority view, then he commits the fallacy of *appeal to authority*, the majority being his authority. For he places the indirect evidence of the majority verdict ahead of the direct evidence of courtroom testimony.

Traditional Wisdom

Another interesting variety of *appeal to authority* is **traditional wisdom,** which trades on the psychological fact that the past and the familiar have as secure a hold on us as the opinions of others.

But traditional wisdom should not be accepted automatically. It's true that the old have more experiences to draw on than the young, so that their view of a problem often carries special weight. However, it is fallacious to suppose that the opinions of an older *generation* are based on more experiences than those of the current generation. In fact, just the reverse is true; those alive today have more experiences to draw on than did past generations, for knowledge tends to be handed down from generation to generation and thus on the whole to increase. (Much that is false is handed down, too, but no one ever said thinking correctly is easy.)

Nevertheless, the fact that something has always been done a certain way seems to be a sufficient reason for many people to continue doing it that way. Here is Senator Sam Ervin of North Carolina, telling how he replied to women who were in favor of the Equal Rights Amendment to the Constitution.[4]

> I tell them, "Why ladies, any bill that lies around here for 47 years without getting any more support than this one has got in the past *obviously* shouldn't be passed at all. Why, I think *that affords most conclusive proof that it's unworthy of consideration.*"

It's hard to imagine a more clearcut case of *traditional wisdom.* But most cases are not so clearcut. The appeal to tradition often is concealed or half-hearted. Here is an example from an article on judicial abuse of migrant laborers in New Jersey.[5] Richard A. Walsh, deputy state public defender, in reply to the charge that migrants were being deprived of due process of law, is quoted as saying:

> It's not right, it's unjust and we know it, *but that's the way the system works down here.*

---

[4] Quoted in the *New York Times Magazine,* 20 September 1970.
[5] *New York Times,* 17 August 1970, p. 34.

This was a halfhearted use of *traditional wisdom* because Mr. Walsh never quite said that past practice constituted an excuse, but, in the absence of any great effort to correct the admitted injustice, the last clause does function to excuse that injustice.

2.   *Two Wrongs Make a Right*

The fallacy **two wrongs make a right** is committed when someone attempts to justify an apparently wrong action by charging his or her opponent with the same or some equally wrong action. The idea is that if the "other side" does it, or some comparable evil, then it's all right if we do also.

Here is a rather mild but otherwise typical example, concerning half-hearted attempts by the two major political parties to find qualified black lawyers to serve as judges in the South.[6]

> Georgia Republicans say they don't know of a single black Republican lawyer who could be appointed to a judgeship. They add smugly that if the Democrats couldn't find a Negro judge in all those years, how can anybody expect the Republicans to find one now?

The fallacy here is setting up the Democrats as a standard of conduct. Past Democratic errors in no way justify current Republican errors.

Like many other fallacies, *two wrongs* seems plausible because of its resemblance to a more sensible way of reasoning, in this case to the plausible idea that we are sometimes justified in fighting fire with fire, or in getting our hands as dirty as our opponents. A good example is the killing of someone in self defense; we're justified in fighting one evil (the taking of our own life) with what otherwise would be another evil (the taking of our attacker's life).

So the fallacy *two wrongs make a right* is not automatically committed every time one apparent wrong is justified by appeal to an opponent's wrong; the crucial question is whether the second wrong indeed is necessary to fight or counteract the first wrong.[7] In the case of justified self defense against physical attack, the evil of killing the attacker is necessary; in the case of Georgia Republicans who didn't look very hard to find black judges, that evil was not necessary or even helpful in fighting any evil—on the contrary, it simply added another evil to all those already existing.

Common Practice

Elected officials are often "excused" for doing wrong on the grounds of **common practice.** It has been argued, for instance, that we shouldn't have

---

[6] "Picking Judges in Georgia," *New Republic,* 15 August 1970.

[7] Overlooking the issue of retributive justice. If retributivists are right, then we're sometimes justified in inflicting harm (punishment) on those guilty of harming others, even though in doing so we fail to fight the original harm.

punished Richard Nixon, because he only did what other presidents (Johnson, Kennedy) did and got away with. (Compare "Why punish Nixon for doing what other presidents have done?" with "Why punish this guilty mafia boss for doing what other criminals have done and gotten away with?") But if common practice is allowed as a defense for wrongdoing, the result will be an inevitable increase in wrongdoing. To reduce wrongdoing by our elected representatives, we must insist that wrongdoing is not excused by common practice.

3. *Irrelevant Reason*

Traditional textbooks often discuss a fallacy called **non sequitur** ("it does not follow"), usually described as a fallacy in which the conclusion does not follow from the given premises. In this sense, any fallacy in the broad category *invalid inference* can be said to be a *non sequitur*.

Other writers use *non sequitur* to describe those arguments in which the "evidence" in the premises is *totally irrelevant* to the conclusion, and not, as is sometimes the case with such fallacies as *ad hominem* and *appeal to authority*, relevant but insufficient to establish the conclusion.

Let's replace the ambiguous term *non sequitur* with the expression **irrelevant reason,** to refer to reasons or premises that are or come close to being totally irrelevant to a conclusion, provided another fallacy name (for instance, *ad hominem* argument) does not apply.

A newspaper columnist, for instance, was guilty of this fallacy when he argued that prices had gone much too high by pointing out that the average housewife spends at a rate of $20 per hour at the supermarket, while her husband earns only $2.95 per hour. The rate of speed at which a housewife spends money is completely irrelevant to the charge that prices are too high. A person may spend a third of his or her yearly salary on a new automobile, or an entire year's salary merely as down payment on a house. But this tells us nothing whatever about whether automobile or house prices are rising too rapidly, or even rising at all.

Politicians often employ this fallacy when their arguments are weak, or too controversial. Thus, in a discussion of a particular public housing bill, a congressman went on and on about the need for more housing for the citizens of this great country, while saying nothing about the merits of the bill in question, confident that some of his listeners would fail to notice the irrelevance of his remarks to the real question at issue. For the issue was not whether we ought to have good housing at all, but whether the bill before the House was the right one to accomplish that goal.

During the Vietnam War, politicians sometimes replied to charges that the United States had no business in Vietnam, either morally or to satisfy our national interests, by arguing that such talk only prolonged the war by making the enemy believe America's will to fight was declining. This reply in all likelihood was true, but it was utterly irrelevant to the question of our justification for being in Vietnam.

(It should be noticed that a reason is not automatically irrelevant just because it is false. For instance, the old idea that masturbation causes insanity is false, but it isn't irrelevant to the question whether a person should or shouldn't engage in that practice, because if true it would be a good reason not to masturbate.)

4.   Ambiguity

A term or phrase is **ambiguous** when it has more than one meaning. Most English words are ambiguous, but their ambiguity usually does not cause problems. The English word "snow," for instance, can be used to refer to the flaked form of H_2O or to the "recreational" drug cocaine. But in most cases in which this word is used, it is clear from the context which meaning is intended.

However, some uses of ambiguous terms are far from harmless. When the ambiguity of a word or phrase leads to a mistaken conclusion, we have the fallacy of **ambiguity** (also, and more accurately, called the fallacy of **equivocation**).

Here is an example of the fallacy of *ambiguity* from a Rowland Evans and Robert Novak column (30 June 1970):

> His [Nixon's] claim that his new Administration really intends to fulfill [William] Scranton's *evenhanded policy* between Israel and the Arab states . . .

The expression "evenhanded policy" here could mean either a policy halfway between the Arab and Israeli positions or a fair policy. By describing the Scranton policy as "evenhanded," Evans and Novak entice support for it from those who favor a "halfway" policy as well as from those who will endorse any policy they consider "fair." The columnists also mask the fact that labeling a policy "even-handed," even if accurate in one or another sense of that term, does not provide grounds for adopting it. (In defense of Evans and Novak, it should be pointed out that the Scranton policy was widely referred to as "evenhanded." They were just passing on the ambiguous label.)

It is he that sitteth upon the circle of the earth.
—Isaiah 40:22

Ambiguity: *Almost any statement can be interpreted in various ways if we have a mind to do so. The Bible is a happy hunting ground for those intent on taking advantage of the ambiguity of natural languages because many people take what it says to be the word of the Ultimate Authority on most important issues. The above passage from Isaiah once was used to prove that the earth is flat, but after Copernicus, Kepler, and Newton to prove that it is a sphere.*

Here is an excerpt from a 2 May 1969, speech by Vice President Spiro Agnew. Notice that the *ambiguity* occurs in an aside, which makes it just that much more likely to slip by undetected:

Aside from the small point that our primary and secondary schools should strengthen their curricula in civics . . . so that even our youngest children learn that civil rights *are* balanced by civil responsibilities . . .

This passage can be taken to say either that (1) we should teach children the moral truth that there is a responsibility (duty) corresponding to every right, or that (2) in the United States our civil rights *in fact* are upheld and balanced by our civil responsibilities. Many minority groups (American Indians, chicanos, Jews, blacks, Puerto Ricans) would vehemently deny the second interpretation. But if attacked, Agnew just had to switch to the first meaning—that civil rights and civil responsibilities are supposed to balance—to win the argument.

Studied ambiguity is the perfect device for protecting oneself from legitimate attack: simply shift meanings at the opportune moment.

So long as the economic system meets these demands [for more jobs, higher income, more consumer goods, and more recreation], and so long as the demands take these forms, the perennial questions about *power* and *control* need never be asked. Or, better, those whose demands are being met can be congratulated on having "power," *for what is power but the ability to have one's demands met?*
—Ben Wattenberg, *The New America,* p. 49

Ambiguity *(very subtle): Do we have power if we have the ability to get* all *of our demands met, some* met, *or even* one? *Just about everyone has some power. The political question Wattenberg evaded is whether average Americans (or Wattenberg's* real majority*) have power equal to their numbers—Wattenberg's opponents don't deny members of the middle class have power, they just deny they have their fair share.*

While becoming wary of ambiguous locutions, we don't want to lose sight of their usefulness. Ambiguity has many useful purposes. For example, along with vagueness, it greases the skids of social intercourse. Benjamin Disraeli, nineteenth-century British Prime Minister, used ambiguity to soften his reply when someone sent him an unsolicited amateur manuscript: "Many thanks; I shall lose no time in reading it," a response similar to that of H. L. Mencken's: "Thanks for your letter. You may be right."

5.   *Slippery Slope*

The fallacy of **slippery slope** consists in objecting to a particular action on the grounds that once an action is taken it will lead inevitably to a similar but less desirable action, which will lead in turn to an even less desirable action, and so on down the "slippery slope" until the horror lurking at the bottom is reached. (Members of the Texas State Legislature sometimes refer to this fallacy as "the camel's nose in the tent," since once the camel's nose enters, the rest, it is alleged, will follow close behind.)

According to a slightly different version of *slippery slope,* whatever would justify taking the first step over the edge also would justify all the other steps. But, it is argued, the last step is not justified, so the first step is not either.

People frequently argued against Medicare in the late 1960s on the grounds that it was socialized medicine for the aged and would lead to socialized medicine for all, and then to socialized insurance of all kinds, socialized railroads, airlines, and steel mills. It was also argued that whatever justified socialized medicine for the aged justified it for everyone, and justified as well socialized railroads, and so on, "down the slope" all the way to a completely socialistic system.

The fallacy of the slippery slope is committed in this example if you accept *without further argument* the idea that, once the first step is taken, the slide all the way down is inevitable. In fact, the first step sometimes does and sometimes does not lead to more steps. Even in Great Britain, under socialist governments, the economy did not become fully socialized. Further argument is needed to determine the facts in particular cases like that of Medicare.

A Quick About-Face

Perhaps intimidated by flak from Capitol Hill, the Social Security Advisory Council has backed away from a proposal to increase the maximum pay subject to Soc-Sec taxation from $14,000 to $24,000 to keep the plan on a pay-as-you-go basis. Instead, it has recommended shifting the cost of medicare to the general fund.

The proposal, if adopted, would begin the process of transforming Social Security into an out-and-out welfare program. Once we start in that direction, where do we stop?

—*New York Daily News,* 21 January 1975

Slippery slope, *a favorite of the* New York Daily News.

The variations on slippery slope are almost limitless. Two, the **Balkanization theory** and the **domino theory,** have been employed quite frequently in recent years.

The Balkanization Theory

The *Balkanization theory* was employed during the Nigeria–Biafra civil war. People argued then that we could not permit Biafra to break away from Nigeria because such a break would produce a chain reaction in which every tribal group in Africa would attempt to gain independence, thus "Balkanizing" Africa. But there was little or no evidence to support such conjecture (ignoring the fact that an independent Biafra would have been larger in population than over half the nations in the world, so it would hardly have exemplified "Balkanization"). Wars of secession usually occur because of internal pressures, not because of successful attempts in other nations. The Biafran attempt to gain independence is itself a case in point, since it came after secessionist attempts elsewhere in Africa (as in the Congo—now known as Zaire) had failed.

The Domino Theory

The classic case of the use of the *domino theory* is, of course, Vietnam (Indo-China). Everyone seems to have used it at one time or another, starting with the French:[8]

> Once Tongking [Northern Indo-China] is lost, there is really no barrier before Suez.

The Americans then joined in, one of the first being John Foster Dulles:[9]

> If Indo-China should be lost, there would be a chain reaction throughout the Far East and South Asia.

Here is William P. Bundy:[10]

> If South Vietnam falls, the rest of Southeast Asia will be in grave danger of progressively disappearing behind the Bamboo Curtain, and other Asian countries like India and even in time Australia and your own [country—Japan] will in turn be threatened.

Even Bob Hope got into the act:[11]

---

[8] General Jean de Lattre de Tassiguy, general in charge of French forces in the Far East, 20 September 1951. This, and several of the examples which follow, are mentioned in the book *Quotations Vietnam: 1945–1970*, compiled by William G. Effros (New York: Random House, 1970), Chapter Three.

[9] Secretary of State under Eisenhower, 5 April 1954.

[10] Assistant Secretary of State for Far Eastern Affairs under President Johnson, 29 September 1964, in Tokyo, Japan.

[11] Anthony J. Lukas. "This Is Bob (Politician-Patriot-Publicist) Hope," *New York Times Magazine*, 4 October 1970, p. 86.

Everybody I talked to there [Vietnam] wants to know why they can't go in and finish it, and don't let anybody kid you about why we're there. If we weren't, those Commies would have the whole thing, and it wouldn't be long until we'd be looking off the coast of Santa Monica [California].

All of these versions of the *domino theory* reveal the simplistic attitude that is characteristic of *slippery slope* in any of its variations, the attitude that once the first step is taken, the rest are inevitable. But sometimes that first step will lead to others, sometimes it won't. We must examine each case individually for the details that make all the difference. If we fail to do so, we reason fallaciously.

Summary of Fallacies Discussed in Chapter Two

1. *Appeal to authority.* Improper appeal to authority.

   Example: Taking the word of power industry executives that nuclear power plants are safe.

   a. *Popularity:* Appeal to the crowd as the authority.

   Example: Spiro Agnew's characterization of man as wrong in buying an Edsel because Edsels were a sales flop.

   b. *Traditional wisdom.* Appealing to the past as an authority.

   Example: Senator Ervin's statement that Congress's 47-year failure to act on a proposed equal rights amendment was a conclusive reason for rejecting that amendment.

2. *Two wrongs make a right.* Defending a wrong by pointing out that one's opponent has done the same (or an equally wrong) thing.

   Example: An Associated Press report that implied it wasn't so bad that we killed lots of civilians in Vietnam, since the enemy (the Viet Cong) did so also.

   a. *Common practice.* Claiming that something is not wrong, or at least is excusable, because it is commonly done.

   Example: Excusing Richard Nixon's errors on the grounds that U.S. presidents commonly make them.

3. *Irrelevant reason.* Use of evidence entirely irrelevant to a conclusion.

   Example: Arguing that prices are too high because the average housewife spends at the rate of $20 per hour at the supermarket.

4. *Ambiguity.* Use of ambiguous locutions to mislead (or which in fact mislead).

   Example: Using the ambiguous *Isaiah* phrase, "It is he that sitteth on the circle of the earth" to claim the Bible tells us the earth is a sphere.

5. *Slippery slope.* Failure to see the first step in a possible series of steps does not inevitably lead to the rest.

   Example: Claims—unargued for—that Medicare would inevitably lead to complete socialism.

   a. *Balkanization theory.* The conclusion that the break-up of one nation into parts will inevitably result in the break-up of others.

      Example: The belief that if Biafra successfully broke from Nigeria, all sorts of tribal groups in Africa would try to establish independent nations.

   b. *Domino theory:* The conclusion that if *A* falls, so will *B*, then *C,* and so on.

      Example: The belief that if South Vietnam goes Communist, so will Laos, Cambodia, Thailand, the rest of the Far East, and so on.

Exercise I for Chapter Two

Which of the fallacies discussed in Chapter Two occur in the following passages? (Some may contain no fallacies.) Explain the reasons for your answers. (For instance, if the fallacy is *ambiguity,* show the different senses that are involved and how they lead to confusion; if the fallacy is *appeal to authority,* show what is unwise about this particular appeal—why we should not listen to this particular authority this time.) Remember that fallacy categories sometimes overlap, and that a given item may contain more than one fallacy. Remember also that the material is quite controversial and thus open to differing interpretations. So your *explanations* are more important than the fallacy labels you put on an argument. [Starred items (*) are answered in a section at the back of the book.] p 269

*1. *Article in college newspaper:* A committee on teaching evaluation in colleges is the coming thing. *popularity*

2. *President Ford, 28 August 1974, soon after taking office:* The code of ethics that will be followed by those in my administration will be the example I set. *No Fallacy.*

3. Texas Observer, *16 March 1973 (quoting State Senator Walter Mengden):* The base cause of inflation is an unbalanced federal budget . . . "If the rate of inflation becomes too excessive, the result of this inflation is that the economy will stop . . . because the dollar will be losing value so fast people will stop exchanging goods of real value for dollars. . . . Now this isn't conjecture; this has happened before, many times. . . . If you don't control inflation, . . . you will destroy the economy, and in a few weeks there will be no food to buy, little water, no electricity and services, and there will be such panic and disaster that some hard-pants general is going to move in and say, 'I am now running the show,' and the Army or somebody like him will take over, and that's the end of the Constitutional Republic. And that's what's going to happen if we don't control inflation." *domino theory – slippery slope.*

*4. Hartford Courant, *20 December 1972, in an article on the possibility of women priests in the Catholic Church:* Citing the historic exclusion of women from the priesthood, however, the study [of a committee of Roman Catholic bishops] said ". . . the constant tradition and practice, interpreted as of divine law, is of such a nature as to constitute a clear teaching of the Ordinary Magisterium [teaching authority] of the Church." *Traditional wisdom*

*5. *Associated Press dispatch on the atmosphere in Vietnam before the American massacre of civilians at My Lai 4:* In Vietnam the killing of civilians was a practice established by the Viet Cong as a major part of the war long before the first U.S. ground troops were committed in March 1965.
2 wrongs, or common practice

6. *Beginning of a book review:* Erich Segal's *Love Story*—*Romeo and Juliet* it isn't. But who cares. It's guaranteed to give you a good cry now and then. And it couldn't have gotten off to such a flying start for nothing. Everybody is going to be reading this novel, so you better go down to your nearest bookstore and pick up a copy. *Popularity.*

7. It's all right for President Ford to impound funds voted by the Congress. Every recent president—Nixon, Johnson, Kennedy—did so. In fact, Nixon did so on a grand scale. *common practice*

8. Hartford Courant, *21 December 1970, AP story on Soviet efforts to crush political dissent in Russia:* Minister of Culture Yekaterina Furtseva publicly berated an American correspondent for "poking his nose into our internal affairs" when he asked a question related to the case of disgraced novelist Alexander Solzhenitsyn. "If you cannot punish the killers of your government leaders, you have no right to be interested in such questions," the [Soviet] culture minister retorted. *irrelevant reason.*
(justification ...)

9. *Mike Royko,* Chicago Sun-Times, *30 June 1978, commenting on the very bad publicity Senator Edward Brooke, Massachusetts, was getting because of the way he was handling his divorce:* What Brooke did was try to cheat his wife out of some money when they made a divorce settlement. In other words, he did what tens of thousands of desperate American men do every year. And for this perfectly normal effort at survival, his career is threatened with ruin. . . . I'm not siding with Brooke against his wife. I have no idea who was in the right or wrong. But lying during a divorce case is not unusual. If anything, it is the rule. Most people who come to divorce courts lie their heads off. *common practice*

10. *New Jersey State Attorney George F. Kugler, Jr.,* New York Times, *17 August 1970:* "I'm not saying there are no abuses." . . . but [he] added that the problem of obtaining justice for poor persons was a problem everywhere in the U.S. *common practice, 2 wrongs,*

11. Houston Post, *28 February 1977:* Feminist attorney Florynce Kennedy says Uganda's President Idi Amin is an "outstanding" figure. Kennedy told a Yale Law School conference that much of the public criticism of Amin can be traced to the attitude that "if a black person is in charge of a

country, he isn't really supposed to be in charge." Commenting on charges that Amin has directed the killing of thousands in his country, she declared, "Sovereign governments are in the process of killing people all the time." *ambiguity—'outstanding'! common practice.*

12. St. Louis Globe Democrat, *on proposed amnesty for Vietnam war draft resistors:* There has never been a general or unconditional amnesty in American history. Never. Not once. There's a point that pro-amnesty advocates try to gloss over through vague allusions to "generous" amnesty by past Presidents. But the fact is, either something has always been required of those who received amnesty—an oath to the Union, a return to military units, completion of sentence—or else only a few persons out of many have received pardons because of special circumstances. (Quoted in Ronald Munson, *The Way of Words,* Boston: Houghton Mifflin, 1976.) *traditional wisdom*

*13. *John P. Roche, political column, October 1970:* Every society is, of course, repressive to some extent—as Sigmund Freud pointed out, repression is the price we pay for civilization. *ambiguity*

14. *Arthur Schlesinger, Jr., supporting Senator McGovern's candidacy for President, in the* New Republic: Though a country boy, he [McGovern] has immersed himself in the problems of the cities. In New York, for example, he has the support of Democratic leaders . . . ; indeed, Prof. Richard Wade, our leading urban historian, is managing his campaign. *appeal to authority; ambiguity—'leading'*

15. *Remark by a Yale University alumnus now a lawyer for Yale, quoted in* Psychology Today, *February 1978, in an article about a class action suit by Yale female students about "fuck or fail" propositioning of female students:* Those kooks don't know what they're doing. Besides, what are they complaining about? The same thing happens all the time to secretaries. *2 wrongs.*

Momma by Mell Lazarus. Courtesy of Mell Lazarus and Field Newspaper Syndicate.

16. (In this case, the question is what fallacy Momma failed to perpetrate on her son.) *equivocation*

17. *William Safire,* New York Times, *16 September 1976, discussing Daniel Schorr's leak of the Pike Report on the CIA to the* Village Voice: Too many editorialists at first missed the significance of all that was at stake, and the Congressmen sensed that weakness and moved in. "If Schorr didn't

do anything wrong," one of the committee members asked me, "why did CBS suspend him?" *no fallacy. evidently—"is wrong", appeal to authority*

*18. *Nat Hentoff in the* Village Voice, *3 March 1975:* City College [of New York] is hardly unique [it censured five history professors for what Hentoff believed to be an exercise of their rights to free speech], among schools of higher education, in its ambience of ignorance of the functions of the First Amendment. It is an ignorance which leads inexorably to contempt for total free speech. *Slippery slope?*

19. *1874 popular magazine article:* Louis Agassiz, the greatest scientist of his day, examined Darwin's claims for his theory of evolution very carefully and finally decided that it could not be true that man was descended from the ape and its earlier animal ancestry. Within six months the greatest German biologists, and the most learned anthropologists now living, have declared that the Darwin theory of the origin of man could not be true. In spite of the opinions of these, the . . . leading investigators of the century, the theory of Darwinism is being taught in the universities of America. There is such a thing as a little knowledge leading to a great error, and this is an example. (Quoted in Richard L. Purtill, *Logic: Argument, Refutation, and Proof,* New York: Harper & Row, 1979.) *appeal to authority, popularity*

20. *Re-creation of conversation between two Howard Samuels' campaign workers:*
    Susan: Look, we've got Howard Samuels scheduled to appear at the orphans' home from 10:00 to 12:00 tomorrow. But kissing babies is a waste of time. Let's use that time to make some TV spots.
    Ted: But campaigners always pose with little kids. It's my decision, and I say he goes to the orphanage. *common practice, traditional wisdom,*

21. *Ad against smoking:* 100,000 doctors have quit smoking cigarettes. (Maybe they know something you don't.) *appeal to authority,*

22. *Lewis Carroll in* Through the Looking Glass: "You couldn't have it if you *did* want it," the Queen said. "The rule is jam tomorrow and jam yesterday—but never jam *today.*"
    "It *must* come sometimes to jam today," Alice objected.
    "No it can't," said the Queen. "It's jam every *other* day: today isn't any *other* day, you know." *ambiguity, equivocation.*

23. *Vivekanada:* There is no past or future even in thought, because to think it you have to make it present. (Quoted in Henry C. Byerly, *A Primer of Logic,* New York: McGraw-Hill, 1978.) *equivocation,*

24. *Benedetto Croce in* Philosophy of the Practical: The Inquisition must have been justified and beneficial, if whole peoples invoked and defended it, if men of the loftiest souls founded and created it severally and impartially, and its very adversaries applied it on their own account, [funeral] pyre answering to pyre. *traditional wisdom.*

25. *William Shakespeare in* As You Like It: Why, if thou never wast at court, thou never sawest good manners; if thou never sawest good manners,

then thy manners must be wicked; and wickedness is sin, and sin is damnation. Thou art in a parlous state, shepherd. *domino theory*

26. *Perry Weddle,* Argument: A Guide to Critical Thinking: Last April, CBS News aired a heretical program, "You and the Commercial," the most eloquent electronic statement to date on the manipulative aspects of advertising. The program's accuracy was fully demonstrated when the masters of unfairness and deceit, the advertising industry, roundly attacked the program as being "unfair and deceptive."

27. Houston Post, *30 September 1972:* The U.S. has supported UN economic sanctions against Rhodesia as an alternative to a violent solution to the controversy over independence for the white minority ruled country. We were criticized when Congress exempted from the sanctions our imports of such strategic materials as chrome ore. This act, open and official, gave rise to criticism that we were ignoring the UN sanctions. The fact is that far more extensive trade with Rhodesia has been carried on by industries in other countries whose governments ostensibly observe total embargoes. *2 wrongs.*

28. *St. Augustine in* De Libero Arbitrio: See how absurd and foolish it is to say: I should prefer nonexistence to miserable existence. He who says, I prefer this to that, chooses something. Nonexistence is not something; it is nothing. There can be no real choice when what you choose is nothing. *is Fallacy,*

29. *From the* Houstonian, *campus newspaper of Sam Houston State College, 23 April 1976, in a letter arguing that Jesus Christ really existed which cites the ancient authors Tacitus and Josephus before presenting this argument:* Besides these two authors of ancient times, the existence of Jesus is documented in a much more modern source: *Encyclopedia Britannica.* The latest edition . . . uses 20,000 words in describing this person Jesus. His description took more space than was given to Aristotle, Cicero, Alexander, Julius Caesar, Buddha, Confucius, Mohammed, or Napoleon Bonaparte. These are just three pieces of literature, of which there are many, that document the historical presence of Jesus Christ. *appeal to authority*

30. *Column by John Cunniff, July 1970:* Do Americans eat well in comparison with other nations? Millions of Americans still have poor diets, but generally speaking most Americans can afford to eat well. In the U.S. and Canada less than 20 percent of all "personal consumption expenditures" are for food. In less developed countries, the figures are much higher. *No Fallacy,*

*31. *Nicholas von Hoffman,* New York Post, *1 October 1974:* The trouble with such propositions [that there was another gunman in the Robert Kennedy murder] is that . . . they are seldom able to give us much of a clue as to who the "real" killer may be. It is for that reason that nobody has been able to discredit the Warren Commission report. If Lee Harvey Oswald didn't murder President Kennedy, then who did? *irrelevant reasons*

32. *From a magazine article:* The Socialist Workers Party (Trotskyist) has launched a hue and cry for "special measures" to apprehend the persons

responsible for the February 4 bombings of their Los Angeles headquarters. The SWP has accused the L.A. police of foreknowledge of the incident, collusion with the CIA, and laxity in performing their investigations. Such a situation is ironic in several respects.

First, it is somewhat out of character for the SWP to be condemning terrorism. Trotsky conducted the infamous "red terror" which allowed Lenin to consolidate power after the Bolshevik revolution; and though the SWP does not find terror to be tactically advisable in the U.S. at the present time, it is affiliated with South American terrorist groups and has no opposition to using terror here in the future when conditions change. *irrelevant reason*

33. *E. F. Schumacher, famous economist, in an article in* Atlantic, *April 1979:* . . . Fifteen months [after I had advised that rural India should have a technology intermediate between the hoe and the tractor] an all-India conference on intermediate technology was arranged. (They still didn't like the term ["intermediate"], so they called it appropriate technology. That's all right: when I come to India and somebody says, "Oh, Mr. Schumacher, I don't believe in appropriate technology," I just look him straight in the face and say, "Oh, that's splendid. Do you believe in inappropriate technology?") *irrelevant reason,*

Exercise II for Chapter Two

Find examples in the mass media (television, magazines, newspapers, radio) of fallacies discussed in Chapter Two, and explain why they are fallacious.

Questionable cause? *It's dangerous to conclude that* A *is the cause of* B *just because* B *follows* A.

Chapter Three

Invalid Inference—II

It don't even make good nonsense.

—Davy Crockett, remarking on a statement by President Andrew Jackson

Two wrongs don't make a right, but three do.

—Unofficial slogan of American military in Vietnam

Let's continue our discussion of the more important fallacies in the broad category of invalid inference.

1. Ad Hominem Argument (Argument to the Man)

The fallacy of **ad hominem argument,** sometimes called the **genetic fallacy,** consists of an irrelevant attack on an opponent, rather than his or her argument.

Senator Jennings Randolph was guilty of *ad hominem* argument in a U.S. Senate debate on the proposed Equal Rights Amendment to the U.S. Constitution (ERA) requiring equal protection of the law without regard to sex (26 August 1970), when he dismissed women's liberationists, and thus their arguments, with the remark that women's liberationists constituted a "small band of bra-less bubbleheads." This may have been good for a laugh in the almost all-male Senate, but it was irrelevant to arguments the women's rights representatives had presented. Randolph attacked *them* (through ridicule) rather than their arguments. So he argued fallaciously.

Al Capp, the creator of Li'l Abner, frequently used ridicule, and thus *ad hominem* argument. Students leaving in protest during one of his addresses once prompted Capp to remark:[1]

Hey! Don't go! I need an animal act! You with the beard! Why don't you walk on water?

In ridiculing women's liberationists as "bra-less bubbleheads," Senator Randolph resorted to namecalling, on a rather low level. But *ad hominem* namecalling need not be so crude. Here is an example with a good deal of literary merit, representing Vice President Spiro Agnew at his very best:[2]

---

[1] Reported in the *Hartford Courant,* 6 September 1970.
[2] From a speech delivered in New Orleans, 19 October 1969.

A spirit of national masochism prevails, encouraged by an effete corps of impudent snobs who characterize themselves as intellectuals.

Agnew attacked his intellectual opponents without bothering to consider their arguments. Now here is *Time* magazine reporting on Yale chaplain William Sloan Coffin, Jr., and the New Haven Black Panther murder trial.[3]

The climate was such that Yale chaplain William Sloan Coffin, Jr., saw no unreason in characterizing the murder trial as "legally right but morally wrong." ... How to explain such logic? The answer is that the New Haven Panthers have ample white guilt going for them at Yale.

Time's argument was *ad hominem* because it attacked Coffin himself through his motives and not his argument. *Time* gave a psychological motive (white guilt) for Coffin's alleged error in reasoning, rather than an argument to demonstrate that he in fact reasoned incorrectly. Even supposing *Time* was correct in saying that a motive of white guilt was at work, what is wrong with Coffin's idea that the murder trial was "legally right but morally wrong"? *Time* erred in failing to answer that question, thus failing to support its implication that the statement is illogical.

Attacks on Character or Credentials May Be Cogent

Lawyers who attack the testimony of courtroom witnesses by questioning their character or expertise are not necessarily guilty of *ad hominem* argument. For courtroom witnesses, doctors, auto mechanics, lawyers, and other experts often present opinions against which we, as nonexperts, are unable to argue directly. The best we can do is try to evaluate their honesty and judgment. Thus, testimony that a psychological expert has been convicted of perjury, and spends more time testifying in court than on any other job, would be good reason to prefer the conflicting opinion of an expert for the other side.

In these cases we certainly do not prove that expert opinion is incorrect. At best, character attacks provide grounds only for canceling or disregarding the opinion of an expert, not for deciding that that opinion is false. If a doctor who advises operating on a patient turns out to be a quack, it is rash to conclude that no operation is necessary. In disregarding the doctor's opinion, we don't thereby judge it false, but rather in need of other support before we can accept it.

Guilt by Association

One of the more important variations on *ad hominem* arguments is **guilt by association.** Many believe that people are to be judged by the company they keep. But many also hold that you should not judge people by their associates, any more than you judge books by their covers. Which view is correct?

---

[3] *Time*, 4 May 1970, p. 59.

> ### *Does Carter Know It from a Hole in the Ground?*
> —Page one headline in the *Village Voice*
>
> ---
>
> Ad hominem *headline, more common in left- and right-wing publications than in the mass media ones, which tend to stay pretty much in the center politically. (You'll never see this nasty a headline in* Time, Newsweek, *or the* New York Times. *On the other hand, the* Village Voice *comes through with many more juicy "how society really works" articles than any establishment publication.)*

The answer is that it *is* rational under certain circumstances to judge people by their associates. However, only rarely will such judgments have a *high degree of probability* attached to them. In the absence of other evidence, a man frequently seen in the company of different women known to be prostitutes is rightly suspected of being connected with their occupation in a way that casts doubt on his moral character. Similarly, a person who associates frequently and closely with men known to be agents of a foreign government is rightly suspected of being an agent of that government.

But caution is needed in dealing with indirect evidence of this kind. Suspecting that Smith uses the services of prostitutes is different from knowing that he does. (It is, of course, good reason for looking further—assuming we care enough to expend the effort.) The man who frequently associates with prostitutes may turn out to be a sociologist conducting an investigation. The close associate of foreign spies may be a friendly counterspy.

Even so, when decisions must be made and our only evidence is indirect, it is prudent to judge people on the basis of their associates.[4] There is no fallacy in this. The fallacy of *guilt by association* occurs when suspicion is taken to be knowledge, when more direct evidence is available but not used, or when association with that kind of person is not truly derogatory.

> In 1950, Senator Joseph R. McCarthy responded to a doubting question about the fortieth name on a list of eighty-one case histories he claimed were of communists working for the United States State Department by saying, "I do not have much information on this except the general statement of the agency that there is nothing in the files to disprove his Communist connections." (Adopted from the book *Senator Joe McCarthy*, by Richard Rovere.)

---

[4] But doing so sometimes generates serious moral or political problems. For instance, auto insurance companies judge blacks who live in certain big city ghettos to be poor risks on the basis of indirect statistical evidence rather than on more direct evidence concerning particular applicants (because the statistical evidence is much cheaper). But is this fair to a ghetto resident who is a hard-working, bill-paying, careful driver, who in fact is a better than average risk?

Many of McCarthy's followers took this absence of evidence proving that the person in question was not a communist as evidence that he was, which is a variation on the fallacy called *appeal to ignorance (argumentum ad ignorantiam).*

Absence of evidence is not a good reason for believing anything, except in the unusual case where we can be quite certain that if such evidence existed we would have found it (as, say, if someone were to claim that a small planet exists between the Earth and Mars—absence of any evidence of this planet's existence, given all the sky watching that has gone on in the past 10,000 years, *is* good evidence that no such planet exists).

2. *Provincialism*

The fallacy of **provincialism** stems from the natural tendency to identify with a particular group, and to perceive experience largely in terms of in-group versus out-group. This tendency has some good things to be said for it, since our personal well-being often depends on that of our group. But when in-group loyalties begin to intrude on the process of determining *truth,* the result is fallacy.

The tendency toward provincialism often results in normally enlightened people displaying shocking ignorance or prejudice. Here is an example from an American newspaper series on Japan:[5]

The [Japanese] empire supposedly was founded about 600 B.C., but for the next 24 centuries the Japanese people lived in almost complete isolation from *the rest of the world.*

"The rest of the world," of course, meant the Western world. The writer ignored the great influence of China on Japan during much of that twenty-four-century period.

Provincialism is a problem for all of us, including experts. For example, countless psychological experiments conducted on American subjects have reached conclusions that could be shown wrong by observing even a few people from other cultures. The same is true of many commonly held ideas. An example is the widely held belief that lefties write with a hooked motion because the left-to-right direction of English (and most written languages) is unnatural for them, while quite natural for right-handers. Even experts have made this claim. Yet lefties in Israel often write Hebrew (written from right-to-left) with that same hooked motion, while righties do not, a fact experts could discover by just removing their provincial blinders.

[5] *Lawrence* (Kan.) *Daily Journal World,* 8 August 1970.

Provincialism leads us to inflate the importance and size of our own nation at the expense of the rest of the world. China is larger in size than the United States, and has about one-third of the human race within its borders (close to 1 billion *people compared to about 220 million in the United States). In this comic strip, Garry Trudeau pokes fun at our provincial ignorance of the rest of the world.*

Loyalty

In its extreme form, the fallacy of *provincialism* turns into a worse vice, the fallacy of **loyalty.** This is the fallacy of believing (or disbelieving), in the face of great contrary evidence, *because* of provincial loyalty.

The reactions of many Americans to the My Lai massacre in Vietnam are a good example.[6] On reading about My Lai, a teletype inspector in Philadelphia is reported to have said he didn't think it happened: "I can't believe our boys' hearts are that rotten." This response was typical, as was that of the person who informed the *Cleveland Plain Dealer,* which had printed photos of the massacre, "Your paper is rotten and anti-American." Surveys taken after wide circulation of news about the massacre revealed that large numbers of Americans refused to believe "American boys" had done such a thing. The myth of American moral superiority seems to have been a better source of truth for them than evidence at hand. One wonders if any amount of evidence would be sufficient to convince those people who set *loyalty* above the truth. They are like the clerics who refused to look through Galileo's telescope to see the moons of Jupiter because they *knew* Jupiter could not possibly have moons.

Let's end our discussion of *loyalty* and *provincialism* on a lighter note. The *New York Times* (17 September 1970) carried a photo of a smiling President Nixon addressing a pleased-looking audience at Kansas State University. Underneath the photo, the *Times* reported that the President had just noted to the audience that he was wearing a tie with the K.S.U. school colors, purple and white. Having thus made the provincial appeal, the President then had a more receptive audience for serious subjects.

3.   Tokenism

When action is clearly called for but is politically inexpedient, politicians frequently turn to **tokenism.** That is, they make a token gesture (do a very little of what is required) and then shout about it as loudly as they can.

On 31 May 1970, an earthquake in Peru killed about 50,000 people, and left an emergency of major proportions in its wake. (That many people have probably not been killed in the United States in all the earthquakes, hurricanes, and tornados in our history.) Relief aid was desperately needed by the Peruvians. The American response was a trip to Peru by Mrs. Nixon (widely publicized—a picture of Mrs. Nixon hugging a little earthquake victim appeared on page one in many newspapers around the country). But very little effective aid ever reached Peru from the United States.[7] Clearly, our hearts were not really in the relief venture: the American effort was only a token gesture designed to pacify the few in the United States who wanted to aid the Peruvians.

The American relief efforts in Biafra, both during and after the Nigerian war, also exhibited this kind of tokenism. In this case, the American government (under both Johnson and Nixon) seemed perfectly willing to relieve the mass starvation in Biafra, but not against Nigerian government objections. So our government did the "natural" thing and gave token aid to church groups,

---

[6] See Seymour M. Hersh, *My Lai 4: A Report on the Massacre and Its Aftermath* (New York: Random House, 1970), pp. 151–52.

[7] See Roger Glass, *New Republic,* 19 September 1970.

the Red Cross, and UNICEF, the agencies attempting to get food into block-aded Biafra.[8]

The fallacy involved in *tokenism* is mistaking a token gesture for the genuine article. Judging from the lack of complaints from Americans after Mrs. Nixon's visit to Peru, it is reasonable to assume a great many Americans committed the fallacy of *tokenism* at that time.

Doonesbury Copyright, 1973, G. B. Trudeau. Used by permission of Universal Press Syndicate. All rights reserved.

Tokenism. *Note that Clint equates his notion of half-way with fairness.*

---

[8] The fact that this token American aid did save thousands of lives, even if only temporarily, is irrelevant to the charge of *tokenism,* in view of the grisly grand total of over 1 million deaths by starvation.

Professional politicians are not the only ones who attempt to mislead via *tokenism*. Ralph Nader has pointed out that Consolidated Edison of New York paid its board chairman more in one year than it spent on pollution control in five (this was roughly during the period 1965–1970). At the same time, General Motors spent about ten times more on advertising per year than it did on pollution research. Its pollution research budget was about 0.1 percent of its gross annual sales.

The token nature of big business and government actions frequently is masked in large-sounding figures. Average Americans cannot hope to earn a million dollars in an entire lifetime. So when we hear that a large corporation will spend $20,000,000 on antipollution efforts, we are impressed with the apparent size of the venture. We may not notice that the amount is to be spent over a period of years. And we forget, if we ever knew, that the corporation has yearly sales in the billions, and spends millions per year just on its corporate image. (Indeed, much spending on pollution during the period 1968–1979 looked suspiciously like image-building, given the immense fanfare that accompanied each project and the widespread use of antipollution themes in institutional advertising.) Average Americans forget also that the federal government's budget now is measured in hundreds of billions of dollars per year.

It's in the icing

Names Change but Tokenism Never Does

Procter & Gamble is making an all-out effort to eliminate sexist language from company reports and job titles. The firm is focusing its attention on a cake plant being built near Jackson, Tenn. There, "manpower curves" have become "effort curves," "man-hours" are now "effort hours" and "he"—"he/she."

Craftsmen became artisans but that term left the plant's building contractor speechless. Now they're crafters. Other terms have been harder to replace: Foremen are now called first-line supervisors, but they've yet to come up with a suitable replacement for journeyman.

As could be expected, the new terminology is not being taken too seriously by the people actually building the plant. And why should it be? Of the 340 wage earners at the cake factory, only five are women.

—*New Times*, 2 October 1978. © 1978 by New Times Publishing Co. Reprinted by permission.

Corporate tokenism on the women's rights front.

4.   *Hasty Conclusion*

In many textbooks, the fallacies about to be discussed are set apart from those just dealt with and are characterized as **inductive fallacies.** But this standard practice is not very useful. Almost all of the fallacies discussed in this text, including *slippery slope, ad hominem,* and *appeal to authority,* are primarily inductive fallacies; it is rare in daily life to claim deductive certitude for the conclusion of a disputed argument.

The fallacy of **hasty conclusion** is generally described as the use of an argument which presents evidence relevant to its conclusion, but insufficient by itself to warrant acceptance of that conclusion.

A news story on a local flurry of flag-stealing quoted a local citizen:[9]

They took both the flag and the pole. This just thoroughly demonstrates the lack of law and order.

But all by itself, it doesn't. In the best of times there will always be some lawbreaking, especially of this minor variety. The evidence *is* relevant, and more like it might establish the conclusion. But taken alone, it cannot possibly do so.

Now listen to Senator Mike Mansfield, Democrat from Montana, trying, in 1970, to pin the recession label onto the economy:

. . . the country is mired in inflation, unemployment, and war, and . . . whether the term is used or not, these words spell recession.

What he meant was that these conditions *prove* the existence of a recession. But they don't, although rising unemployment is good evidence of a recession. (War, in fact, is indirect evidence, although surely not proof, that an economy is not in recession, since most recent wars have been accompanied by an expanding economy.)

5.   *Questionable Classification*

Hasty conclusion overlaps another fallacy we might call **questionable classification,** or **false classification.** This fallacy occurs when we classify something incorrectly, given the evidence we have or could have. For instance, Senator Mansfield's classification of the 1969–1970 business slowdown as a recession was a questionable one, since the evidence he presented didn't prove the slowdown warranted that label.

Robert Waters reported in one of his newspaper columns that the U.S. Chamber of Commerce had classified 152 U.S. congressmen as "big spenders" because each of them had voted to override President Nixon's vetoes of four

---

[9] *New Britain* (Conn.) *Herald,* October 1970.

bills he had labeled "excessive spending bills."[10] The four bills, for domestic matters, appropriated a total of about 2.5 billion dollars more than the 40.5 billion Nixon had asked for.

But the chamber's classification of these congressmen as "big spenders" was a bit hasty. Many of them had attempted to reduce expenditures for other matters, such as the outer space program, the SST, and ABM, as well as many other military programs. So they weren't necessarily big spenders. They might more accurately have been classified as people who wanted to spend money *differently* than did the Nixon administration. But it would have been politically unproductive to brand them as *spend-it-differently* men, while it was politically expedient to brand them as *big spenders*.

The program of NOW (National Organization for Women—a women's rights group) once included in its list of recommendations for securing equality of the sexes the proposal that facilities be established to rehabilitate and train divorced *women*. They further recommended that the ex-husbands in question, if financially able, should pay for the education of divorced *women*.

But stated this way, their recommendation exhibited *questionable classification* (to say nothing of female chauvinism). The group in need of rehabilitation clearly was not divorced women, but divorced *persons*, or better yet divorced *homemakers*. For if a man happened to be the partner who took care of the home while his wife earned the bread, surely he would be entitled to help in the event of a divorce just as a women would in the same situation. Of all groups, NOW, with its concern for equality between the sexes, should not have classified the needy group as divorced *women*.

This is a particularly interesting example of *questionable classification* because the correct and incorrect classes (divorced homemakers and divorced women) are close to being identical in membership. There are relatively few divorced males in the United States who fit the classification divorced homemaker. Close overlap of this kind is frequent when the fallacy of *questionable classification* occurs, and is a major reason why this fallacy is so common.

But it also is a major reason why avoiding questionable classifications is so important. In some areas of the United States, the overwhelming majority of "deprived children" (whatever that means) are nonwhite (whatever *that* means). Deprived children, as a group, do less well in school than nondeprived children. Hence, nonwhites do less well than whites. But to classify backward students as nonwhites leads naturally to the conclusion that their being nonwhite is the *cause* of their backwardness. And we are all familiar with the way in which this conclusion has been used to defend racial prejudice and segregation in the United States.

6.   *Questionable Cause*

We are guilty of the fallacy of the **questionable cause,** or **false cause,** if we label a given thing as the cause of something else on the basis of insufficient or inappropriate evidence.

---

[10] Robert Waters, "Washington Scene," *Hartford Courant,* 3 September 1970.

The fallacy of *questionable classification* frequently entails *questionable cause*, because we classify partly in order to determine causes. As just stated, once we classify slow learners as mostly nonwhite, it is easy to take the next step and conclude that their being nonwhite is the *cause* of their being slow learners. But even in cases where the *classification* is correct, it does not follow that we have discovered a causal connection; the connection we have discovered may be *accidental*.

Here is an example from the logic-textbook-writer's friend, Spiro Agnew. He was speaking of Lawrence O'Brien, then Democratic Party Chairman who had been Postmaster General under Lyndon Johnson and then became president of a Wall Street brokerage firm after Johnson left office.[11]

> Under his [O'Brien's] adroit management, the firm collapsed, and it is presently being liquidated. Isn't that a splendid credential for a man who would advise the president of his country on economics?

The implication of Agnew's comment is that O'Brien's lack of ability caused the brokerage firm to collapse. Now there is no doubt that the classification is correct; O'Brien does belong in the unenviable class of those who have presided over a business firm as it went under. The question is whether this proves that he was unreliable on economic theory or even as a businessman. In other words, the question is whether the firm went under because he lacked business ability.

And put this way, the answer is obvious; the conclusion is much too hasty. There are many cases of financial disaster presided over by first-rate business people who have at other times proved their business acumen. The Edsel was one of the biggest financial disasters in American business history. But it would be foolish to conclude from its failure that Henry Ford II, the man who rescued the Ford Motor Company from the brink of disaster after World War II and increased Ford's share of the highly competitive automobile market, didn't know how to run a business.

In addition, Agnew was guilty of the fallacy of *suppressed evidence* (to be discussed in the next chapter). O'Brien's firm went under at a time when brokerage firms as a group suffered great losses. His was by no means the only firm that was forced to liquidate. (Indeed, it is ironic that Agnew should have mentioned the matter, since it was commonly charged at the time that Wall Street's losses were the result of economic measures President Nixon instituted to cure the inflation problem.)

Here is another *Newsweek* example of the fallacy of *questionable cause*.[12] *Newsweek* asks concerning the My Lai massacre:

> . . . should the G.I.'s be punished for, in effect, *trying too hard*—by gunning down civilians in a village long sympathetic to the Viet Cong?

---

[11] Reported in *Newsweek,* 31 August 1970.
[12] *Newsweek,* 31 August 1970.

But is it reasonable to say that the *cause* of the massacre was too great effort on the part of the soldiers in question? Firsthand accounts of the massacre contradict such a simplistic view.[13]

Statistical Versions

Statistical fallacies are not discussed until Chapter Five, but let's anticipate a bit and consider one statistical version of the fallacy of *questionable cause*.[14] Dr. K. S. Sitaram, a University of Hawaii mass media researcher, claims that television programs displaying a great deal of violence may *cause* reckless and irresponsible driving. He drew his conclusion after interviewing 293 "bad" drivers (convicted of traffic violations) and 54 "good" drivers, and comparing their tastes in television programs.

But even if bad drivers watch more television violence, this doesn't prove that watching television *causes* bad driving. It may be, for instance, that poor driving and a tendency to watch television violence both are caused by some third element, such as a desire for excitement, so that, say, forbidding bad drivers from watching television violence would have no effect whatever on their driving habits.

Ninety percent of our breakfast cereal comes from Kellogg, General Mills, Quaker Oats or General Foods; it is they who have decided that breakfast cereal and sugar are almost inseparable.

—Jeffrey Schrank, *Snap, Crackle, and Popular Taste* (New York: Delacorte, 1977)

Yes and no. The big four does sell most of our breakfast cereal, but what they decide to sell depends to a great extent on another factor, namely, what sells best to consumers, *who are the ultimate deciders on this matter—witness the many brands of nonsugary cereals on the market, none of which are big sellers. That the big cereal manufacturers are the cause of so much sugar in cereals is thus, to say the least, a case of* questionable cause.

---

7. *Questionable Analogy*

We reason by analogy (as described in Chapter One) for much the same reason that we classify and assign causes, namely to understand and control ourselves and our environment. (In fact, analogical reasoning is a common way in which we reason to causes.)

---

[13] Those who have read no firsthand accounts of the incident will have to rely on the word of this book's author of that of the *Newsweek* writer. Whether in doing so the reader commits the fallacy of *appeal to authority*, given the availability in book form of such testimony, is a question best left to the reader.

[14] *Houston Chronicle*, 18 May 1972.

But analogical reasoning can go wrong, and when it does, the result is the fallacy of **questionable analogy,** or **false analogy.**

A high-fashion hairdresser, Marc Decoster, complained that some of his customers tried to save money by shampooing their own hair before getting a DeCoster set:[17]

> Some are trying to wash their hair at home and then ask why I charge them for a shampoo. So I ask them, *do you bring your own salad to the restaurant?*

Spelled out, DeCoster's analogy is this: Washing your hair at home before getting it set at the beauty parlor is like bringing your own salad to a restaurant before eating their roast beef. It would be wrong to bring your salad to the restaurant, so it's wrong to shampoo your hair first at home. Therefore, claims DeCoster, it's not unfair to charge for the shampoo he doesn't give you, when he does give you a set.

But DeCoster's analogy is not apt. Shampooing your hair at home before going to the hairdresser is more like eating your own salad *at home* before going to the restaurant than it is like bringing your own salad to the restaurant to eat there before eating their roast beef. The two cases he considers thus differ in a relevant way. So the analogy fails.

If we have to teach the Bible account of the creation along with evolution theory, we ought to have to teach the stork theory of creation along with biological theory.

—Response to a demand that the Bible account of creation get equal time with evolution theory in biology classes

---

This is a typical case in which our opinion about whether the fallacy of questionable analogy has been committed depends almost entirely on our world view. Those whose religious convictions lead them to a literal acceptance of the Bible will tend to find this analogy questionable; others will tend to find it apt.

Faulty Comparison

The fallacy called **faulty comparison** (discussed more fully in its statistical form in Chapter Five) is an overlapping neighbor of *questionable analogy.*

A *3-in-1* Oil television commercial pictured a saw oiled with *3-in-1* Oil outperforming an unoiled saw—the intended conclusion being that you should use *3-in-1* Oil on your saws. But the comparison was faulty. It should

---

[15] *New York Times*, 12 December 1971, p. 57.

have shown a saw oiled with *3-in-1* outperforming a saw oiled with some other standard oil brand. Otherwise, all it proves is that oiled saws work better than unoiled ones, not that saws oiled with *3-in-1* Oil work better than those oiled with a competing product. So their faulty comparison gave no "reasons why" you should use their brand rather than another.

Analogy: *Questionable?*

Summary of Fallacies Discussed in Chapter Three

1. *Ad hominem argument.* Attacking the arguer rather than the argument.
   genetic fallacy.
   Example: Senator Randolph dismissing women's liberationists as "a small band of bra-less bubbleheads."

   a. *Guilt by association.* Unfairly judging people by the company they keep or are alleged to keep, or by what their associates say.

   Example: Judging an associate of foreign spies to therefore also be a spy for a foreign country.

2. *Provincialism.* Assuming that the familiar, the close, or what is one's own is *therefore* the better or more important. Also, the failure to look beyond one's own group, in particular to the ideas of other cultures.

Example: The far greater coverage in the United States of American space efforts than of Russian efforts.

a. *Loyalty.* Deciding the truth of an assertion on the basis of loyalty.

   Example: Refusal to believe the overwhelming evidence that U.S. soldiers had shot and killed defenseless women, children, and babies at My Lai 4 in South Vietnam.

3. *Tokenism.* Mistaking a token gesture, usually ineffective, for an adequate effort.

   Example: Accepting General Motors spending of 0.1 percent of its gross annual sales on air pollution research as a genuine effort at pollution control.

4. *Hasty conclusion.* Use of relevant but insufficient evidence to reach a conclusion.

   Example: A newspaper's claim that the theft of a flag and a flagpole "thoroughly" demonstrated a lack of law and order.

5. *Questionable classification.* The incorrect classification of something, given available evidence.

   Example: The classification of those congressmen who voted to override the president's veto of some domestic spending programs as "big spenders," although many of these same congressmen had sought to reduce military expenditures.

6. *Questionable cause.* Labeling something as the cause of something else on insufficient evidence, or contrary to available evidence.

   Example: A magazine's suggestion that Vietnamese civilians were massacred by American soldiers because the soldiers were "trying too hard."

7. *Questionable analogy.* Use of analogy where the cases seem relevantly different.

   Example: DeCoster's analogy between customers washing their own hair at home before going to the beauty parlor and diners bringing their own salad to the restaurant to eat before ordering roast beef, questionable because it would be more like eating salad at home before coming to the restaurant just for the roast beef.

Exercise I for Chapter Three

Determine which fallacies (if any) occur in the following passages, and state the reasons for your answers, following the instructions given for Exercise I of Chapter Two.

1. *Pentagon logic, from* The Progressive *magazine:* Defense Secretary Harold Brown, commenting on the failure of two submarine test firings of the Tomahawk cruise missile: "Failure in the past increases the probability of success in the future." *questionable analogy*

2. *John F. Keenan, New York Off Track Betting Corporation chairman, responding to a question about whether licensed gambling casinos would cut into OTB revenue,* Washington Monthly, *August 1979:* Big business thrives on competition. When night baseball came, they didn't stop sex. *questionable analogy.*

*3. Hartford Courant, *Sunday Parade, 20 August 1972:* [There was] a judge in Salisbury, Rhodesia, who had never driven a car. Someone in his court wanted to know how [he] could rule on motor accidents without first-hand knowledge of driving. "It's really no handicap," the magistrate explained. "I also try rape cases." *questionable analogy*

4. Baltimore Sun, *24 August 1976:* "Jimmy Carter says he'll never lie," [Senator Howard] Baker [R., Tennessee] noted, but he is "the nominee of the party which created more than 1,000 new federal programs and planned them so poorly that they made Washington sound like a dirty word." *questionable classification, or guilt by association.*

5. *Comment in the* Skeptical Inquirer, *Winter 1978, on astronaut Gordon Cooper's belief that some UFO's are space ships from outer space:* What does Cooper do, now that he is no longer with NASA? He is currently employed, appropriately enough, by Walt Disney Enterprises. *guilt by association*

*6. *Adelle Davis, in* Let's Eat Right and Keep Fit: Namecalling, derogatory articles, and adverse propaganda are other methods used to belittle persons refusing to recommend refined goods. We have long been called crackpots and faddists regardless of training or of accuracy in reporting research. The words "quacks" and "quackery" are now such current favorites that you can be fairly sure that anyone using them is receiving benefits from the food processors. *ad hominem argument*

7. *Henry J. Taylor,* Topeka (Kans.) Daily Capital, *July 1970:* . . . The great Declaration of Independence begins: "When in the course of human events . . ." and for the first time in man's history announced that all rights came from a sovereign, not from a government, but from God. . . . *loyalty.*

8. *Letter in the* Huntsville (Texas) Item, *September 27, 1974:* The Chamber [of Commerce] proposes taxing occupancy of the hotels to build occupancy [by advertising for tourists]. If the city adopts this policy, then it should tax bank deposits and use the proceeds to advertise for more bank depositors; it should tax professors' salaries and use the proceeds to try to attract more students; it should tax retail sales and use the proceeds to advertise for more shoppers. *questionable analogy.*

9. *Recreated private conversation:*
Howard: You mean you take this Horoscope business seriously?

Aunt: Yes, of course. Don't you see how today's horoscope fit you to a T?
Howard: Yes, but . . .
Aunt: No buts. There must be something to it. *Hasty conclusion.*

10. *Item from* The Progressive *magazine:* New York State Senator James H. Donovan cited the Crucifixion as a rationale for capital punishment: "Where would Christianity be," he asked, "if Jesus got eight to fifteen years, with time off for good behavior?"

11. *Allan Grant, president of the American Farm Bureau Federation,* Houston Post, *5 October 1976, lamenting the forced resignation of Secretary of Agriculture Earl Butz for telling offensive ethnic jokes:* It's unfortunate and it shouldn't have been said, but most people are guilty of telling ethnic jokes at one time or another. *common practice*

12. *Old puzzle favorite:* To demonstrate the superior quality of his paint, a salesman painted a patch on one side of a farmer's barn with his paint and a patch on another side with a competitor's product. A year later, his paint showed no significant wear, while the other paint had faded and begun to crack. Convinced, the farmer ordered several gallons of the salesman's paint. (We're supposed to figure out how the salesman tricked the farmer.) *question involves, faulty comparison*

*13. *Start of letter from Anita Bryant Ministries arguing for harsh laws against homosexuals:* "When the homosexuals burn the Holy Bible in public . . . how can I stand by silently?" Dear Friend: I don't hate the homosexuals. But as a mother, I must protect my children from their evil influence. . . . *questionable classification*

14. The universe, like a watch, must have a maker. *question analogy.*

*15. Libertarian Review *writer Henry Louis, February 1979, quoting the following scene from an NBC documentary "Reading, Writing, and Reefers," 10 December 1978:*
Edwin Newman: Lisa is 15 now, but she has been smoking marijuana for a long time.
Question: When did you start smoking regularly?
Answer: In the eighth grade.
Question: How much did you smoke?
Answer: About four or five joints a day.
Question: How long have you been smoking four or five joints a day?
Answer: Three years.
Question: What effects did it have on you?
Answer: I liked the high.

Louis constructed the following analogy to express his disagreement with the angry antimarijuana response this scene generated:
Edwin Newman: Lisa is 15 now, but she has been drinking coffee for a long time.
Question: When did you start drinking coffee regularly?
Answer: In the eighth grade.

Question: How much did you drink?
Answer: About four or five cups a day.
Question: How long have you been drinking four or five cups a day?
Answer: Three years.
Question: What effect did it have on you?
Answer: I felt more energetic. *questionable analogy*

16. Hartford Courant, *11 July 1972, UPI story:* A study completed by four University of Rhode Island researchers shows vitamin E may be a key to the secret of youth. . . . The research team said the vitamin . . . may be at work normally in humans to prevent aging. Working with a group of experimental rats, the scientists learned animals deprived of vitamin E seem to age faster and even become senile. Dr. Harbrans Lal of URI said that although the aging process is still a mysterious event, an "interesting relationship" had been found in the rats between the lack of vitamin E and old age.

17. *From the* American Sociological Review, *October 1950:* One of woman's most natural attributes is the care of children. Since the ill and infirm resemble children in being physically weak and helpless as well as psychologically dependent and narcissistically repressed, women are also especially qualified to care for the sick.

*18. *W. A. Wallis and Harry V. Roberts in* Statistics: A New Approach: After the New Hampshire preferential primary in 1952, it was reported that Senator Taft, Ohio, had received a slightly higher percentage of the total vote in a group of 17 cities in which he had not campaigned personally than in a group of 15 cities in which he had. One newspaper jibed that "Senator Taft should have stayed at home." *questionable cause*

*19. *Presidential press conference, 1 July 1970:*
Questioner: Do you feel that in the modern world there are situations when a president must respond against a very tight deadline when he cannot consult with the legislative branch? [The question was general, but in context had specific reference to the "incursion" (invasion) into Cambodia, which was taken without first consulting Congress.]
President Nixon: Well, another good example, of course, is the Cuban missile crisis. President Kennedy had a very difficult decision there and two hours and a quarter before he ordered the use of American men to blockade Cuba, he told the Senate and Congressional leaders. I can assure the American people that this President is going to bend over backwards to consult the Senate and consult the House whenever he feels it can be done without jeopardizing the lives of American men. But when it's a question of the lives of American men, or the attitudes of people in the Senate, I'm coming down hard on the side of defending the lives of American men. *questionable analogy*

20. *Robert Sherrill,* Inquiry, *14 May 1979:* The myth of Franklin D. Roosevelt as the savior of a depressed nation has been pretty thoroughly debunked.

The welfare capitalism of his New Deal, his Keynesian orgy, has left us with a federal government dedicated to waste and corruption and corporate favoritism.

Exercise II for Chapter Three

Find several examples in the mass media (television, magazines, newspapers, radio) of fallacies discussed in Chapter Three, and explain carefully and fully why they are fallacious.

The Village Voice. Reprinted by permission of Edward Sorel.

O! Little Clown of Bethlehem

Complaining about the "commercialization of Christmas," Mike Douglas told his television audience: "Christmas has virtually lost its true religious significance. It's tragic to see the tradition of gift-giving perverted into nothing more than an excuse for stores to run sales." Oddly enough, one of the items on sale in stores this Christmas is Mr. Douglas's recording of "Happy Birthday, Jesus," written by Lee Pockriss and Estelle Levitt. Mr. Pockriss is perhaps best remembered for his "Itsy-Bitsy, Teeny-Weeny Yellow Polka Dot Bikini." In keeping with the Christmas spirit, Mr. Douglas has decided to keep all his royalties from the record.

—from "Daily News," *Village Voice,* 6 December 1977

Mike Douglas's fans don't want to think of him as just another money grubber. So he keeps them happy (fools them?) with a little inconsistency *between words and actions.*

Chapter Four

Fallacious Even If Valid

Arguments, like men, often are pretenders.
—Plato

No executive devotes much effort to proving himself wrong.
—[Laurence J.] Peter's Calculation

The fallacious arguments discussed in the previous two chapters all violated the requirement that cogent reasoning be *valid*. In this chapter, we'll look at some arguments that violate the other two requirements good reasoning must satisfy, and thus are *fallacious even if valid*.

1. Suppressed Evidence

We are guilty of the fallacy of **suppressed evidence** when we violate the requirement of cogent reasoning that our starting points (premises) contain as much as possible[1] of the relevant evidence at our disposal (in particular, not passing over or "forgetting" evidence contrary to what we want to believe). That is, we commit this fallacy when we fail to use relevant information that we should have thought of or known to look for. (Similarly, we argue fallaciously in this way when we suppress, conceal, or otherwise pass over relevant information.)

The United Way used to discourage donations earmarked for individual member charities but has given in to public pressure and now "honors designation" of a particular member charity. This sounds like progress, but it isn't; the suppressed evidence—what the United Way doesn't choose to tell us—is that it subtracts the amount so designated from the amount it would have given that charity anyway. So in fact there is no "designation" honored by the United Way. (Very charitable of them, too.)

As the competitive position of American industrial goods declined during the 1970s, some economic "experts" attributed this decline primarily to rapidly rising gas and oil prices. But this could not possibly have been an important reason for the decline, since America produces more of its own oil than any of its major industrial competitors, who, therefore, were even more at the mercy

---

[1] Up to the point of proof, of course. Every time we flick a switch and thus turn on a light, we have evidence relevant to the "theory" that copper conducts electricity. But with much better evidence having proved the point a long time ago, it would be silly to bother with such evidence now.

of OPEC blackmail than we were. (But didn't the experts in question know this? What does your world view tell you about this?)

Since most of us tend to suppress evidence when it suits our purposes, it's reasonable for us to suspect that others do so also and be on our guard against such practices. And we do need to be on our guard when dealing with rhetoric meant to persuade us. Several television commercials extolling the Shell gasoline ingredient Platformate illustrate this well. In these commercials the automobile using Shell with Platformate always obtained better mileage than autos using gasoline without this ingredient. What was the suppressed evidence? Simply that just about every standard brand of gasoline at the time contained Platformate or a similar ingredient. Thus, Shell pitted its gasoline against a decidedly inferior product most auto owners did not use. The viewer's attention was directed away from this fact by the way the claim was worded and also by the general presentation of the commercial.

Others May Take Advantage of Our Ignorance or Forgetfulness

Other people often trade on our ignorance of or forgetfulness about details in perpetrating the fallacy of *suppressed evidence*. (Those so taken in commit a fallacy only if they should have suspected that evidence was being suppressed.)

The 1969 American Bar Association House of Delegates came out against no-fault auto insurance in part because of:[2]

> the moral values which underlie the almost instinctive feeling that persons guilty of wrongful conduct . . . ought to be required to pay.

We should be on guard when experts argue on matters about which they have a large financial interest (like auto accident lawsuits). In this case, the ABA hoped we would forget that: (1) many accidents involve no moral or legal guilt (for example, accidents caused by mechanical defects or "acts of God"); and, more importantly, (2) the very point of automobile insurance is to spread the risk of accidents, so that the person who has the accident pays no more than anyone else (the insurance company pays, not the person who has the accident).

In early 1971, then Democrat John Connally, ex-governor of oil-rich Texas, testified before the U.S. Senate Finance Committee concerning his nomination as Secretary of the Treasury. He testified that the allegations of his "vast wealth" in oil and gas were false and that his total wealth in oil and gas was $7,240. But when the *New York Times* revealed that Connally had received money from the Richardson Foundation (set up by the late Texas oil millionaire Sid Richardson), Connally admitted he had been paid $750,000 by the Richardson Foundation for services rendered to Richardson's estate.[3]

---

[2] "The ABA: The Rhetoric Has Changed but the Morality Lingers On," *Washington Monthly*, January 1974, p. 23.

[3] For more details, see the *New Republic*, 13 February 1971.

This example illustrates how a person may attempt to conceal evidence while not actually lying. Connally's original testimony conveyed the impression that he had not profited from his proximity to vast oil wealth. And he managed to convey that impression without committing what is politely called an "error of commission" (that is, he did not actually lie). But his suppression of the very kind of information that he knew his questioners were looking for did amount to an "error of *omission*" (that is, he did mislead by omitting information he knew the Committee was seeking).

In cases where inconclusive evidence or reasons are given to us when it would be reasonable to expect something more conclusive—for instance, when some easily obtained fact necessary to prove a point is omitted from an argument—we should suspect that the arguer didn't provide us with the information because he didn't have it (or perhaps, worse, knew it to be false). The question we should ask is why that relevant fact hasn't been given to us.

When the *New York Times* settled a sex discrimination suit for $350,000 (plus promises to hire more women), it tried to reduce its guilt by pointing out that the $350,000 was less than female employees at the *Readers Digest* and NBC received from their suits. But before we can accept this conclusion, we need to know whether there are as many women employed by the *Times* as by these other corporations, so as to calculate average compensation. Since the *Times* didn't provide this needed information, we should suspect that negative evidence was suppressed and therefore not accept their conclusion that they discriminated less. (This turned out to be a suspicion confirmed: in fact, *New York Times* women received more per person than the women at the other organizations, which certainly does not support the *Times* in its claim to have discriminated less.)

Finally, here is H. R. Haldeman, assistant to President Nixon, arguing that President Nixon was *not* isolated from public opinion during the demonstrations in Washington against the 1970 American "incursion" into Cambodia:[4]

. . . President Nixon himself went to the Lincoln Memorial at sunrise on Saturday, May 9, to talk with young people who had come to Washington for that day's demonstrations.

Haldeman conveyed the impression that the president and the "young people" had had a heart-to-heart talk about Cambodia, Vietnam, and foreign policy. But no. The (suppressed) fact is that the President (in what might be called his "Lincoln Memorial Caper") talked mostly about football and surfing.

---

[4] At UCLA, 9 September 1970. Quoted in UCLA *Benchmarks*, Summer 1970. Even if the event had happened precisely as depicted by Haldeman, it still would have amounted just to *tokenism*.

2. *Questionable Premise*

We are guilty of the fallacy **questionable premise** when we violate the requirement of cogent reasoning that we use only warranted premises. (Of course, what a given person finds warranted depends on that person's background information and world view.)

To become a pro at spotting questionable premises, we have to overcome certain natural tendencies and beliefs. Recall the misplaced faith many Americans had—almost to the end—that President Nixon did not take part in the Watergate coverup.[5] Why did they believe this in the face of increasingly strong evidence that he was lying? The answer spotlights several of the natural tendencies we need to hold in check.

In the first place, we all are strongly moved to accept the official "myths" about our own society. And one of those myths is that our leaders, in particular our presidents, do not lie to us (the point of the George Washington cherry tree myth), except perhaps for very high minded reasons (for instance, to keep vital secrets from the enemy). Good thinkers go beyond official myths to formulate more accurate theories as to how their societies function.

Second, when we're young, most of us accept our parents as genuine authorities, perhaps even the best authorities (when we're kids, *we* obviously don't know enough to survive—without their knowledge). Other authority figures, such as religious ministers and especially leaders of nations, receive some of that parental aura by virtue of their positions of authority. Good thinkers learn from experience that authority figures come in all shapes, sizes, and qualitites—our parents and leaders may be brilliant people of sterling integrity, but then again they may not. (Nixon, obviously, was not a leader of sterling integrity.)

Third, our feelings get bound up with issues and personalities, making it hard for us to be objective. (Gamblers know, for instance, that in a stadium sports crowd better odds can be obtained betting *against* the home team.) Thus, the feelings of those who voted for Nixon became bound up with his innocence. It's hard after all, to admit we voted for a liar. Good thinkers learn to give up discredited opinions.

Fourth, we tend to deceive ourselves in ways that favor our own narrow interests. Nixon, like any president, favored certain social and economic interests over others. Selfish desire led some people who had those interests to deceive themselves into believing in his innocence. Those who reason well don't let selfish desires influence their perception of reality.

Fifth, we tend to hang on to beliefs out of tenacity or loyalty, even in the face of contrary evidence. Some diehard Nixon supporters didn't want to become "quitters" or "fair weather friends," and thus believed the president

---

[5]Their fallacy was *questionable premise* because the conclusion Nixon wanted us to draw was that he shouldn't be forced out of office. (Premise: I'm innocent. Conclusion: Don't fire me.) In everyday life, however, it's often difficult to tell premises from conclusions—an argument should be questioned if it contains a questionable *statement*, whether or not we can figure out that it was a premise rather than a conclusion.

long after overwhelming evidence of his guilt was available. Loyalty is a wonderful human trait, but not for finding out the truth about things.

And, finally, most of us simply aren't trained in the art of critical thinking, in particular, in the knack of dredging up from memory old information relevant to current issues. Nixon should have been doubted on Watergate because of his past record (think only of the lies he told in campaigning against, say, Helen Gahagen Douglas in 1950); but even among those Americans who once knew this, there was a tendency to let the past rest. This tendency is the reason why, for instance, a sitting president can campaign for reelection on a platform contradictory to the one on which he originally was elected.

Questionable Facts and Questionable Evaluations

The premises of an argument of an alleged fact may be questionable because it is unknowable in principle (the number of snowflakes that fell in Chicago in the blizzard of '79 is an example) or because it is not known to the speaker in question, even though others may know it. Here is an example of the latter from a Tom Hayden article (*Ramparts*, September 1970) written before his Jane Fonda–California political period:

> Nixon's promise to withdraw from Cambodia did have a temporary cooling effect, but it also blew away many lingering illusions about peace in Asia. The government had served notice to all but the most blind that its intention was to win the war through escalation—even with nuclear weapons, if necessary.

Obviously Mr. Hayden, of all people, was not privy to one of the most intimate secrets of the Nixon administration (whether that administration would or would not use nuclear weapons). He thus stated something as a fact which he could not possibly have known.

An evaluation should be questioned for the same reason we question an alleged fact: lack of an adequate reason for accepting it, in particular, failure of the speaker or writer to provide such a reason. Listen to *Time* magazine (13 July 1970) reporting on the charge made by the National Association for the Advancement of Colored People (NAACP) that the Nixon administration had adopted a ". . . calculated policy to work against the needs and aspirations of the largest minority of its citizens":

> One *accurate* assessment of the controversy was offered by former Attorney General Ramsey Clark, who told the NAACP convention that he "hated to believe" that the Administration was anti-black. "It's not that they are aginners," he said, "but rather they are do-nothingers. They are guilty of neglect, not malice."

Time furnished no evidence for its judgment that Mr. Clark's evaluation was "accurate." Yet the question of its accuracy was of great importance at the time in evaluating the Nixon administration on crucial racial issues. (This quotation is interesting because it illustrates how one word—the word "accurate"—can be used to slant the viewpoint of a whole article and put the reader into a frame of mind receptive to the writer's message. The fact that only one word was used to do the job makes it all the harder to detect the fallacy.)

Some "hardnosed" people have the idea that all evaluations are questionable—that we should always "stick to the facts." But this is nonsense. We must evaluate! Otherwise, we could never use our knowledge as a guide to action, since acting rationally requires acting to accomplish goals, chosen—if we're rational—to obtained valued consequences. No. The fallacy is rather to accept an evaluation without sufficient reason, either of our own or provided by the speaker or writer.

3. Straw Man

One of the important variations of *questionable premise* is the fallacy **straw man**.[6] We are guilty of this fallacy when we misrepresent an opponent's position to make it easier to attack, or attack a weaker opponent or position while ignoring a stronger one.

Politicians running for office frequently use this fallacy, Richard Nixon being a good example. He used *straw man* (along with *ad hominem* argument and another version of *questionable premise*—namely, *false dilemma,* to be discussed soon) as the cornerstone of his rhetorical style in every campaign he waged. In 1950, when he ran for the Senate against Congresswoman Helen Gahagen Douglas, Nixon's speeches and political ads were full of *ad hominem* and *straw man* arguments. Here is an example from a political ad:[7]

> The real import of the contest between Mr. Nixon and Helen Gahagen Douglas is whether America shall continue to tolerate COMMUNIST CONSPIRACIES within our own borders and Government, persist in condoning BUREAUCRATIC PROFLIGACY and appeasing TOTALI-TARIAN AGGRESSION, or whether America shall victoriously resist these deadly dangers.

The later Nixon played down communism in distorting his opponents' positions, preferring instead to associate them in the public eye with the views of "radical liberals," hippies, the youth counterculture, and militant left-wing groups like the Weather Underground. Here is an example from his acceptance speech at the 1972 Republican Convention:

> Let me illustrate the difference in our philosophies. Because of our free economic system, what we have done is build a great building of econo-

---

[6] Should a time-honored name such as this one be replaced by, say, *straw person*, on grounds of reforming sexist features of language? Is the name *straw man* derogatory to women?

[7] For more on early Nixon campaign rhetoric, see the October 1973 article on Helen Gahagen Douglas in *MS* magazine, and the book *The Strange Case of Richard Milhous Nixon* (New York: Popular Library, 1973) by former Congressman Jerry Voorhis, Nixon's opponent in 1946.

mic wealth and might in America. It is by far the tallest building in the world, and we are still adding to it. Now, because some of the windows are broken, they say tear it down and start again. We say, replace the windows and keep building. That's the difference.

The "they" was the radical left; Nixon wanted voters to think the position of his opponent, George McGovern, was just like that of the radical left, because Nixon's version of the radical left position was so easy to caricature and then attack. Nixon rarely mentioned the specifics either of McGovern's program or actual record. The straw McGovern was, after all, such an inviting target.

Why are *ad hominem* argument and *straw man* so powerful in the hands of a skilled practitioner like Richard Nixon? One reason is that voters rarely do the small amount of work necessary to discover that the position attacked is a straw one—a distortion of the position actually held. Those who fail to follow through on the facts are condemned to be easy marks for the clever politicans who hawk *straw man* and other fallacies as their stock in trade.

From a May 1979 *Atlantic* magazine article by Walter Berns arguing against the Equal Rights Amendment (ERA):

A twenty-seventh amendment, which would provide full representation in the House and Senate for Washington, D.C., is defended on grounds that to oppose it is racist. And now the twenty-eighth, or Equal Rights Amendment, is recommended to recalcitrant states on the basis that to resist it will invite economic reprisals [against states that did not ratify the amendment].

The fallacy straw man *is committed not just when conclusions are distorted but also when reasons for espousing those conclusions are mangled. Failing to achieve passage of the Equal Rights Amendment on the basis of fairness or justice, their reasons for championing ERA, equal rights advocates tried economic force to push hesitant states into ratifying ERA (considerations of fairness rarely are sufficient alone to bring about social change). But there is a great deal of difference between the reasons a person gives in the sense of justifications for holding a view and reasons in the sense of motivators to action. Analogy: A mother might tell her daughter to clean up her room because it's fair for everyone to pitch in and do part of the work but, when that fails, tell the child that if she doesn't clean up her room she'll have to stay in it all evening and miss her favorite television programs.*

Exaggeration

The fallacy of the *straw man* is perpetrated by distorting the argument of one's opponent and then attacking that distorted version. However, distortion itself is not necessarily bad or fallacious. In the form of *exaggeration,* for instance, it is a time-honored literary device used by most great writers for satirical or poetic effect. Great satirists, such as Jonathan Swift, use exaggeration in order to shock people into seeing what they take to be man's true nature, and in an attempt to reduce that strange gap in most of us between mere belief and belief that serves as an impetus to action.

So exaggeration in itself is not fallacious. The purpose of the exaggeration determines whether or not a fallacy is committed. A satirist who exaggerates the evil in human nature doesn't intend us to believe that human beings are as bad as he portrays them. He exaggerates to help us realize the actual extent of human evil. But when his intent is to make us believe that the exaggeration is literally true, then the **exaggeration** version of the fallacy *straw man* enters into the picture.

Exaggeration can be accomplished easily, with a single word or a short phrase, so it often slips by unnoticed. Here is an example.[8]

> Since the beginning of a *massive* airlift on January 23, the United States has flown 113 jeeps and trucks to Nigeria.

The airlift was intended to help overcome the truly massive starvation following the collapse of the Biafran attempt to gain independence from Nigeria. Those threatened with starvation numbered in the millions. So the 113 airlifted jeeps and trucks could hardly be said to represent a massive airlift. (We flew more material into Berlin every day for several months during the 1948 Russian blockade of the ex-German capital.) The word "massive" was used to exaggerate the importance of what was in fact a miniscule effort to reduce Biafran deaths by starvation.

In the case of Richard Nixon, he got where he got by . . . dogged and intelligent perserverance: *ten million* town hall appearances for local candidates over a period of 20 years.

—William F. Buckley, Jr., *New York Post,* October 1974

We don't want to be foolishly strict in labeling items fallacious. Obviously, Buckley did not intend readers to take the ten million figure literally. So he is not guilty of the fallacy of exaggeration, *although he surely did exaggerate. He used exaggeration to impress on us that in 1972 Nixon made an unusually large number of appearances for local candidates, and in fact Nixon did do just that.*

---

4.   *False Dilemma*

Strictly speaking, the fallacy **false dilemma** (also called the **either-or-fallacy**) occurs when we reason or argue on the assumption that there are just

---

[8]*New York Times,* 15 February 1970, p. 10.

two plausible solutions to a problem or issue, when in fact there are at least three.[9] However, it's convenient to stretch the term *false dilemma* to cover *false trilemmas,* and so on.

Here is the lead-in blurb for an article "Society and Sex Roles" (*Human Nature,* April 1978):

Economics, not biology, may explain male domination.

This statement suggests that there are just two possibilities: either biology explains male dominance, or economic success does so. And it suggests that the second possibility, economic success, "may" (weasel word) be the true explanation of male domination. Yet there are many other possibilities, such as social custom, religious conviction, and various *combinations* of economic and biological factors. By tempting us to think of the cause of male domination as either economics or biology, the quote leads us to overlook other possibilities and thus to commit the fallacy of *false dilemma.*

Which brings to mind the familiar question whether it is differences in heredity or in environment (nature or nurture) that are responsible for individual differences in intelligence. Put as a question of heredity *or* environment, the problem becomes a *false dilemma,* because it should be clear by now that heredity and environment both shape intelligence. The sensible question to ask is not whether heredity or environment is responsible but rather how much effect each of these has on intelligence.

Arguments or statements posing *false dilemmas* often mask the fact that they contain a dilemma of any kind, so that noticing their fallaciousness takes watchfulness. Here is an example, a 1978 statement by Harvard President Derek Bok:

If you think education is expensive, try ignorance.

This has lots of truth to it, of course; some sort of education is certainly more valuable than no education at all. But Bok's statement, in particular because uttered by the president of Harvard, invites us to think that our choice is either formal education or ignorance. So it invites us to accept the *false dilemma* of either getting a formal education or remaining ignorant—omitting the alternative of *informal* education.

5.   Begging the Question

When arguing, it is impossible to provide reasons for every assertion. Some of what we say or do must go unjustified, at least for the moment. But if, in the course of a discussion or debate, we endorse without proof some form of the

---

[9]*False dilemma* is a species of *questionable premise* because any statement that sets up a *false* dilemma ought to be questioned.

very question at issue, we are guilty of the fallacy generally called **begging the question.**[10]

Political arguments frequently beg questions at issue. For example, in 1972, an expert in Massachusetts testified against legalizing abortion, arguing that abortion is wrong since a baby shouldn't have to suffer because of the selfish desires or the illness of the mother. By calling the fetus a *baby,* the arguer implicitly asserts that it is a human being—a hotly debated issue in the abortion controversy.

Questions are begged in different ways. One of the most common is to mask what is happening (perhaps from ourselves) by asserting the question to be begged in different words. Here is an example excerpted from a recent magazine interview:

BOOTH
Drawing by Booth; © 1975 The New Yorker Magazine, Inc.

"Having concluded, Your Highness, an exhaustive study of this nation's political, social, and economic history, and after examining, Sire, the unfortunate events leading to the present deplorable state of the realm, the consensus of the Council is that Your Majesty's only course, for the public good, must be to take the next step."

Question-begging *advice, following oracular rule number one: make pronouncements as vague as possible to minimize the chance of being wrong.*

---

[10] The fallacy *begging the question* falls into the category *fallacious even if valid* because arguments that beg the question can be cast into the form $p \therefore p$, or p and $q \therefore p$, both of which are valid. And it falls into the category *questionable premise* because a statement questionable as a conclusion is equally questionable as a premise.

Question: Why do you think Argentina will go socialist?
Answer: Because of the force of "world historical circumstances."

In other words, we're told that the circumstances in the world today that will lead Argentina to socialism are the historical circumstances in the world today that will lead Argentina to socialism.

Question-begging occurs frequently in disputes between partisans of extremely different positions. Thus, the rejoinder "But that amounts to socialism!" often is heard in disputes over public medical care, even though the other side is perfectly aware of this fact, and may even be attracted to the proposal precisely because it *is* socialistic. To avoid *begging the question,* the antisocialist must present *reasons* for rejecting anything that smacks of socialism.

Evading the Issue

A similar fallacy sometimes misdiagnosed as *begging the question,* is that of **evading the issue** altogether. One way to do this (whether on purpose in arguing or by accident in reasoning) is to *wander from the point* long enough to distract attention from the fact that the issue has been evaded. Another is to seem to address the issue while really just pussyfooting around it.

In 1978, when University of Maryland President John Toll vetoed the appointment of Professor Bertell Ollman, a Marxist, as chair of the College Park campus Department of Government and Politics, academic freedom became an explosive issue in that year's Maryland race for governor, the kind of issue smart candidates like to duck. The Republican candidate, J. Glenn Beall, did so by announcing, "It's not a political decision: it's a matter for the University President and the Board of Regents to decide." But his Democratic Party opponent, Harry Hughes, did him one better and came out with this evasive reply: "I strongly support the principle of academic freedom. If I were presented with such an appointment, I would discuss the subject with the University President, get fully briefed, before making any comment."

6. Inconsistency

The fallacy of **inconsistency** consists in arguing or reasoning from inconsistent (contradictory) premises. Obviously, if two premises contradict each other, one of them must be false. So even if the argument in which they occur is *valid,* we commit a fallacy in accepting its conclusion. (Similar remarks apply to the case in which we reason to inconsistent conclusions.)

Politicans are famous for being inconsistent, but their inconsistency usually is not overt, explicit, or even exact. Perhaps this is true because they rarely speak with enough precision to be 100 percent inconsistent. At any rate, they frequently are more or less inconsistent in several different ways. One way is to say one thing at a particular time and place and something quite different at another time and place (without either justifying the change or retracting the former statement).

Here is Senator Hiram Fong (Republican, Hawaii) supporting a 1970 Post Office reorganization bill.[11]

This bill will eliminate politics from the Post Office Department as we have seen it operate.

But in 1976, when questioned about his nomination of Hung Wai Ching, Hawaii Finance Committee Chairman for President Ford, to serve on the Postal Service board of governors, Fong talked out of the other side of the mouth: "That's politics. He's worked very hard for the [Republican] party."

Zigzaggers make touchdowns.
—Gerald Ford, answering a charge of being inconsistent, quoted in *New York Review of Books,* 16 October 1975.

President Ford answering a charge of inconsistency *with a* questionable analogy.

Politicians often are forced by circumstances to commit the fallacy of *inconsistency* when, by rising in office, they come to represent different constituencies with different viewpoints. Similarly, they often commit this fallacy in order to "keep up with the times"; what is popular at one time often is unpopular at another.

Lyndon Johnson's position on civil rights legislation illustrates both of these. As a congressman and for a while as a senator from Texas, he consistently voted and spoke *against* civil rights legislation. But when he became a power in the Senate his tune modified, and as president it changed completely. Here are two quotes that illustrate Johnson's fundamental *inconsistency over time* on the question of race and civil rights legislation. The first statement was made in 1948 at Austin, Texas, when he was running for the Senate:

This civil rights program [part of President Truman's "Fair Deal"], about which you have heard so much, is a farce and a sham—an effort to set up a police state in the guise of liberty. I am opposed to that program. I have fought it in Congress. *It is the province of the state to run its own elections.* I am opposed to the antilynching bill because the federal government has no more business enacting a law against one form of murder than another. I am against the FEPC [Fair Employment Practices Commission] because if a man can tell you whom you must hire, he can tell you whom you cannot employ.

---

[11] Quoted in the *Chicago Sun Times,* 14 August 1976.

But in 1964 Johnson was president of the United States. He had a larger constituency, and, equally important, the average American's views on race and civil rights were changing. In that year Congress passed an extremely important civil rights act *at his great urging*. And in 1965 he delivered a famous speech at the predominantly black Howard University, in which he said in part:

> . . . nothing in any country touches us more profoundly, and nothing is more freighted with meaning for our own destiny than the revolution of the Negro American.
>
> In far too many ways American Negroes have been another nation, deprived of freedom, crippled by hatred, the doors of opportunity closed to hope.
>
> In our time change has come to this nation, too. The American Negro, acting with impressive restraint, has peacefully protested and marched, entered the courtrooms and the seats of government, demanding a justice that has long been denied. The voice of the Negro was the call to action. But it is a tribute to America that, once aroused, the courts and the Congress, the President and most of the people, have been the allies of progress. . . . we have seen in 1957 and 1960, and again in 1964, the first civil rights legislation in this nation in almost an entire century.
>
> As majority leader of the United States Senate, I helped to guide two of these bills through the Senate. And as your president, I was proud to sign the third. And now, very soon *we will have the fourth—a new law guaranteeing every American the right to vote.*
>
> No act of my entire administration will give me greater satisfaction than the day when my signature makes this bill, too, the law of this land.

And on 6 August 1965, he did sign the Voting Rights Act into law. But he didn't explain why it was no longer ". . . the province of the state to run its own elections." He didn't explain his about-face on civil rights legislation.

Organizational Inconsistency

Large organizations such as governments generally have several different people who can "speak for" the organization. Perhaps we can think of an organization as being guilty of *inconsistency* when different authorized representatives—speaking for the organization—contradict each other, or where there is a contradiction between the organization's announced policies and its actual practices.

The executive branch of the United States then becomes guilty of the fallacy of *inconsistency* when the president says (or does) one thing while responsible representatives of his administration say (or do) another. Here are some examples.

At about the time President Johnson was stressing his policy against enlarging the Vietnam War, his Assistant Secretary of State, William P. Bundy, stated (on 18 June 1964):

We are going to drive the Communists out of South Vietnam even if that eventually involves a choice of attacking countries to the north. If Communist forces get the upper hand in Laos, the only response we would have would be to put our own forces in there.

Inconsistency Between Words and Actions

Another common variety of *inconsistency* is to *say* one thing but *do* something else. During the 1976 campaign, Jimmy Carter and his representatives kept assuring us that Carter would appoint "fresh talent" if elected. Here, for instance, is the then campaign manager Hamilton Jordon:

If we end up appointing people like Cyrus Vance and Zbignew Brzezinski, we will have failed.

So after winning election, Carter appointed Vance Secretary of State and Brzezinski head of the National Security Council. (His other appointments tended to be equally stale "fresh talent," like James Schlesinger as energy chief.)

When Gerald Ford, chosen by Richard Nixon as his successor, became the first unelected president, he assured the American people he would not run for president in 1976. But when the time came, he ran, an inconsistency between his words and actions that hardly caused a ripple.

During the hearings held before Ford's confirmation as vice president, he was asked: "If a president resigned his office before his term expired, would his successor have the power to prevent or to terminate any investigation or

© 1975 Jules Feiffer.

This Feiffer cartoon illustrates an inconsistency between our words and actions *in Chile. If we say we interfered in Chile at one time to "preserve opposition news media and political parties" then we ought to have been prepared to do so again in like circumstances. We weren't, leading Feiffer to conclude that our stated reasons were window dressing to conceal our real reasons. This is often the case where there is an inconsistency between words and actions, which is why spotting such inconsistency is so important.*

Humorous use of inconsistency between words and actions.

criminal prosecution charges against the former president?" His reply was: "I do not think the public would stand for it," a clear indication that he would not use such power. And then, eleven days before issuing the pardon, when asked if he intended to pardon Mr. Nixon, he replied that until legal procedures had been undertaken, ". . . I think it's unwise and untimely for me to make any commitment." In the absence of an explanation of his change of mind, it's clear that President Ford was guilty of the fallacy of *inconsistency* when he pardoned Richard Nixon.

Of course, high government officials are not the only ones whose words are inconsistent with their actions. Cigarette smokers who argue against legalizing marijuana on the grounds that marijuana is unhealthy are inconsistent in this way. And so are those women's liberationists who argue against different "roles" for each sex, yet play the feminine role when it's in their interest to do so (for instance, expecting men to pay on dates, drive on long trips, buy them expensive engagement rings, or spank errant children).

For a change of pace, let's look at a case of *inconsistency* from one of the fringes of science. In this book *The Lunar Effect: Biological Tides and Human Emotions* (Garden City, N.Y.: Doubleday, 1978), Arnold Lieber, M.D., implies (on page 16) that the effect of the moon's gravitational force on the earth (the "lunar effect") is obvious in terms of overt behavior (witness the fact, he says, that nearly everyone is aware that inmates of mental institutions act strangely during the full moon). But then he states (on page 18) that the lunar effect is so small that it requires a large sample to reveal, thus contradicting what he'd said two pages back.

This Peanuts comic strip illustrates another way in which we tend to be inconsistent. Linus is all for a generality (he loves humanity in general), but not the individual cases that fall under it (he doesn't love individual people).

7. False Charge of Fallacy

Let's now clear up an important point that may be bothering some readers. A person who makes a certain statement at one time and a contradictory statement later is not automatically guilty of the fallacy of *inconsistency*. That person may have rational grounds for a change of mind.

Take the person who argues, "I used to believe that women are not as creative as men, because most intellectually productive people have been men; but I've changed my mind because I believe now (as I didn't them) that *environment* (culture, surroundings), and not native ability, has been responsible for the preponderance of intellectual men." Surely, that person cannot be accused of *inconsistency*, since he (or she!) has explained the change of mind, as, say, Lyndon Johnson did not explain his switch on the race question.

Consider the charge that the philosopher Bertrand Russell was guilty of *inconsistency*. Soon after World War II, he advocated attacking the Soviet Union if the Russians failed to conform to certain standards, and yet in the 1950s he supported the "better Red than dead" position. Russell *would* have been guilty of *inconsistency* if he had not had, and stated, what he took to be good reasons for changing his mind about how to deal with the Russians. He felt, and stated, that Russian acquisition of the atomic bomb made all the difference in the world. Before they had the bomb, he believed it to be rational to deal with them in ways that became irrational after they had acquired such great power. Hence, Russell was not guilty of the fallacy of *inconsistency*.

On the contrary, it is his critics who are guilty of a fallacy, which we might as well call the **false charge of fallacy.** (Of course, falsely charging a person with *any* fallacy, not just *inconsistency*, makes one guilty of a *false charge of fallacy*.)

Exercise item from the second edition of a textbook on logic and contemporary rhetoric:

Newspaper Story: Thor Heyerdahl has done it again, crossing the Atlantic in a papyrus raft designed according to ancient Egyptian tomb carvings. Landing in the Western Hemisphere on the island of Barbados, he was greeted by the Barbados Prime Minister, Errol Barrow, who declared, "This has established Barbados was the first landing place for man in the Western World."

The correct answer was supposed to be hasty conclusion, *but a student from Barbados pointed out that the prime minister was known for his sense of humor. Another* false charge of fallacy.

Summary of Fallacies Discussed in Chapter Four

1. *Suppressed evidence.* The omission from an argument of known relevant evidence (or the failure to suspect that relevant evidence is being suppressed).

   Example: The failure of Shell Platformate commercials to indicate that most other standard brands of gasoline contain the ingredient Platformate.

2. *Questionable premise.* The use of questionable evidence to reach a conclusion.

   Example: President Nixon's many statements from June 1972 to the time of his resignation that he had no part in the Watergate coverup.

3. *Straw man.* Attacking a position similar to but significantly different from an opponent's position.

   Example: Richard Nixon branding his opponent, Helen Gahagen Douglas, as a pinko.

   a. *Exaggeration.* Distortion by exaggeration.

      Example: Characterizing the sending of 113 jeeps and trucks to Nigeria as a "massive airlift."

4. *False dilemma.* Erroneous reduction of alternatives or possibilities, usually a reduction to just two.

   Example: The statement implying that male domination is due to economics or biology, omitting all sorts of other possibilities.

5. *Begging the question.* Asserting without justification all or part of the very question at issue.

   Example: Answering the question why Argentina will go socialist by saying it's because of "world historical circumstances."

   a. *Evading the issue.* Ignoring all or part of an issue.

      Example: Maryland gubernatorial candidate Harry Hughes ducking the issue of hiring a Marxist professor by stating he'd consult with the university president.

6. *Inconsistency.* The use or acceptance of contradictory statements to support a conclusion or conclusions. These statements may be presented (1) by one person at one time; (2) by one person at different times (without explaining the contradiction as a change of mind and providing evidence to support the change); or (3) by different representatives of one institution. It also is committed by someone who *says* one thing but *does* another.

Example: Lyndon Johnson's stand on racial questions as a candidate for the U.S. Senate and his stand on racial questions as president of the United States.

7. *False charge of fallacy.* Fallaciously charging someone with a fallacy.

Example: The charge that Bertrand Russell was *inconsistent* in advocating the use of force against the Russians at one time, while adopting a "better Red than dead" position at another; Russell explained this switch several times as being due to changing circumstances.

Exercise I for Chapter Four

Determine which fallacies (if any) are committed by the following, and carefully explain why you think so. (Some of these contain fallacies discussed in previous chapters.)

*1. *Rowland Evans and Robert Novak in a political column, August 1970, on Hanoi's opposition to Mideast ceasefire proposals and the Soviet-West Germany treaty; the statement was used later in drawing further conclusions:* Apart from again revealing their ideological differences with Moscow, the North Vietnamese are venting morbid premonition in Hanoi that the Kremlin may yet forcibly end the Vietnam war short of total victory. *questionable premise*

2. *Soviet sociologist Geunadi Gerasimov (quoted in* Village Voice, *5 May 1975, p. 19):* . . . communism will replace capitalism because private ownership of the means of production is obsolete. *questionable evaluation, begging the question*

3. a. *Spiro Agnew, Cleveland, Ohio, 20 June 1970:* We are not going to heed the counsel of the Harrimans and Vances and Cliffords [important Democrats], whom history has branded as failures. . . .

   b. *Lawrence O'Brien, Democratic National Chairman, Washington, D.C., in reply to the above:* You'd think that of all people, Mr. Agnew would know the difference between a donkey and an ass. *ad hominem?*

*4. *Explanation of why Senator McGovern went from about even to approximately 20 percent ahead of Senator Humphrey in the 1972 California primary:* One factor is that McGovern was on the rise; he had momentum. *evading the issue, or begged the question*

*5. *Radio announcer:* President Nixon today announced another troop withdrawal of 25,000 men from Vietnam, and pointed out that he would continue to confound his critics by continuing his scheduled withdrawal of troops. He also reemphasized the importance of our defense of the Saigon Government, pointing out that the prestige of the United States is at stake: We simply cannot afford to let the Communists take over in Vietnam. *inconsistency*

6. *From the television show,* The Advocates, *a December 1972 story on a proposed "shield law" granting reporters immunity from prosecution if they refuse to reveal their sources to the police or courts:* Contempt of court is a crime for an ordinary citizen. Since it is a crime for every citizen, it ought to be a

crime for a news reporter who refuses to disclose his sources to a court which has subpoenaed him. *suppressed Evidence*

7. San Francisco Chronicle, *28 March 1972:* "I'm all for women having equal rights," said Bullfight Association president Paco Camino. "But . . . women shouldn't fight bulls, because a bullfighter is and should be a man." *inconsistency*

8. *Editorial, Hartford Times, 11 September 1970, on the topic of an extra twenty minutes of school time for teachers; the extra time was objected to by the teacher's union:* Insisting that teachers be in school [twenty minutes] longer than children may seem to some teachers like a factory time-clock operation, but it probably troubles the conscientious teacher far less than those who leave school at the final bell. *questionable premise. Just cause you stay long doesn't mean you are better teacher.*

*9. *Nutrition expert Frederick Stare, answering the charge that flaked dry cereals —Wheaties, Corn Flakes, and the like—are not sufficiently nutritious* (New York Daily News, *5 August 1970):* Stare said cereals with milk "provide approximately the same amount of protein and calories as a bacon-and-eggs breakfast. And they also provide substantially more calcium, riboflavin, niacin, thiamin, and iron and substantially less saturated fat. . . . Popeye's spinach doesn't begin to compare with the over-all nutritional worth of breakfast cereal—any cereal. . . ." *suppressed evidence*

10. New York Times, *10 March 1972, story on the alleged bribe involved in the ITT $400,000 contribution to the 1972 Republican National Convention:* Inquiry here indicates that, although there may be no actual "rejection" of the ITT-Sheraton commitment—since that might be construed as a confession of guilt and wrongdoing—Republican party leaders in Washington are urging the local fund raisers and convention planners to "get out from under" the ITT arrangement as quickly as can be done.

*11. *Aristotle:* Oh my friends! There are no friends. *no Fallacy.*

12. *From student comments on a claim made in the second edition of this text:* . . . Value judgments . . . ought to be left to the editorial page, where readers recognize that what they read is based primarily on value judgments and not on strenuous attempts to discover the facts. *question premise, last statements*

13. *Letter from Robert Rodale touting his* Complete Book of Minerals for Health: . . . That's just one small part of the story of these magnificent elements called minerals—the cornerstones of good health. The fact is, minerals are every bit as important to you as are your vitamins. Good health cannot exist without *both!* But still, many doctors and nutritionists continue to relegate minerals to some minor status. *suppressed evidence*

14. *Private conversation:*
    Miana: You'll be rich some day, How.
    How: What makes you think so? *questionable evaluation.*
    Miana: You were born for it.

15. *Lyndon B. Johnson:* I believe in the right to dissent, but I do not believe it should be exercised. *inconsistency*

*16. *George Meany, American Federation of Labor President,* New York Times, *31
     August 1970:* To these people who constantly say you have got to listen to
     these younger people, they have got something to say, I just don't buy
     that at all. They smoke more pot than we do and if the younger genera-
     tion are the hundred thousand kids that lay around a field up in Wood-
     stock, N.Y., I am not going to trust the destiny of the country to that
     group. *ad Hominem*

17. *From a private conversation: Aunt:* I asked the doctor why my mouth was so
    dry, and he said it was because my salivary glands are not producing
    enough saliva. Some doctor. *Begging the question*

18. *John F. Kennedy:* Why, some say, the moon? Why choose this as our goal?
    They may [as] well ask why climb the highest mountain? Why thirty-five
    years ago fly the Atlantic? Why does Rice play Texas? *questionable analogy*

19. *From Ohio State University* Lantern *story "Study of Pot Uses Eyed":* Mari-
    juana may be used to treat glaucoma and cancer patients if legislation
    introduced Wednesday before the Ohio Senate is passed. Under the bill,
    a research program would be set up to study the medicinal uses of
    marijuana as it affects . . . glaucoma patients.

    . . . OSU glaucoma specialist, Dr. Paul Weber, is . . . against the bill.
    "There is no question in my mind that marijuana eases eye pressure, but
    not enough studies have been done," Weber said. *inconsistency or no fallacy*

20. *Evans and Novak column:* More serious, however, was [University of
    Michigan President Robben] Fleming's acceptance of a 10 percent Ne-
    gro enrollment goal, the major demand of the March student strike.
    Substantive arguments against the 10 percent quota . . . are formidable.
    To raise black enrollment from the present 3.5 percent would leave
    precious little in scholarship funds for poor white students.

21. *Note from* High Times *magazine:* Even though they contain an illegal
    drug, Psilocybe mushrooms are legal in Great Britain, held the Reading
    Crown Court. . . . Judge Blomefield reasoned: "Psilocybin is a chemical;
    these mushrooms are mushrooms."

22. *Re-creation of conversation between patient and psychiatrist:*
    Patient: Doctor, my wife left me four months ago, and I've been shot
    ever since. I'm beginning to wonder. Will I ever pull out of this?
    Shrink: It's normal to feel a lot of anxiety and depression after a severe
    loss. But let me assure you that everyone does recover from this sort of
    thing. So you will too. . . . Unless, of course, the trauma has been so
    severe that the ego is shattered.

*23. *David Ogilvy in* Confessions of an Advertising Man *(New York: Atheneum,
     1963), p. 32:* I always showed prospective clients the dramatic improve-
     ment that followed when Ogilvy, Benson and Mather took accounts away
     from old agencies—"in every case we have blazed new trails, and in
     every case sales have gone up." [The period referred to was roughly the
     postwar period 1946 through 1962.]

*24. *From "Intelligence Report," by Lloyd Shearer,* Parade, *5 November 1978:* This past September, [Bob Hope] refused to cross a picket line at the Chicago Marriot Hotel, where 1500 guests were waiting for him at a dinner of the National Committee for Prevention of Child Abuse. W. Clement Stone, the insurance tycoon who contributed $2 million to the Nixon campaign fund in 1972, tried to negotiate a temporary halt of picketing so that Hope could enter the hotel. When Stone failed, Hope returned to the Drake Hotel, where he videotaped a 15 minute spot to be shown at the dinner. Hope, who belongs to four show business unions, later explained that he had crossed a picket line many years ago and subsequently had to apologize to labor leader George Meany. He promised then never to cross another.

25. Public school textbooks inculcating the idea that the United States is a peace-loving nation point with pride to the fact that the border between the United States and "our friendly neighbor to the north," Canada, is the longest unprotected border in the world.

26. *Wayne W. Dyer in* Your Erroneous Zones *(New York: Avon Books, 1977):* Here is a logical exercise that can forever put to rest the notion that you cannot take charge of your own emotional world.
MAJOR PREMISE: I can control my thoughts.
MINOR PREMISE: My feelings come from my thoughts.
CONCLUSION: I can control my feelings.
Your major premise is clear. You have the power to think whatever you choose to allow into your head. . . . You alone control what enters your head as a thought. If you don't believe this, just answer this question, "If you don't control your thoughts, who does?" Is it your spouse, or your boss, or your momma? . . .

27. *William Harsha in the* Congressional Record: The city of Boston, the city of Philadelphia, the city of Chicago, the city of New York, all have rapid rail transit systems, and they have the highest congestion and traffic tieups in the country. Rail mass transit has not solved their problems. It is not the solution . . . to the problem.

28. *Synopsis of article by Howard Smith and Brian Van derHorst in* Village Voice *(18 October 1976):* Sri Swami Swanandashram, Hindu holy man from India, after criticizing other Hindu swamis [for instance, Maharishi Mahesh Yogi of TM fame, Swami Muktananda, Sri Chimnoy, and Baba Ram Dass (Richard Alpert)] for making lots of money in the United States from their teaching: "They should have no house, no foundation, no bank accounts. . . . Our laws strictly forbid selling spirituality. But that's what they're doing." When asked what will happen when *he* starts making money, his chosen ally, the Divine Mother Swami Lakshmy Devyashram Mahamandaleshwari, responded: "Money itself is not bad. It's how it's used. Money should all be given away to schools, hospitals, and needy children, or something. It shouldn't be held on to." When asked if it wasn't against their own rules to criticize anyone else's spiritual path, that each must find his own way, Swami Swanandashram answered:

"Oh, yes, it's true. Nobody is supposed to do it. But I'm in America. In India we wouldn't criticize. But we are not actually criticizing here. When they are deviating from the real path, we are just telling the truth."

29. *Ad for Conoco in* New York Review of Books *(17 May 1979) complaining about efforts to get more land put off limits for oil drilling, arguing that we can have both the oil and conservation:* For example, more fish are being caught in the Gulf of Mexico today than before the Gulf became the most drilled body of water in the world. And at the Aransas National Wildlife Refuge in Texas, where Conoco has been producing oil and natural gas for 35 years, there are more rare whooping cranes than when we started.

30. A magazine article (*New Times*, 30 May 1975, p. 13) on the Catholic Church reported its efforts to reduce the divorce rate among Catholics by instituting rules that prospective couples must satisfy to gain the Church's blessing for their marriage. A church spokesman stated that the right to marry is a natural right, but restrictions are justified when the proposed marriage "poses a threat to the common good of society."

31. *Senator Jacob Javits, Republican New York, 5 October 1971, on Senator Mike Gravel's amendment to cut off funds for bombing Indochina:* I have decided to vote against the amendment [which he then did], because on balance, I think it would be a mistake to single out this one aspect of U.S. military activity in Indochina. . . . I want to make it clear that my decision to vote against the Gravel amendment in no way lessens my deep, anguished concern over the continuing ravage being rained on civilians throughout Indochina through the massive U.S. bombing program. I want this war to end now.

32. *House Appropriations hearings on the 1971 supplemental, pp. 609–610, released 8 December 1970. Reported in* I. F. Stone's Bi-Weekly, *28 December 1970:*
   Congressman Frank T. Bow, Republican, Ohio: How did this so-called leak get out with regard to Kent State?
   FBI Director, J. Edgar Hoover: That did not come from the FBI. But it did cause me great concern. The first time I knew of it was when the Akron Beacon-Journal had a great headline—it is part of the Knight chain of newspapers—saying "FBI: No Reason for Guard to Shoot at Kent State." I knew this was untrue. We never make any conclusions. . . . These were certainly extenuating circumstances which caused the guard to resort to the use of firearms. Perhaps they were not as completely trained as they should have been, but certainly some stated they feared for their lives and then fired; some of the students were throwing bricks and rocks and taunting the National Guardsmen.
   Congressman Bow: Do you mind this being on the record?
   Hoover: Not at all.

33. *Thomas A. Porter, Dean, School of Arts and Sciences, Central Connecticut State College, in a November 1970 report titled "School of Arts and Sciences: 1970–*

1980": Each department of the school should begin at once to plan how to utilize various instructional patterns and/or new instructional techniques so as to make quality instruction available to all students who seek it. The problem of closing students out of classes which they want and need can only become more serious as our enrollments increase. Efforts in this direction by departments may include the creation of large lecture classes (not always at the lower division level) and utilization of TV, auto-instructional labs, and other technological aids. It can be argued, of course, that this approach sacrifices individual communication between faculty and student and dehumanizes education. On the other hand, nothing sacrifices communication so much as being closed out of a class entirely.

34. *Naval Investigative Service director, reported to AP, 3 January 1971:* A Naval Investigative Service office will not initiate any investigation . . . when the prediction [prediction? provocation?] for the investigation is mere expression of views in opposition to official U.S. policy. . . . Nothing herein is intended to inhibit or preclude normal reporting of information . . . on those individuals whose expressed controversial views may be adjudged to have a potential for embarrassment to the Department of the Navy.

35. *Testimony before the Senate Foreign Relations Committee, 24 November 1970, reported in* I. F. Stone's Bi-Weekly, *14 December 1970:*
    Senator Church: What do you expect the bombing will accomplish?
    Secretary Laird: The bombing, I think, will stop the violation of these understandings [that the United States could fly unarmed reconnaissance planes over North Vietnam unmolested].
    Church: Has the bombing in the past ever caused the enemy to acquiesce in our demands or to make concessions?
    Laird: Yes it has.
    Church: It has? When did it have that effect in the past?
    Laird: Well, the last protective reaction flight [i.e., bombing] that was flown in the North was in May, and after that strike there was an indication by the other side that they would abide by those understandings, and they did until the month of November when they shot down an unarmed reconnaissance plane. . . .
    Church: Was this the only attack upon a reconnaissance plane that occurred or were there a series of attacks on reconnaissance planes?
    Laird: We had attacks upon our planes, Senator Church. But this was the first plane shot down.

Exercise II for Chapter Four

Find examples in the mass media of fallacies discussed in Chapter Four and carefully explain why they are fallacious.

Within the next six months, there will be a spectacular rash of UFO sightings over California. Within hours after the first reports, there will be inexplicable blackouts in the San Francisco Bay area.

Within the next two years, Russian scientists will receive powerful radio signals from space—proof that an alien civilization is attempting to communicate with us.

We will accidentally discover the ruins of Atlantis deep in the sea between Cyprus and Turkey. Finely preserved tablets containing complicated symbols will reveal that the inhabitants of Atlantis were highly intelligent in mathematics and language. Several types of highly sophisticated construction tools will be found.

Prominent researchers and scientists will announce that they have proof that the Loch Ness Monster is a living creature. Photographs and recordings will be studied and they'll solve this ancient mystery.

The stock market will hit an all-time high in April [1979].

A new planet will be discovered by the Venus space probe.

The rise in the market will be coupled with the end of inflation.

. . . Researchers will discover the aging process can be stopped by eating a fruit found in the Amazon jungle.

It will be revealed that the Food and Drug Administration has been keeping anticancer drugs off the market. After the scandal breaks and the drugs become available, cancer will cease to be a major health problem.

Ugandan dictator Idi Amin will be assassinated March 13.

President Carter will be injured in a hang-gliding accident between April 8 and 10.

The predictions on the left (above) were made by the famous metal-bending watch-starter, Uri Geller ("FAMED PSYCHIC") in the National Enquirer, *9 November 1976. The predictions on the right were made (for the year 1979) by psychic Jack Gillen, described by the* National Enquirer, *2 January 1979, as having "correctly predicted the 1974 crash of the Turkish airliner near Paris." None of their predictions have so far turned out to be true. Not that alleged psychics don't sometimes make correct general predictions— predictions with no exact dates, places, or other hard-to-predict details. But anyone with half a brain can do that. A true psychic should have a much better batting average than the rest of us. Their "stats" should reflect their powers, just as do the stats of professional athletes. No alleged psychic has ever consistently predicted the sorts of things normal people find really hard to predict (the stock market, horse race winners, state lottery winners, the next card in a money game of poker), the things any of us could make a fortune predicting. Of course, the literature on the "paranormal" is full of experiments by university scientists proving that some people have predicted consistently under the given laboratory conditions. But considering the contrary evidence available (see, for instance, almost any issue of the* Skeptical Inquirer—*say, Winter 1978), wake me up when Jeane Dixon or Uri Geller, or any psychic, breaks the bank at Atlantic City.*

Chapter Five

Statistics and Fallacies

There are lies, damn lies, and statistics.
—Benjamin Disraeli

Figures don't lie. But liars figure.
—Old saying

Statistical fallacies are just fallacies in which numbers play a central role. Nevertheless, they merit special attention because so many of us are more likely to fall for statistical fallacies than for the nonstatistical variety.

1. Suppressed Evidence and Biased Statistics

The statistical fallacy most frequently encountered is simply the suppression of known and relevant data (a variation on the fallacy of *suppressed evidence*). When positive statistics are reported but negative ones suppressed, the fallacy is said to be that of **biased statistics.**

Republican victory claims in the nationwide 1970 U.S. Senate races furnish a typical example. These claims were based on the fact that in off-year elections (years when no president is being elected), the party of the incumbent president almost always loses Senate seats. In the 1970 elections, the Republicans *gained* two Senate seats.

In this case, the suppressed evidence was quite simple. In the first place, Republicans suppressed the fact that a victorious presidential candidate usually carries a comfortable majority of senators of his own party along with him and that the larger the majority, the greater the loss two years hence (on the average). But in 1968, President Nixon, elected by the tiniest of margins, failed to carry a Republican Senate in with him. So only a very small Republican loss would be expected in any case.

Even more important is the suppressed fact that twenty-five Democrats and only ten Republicans were up for reelection, due to the Johnson landslide of 1964. Such an imbalance of risk is almost unprecedented. Once we take it into account, the Democratic showing begins to look quite respectable, and Republican claims of victory out of order. Having risked fifteen more seats, it is not surprising the Democrats lost two more races than did the Republicans.

And, finally, the two-seat improvement looks even less like a victory when it is observed that two of the Democratic losses (those in New York and Connecticut) may have resulted from unusual three-way races which hurt the Democrats more than they did their opponents. (Notice again that this fallacy could not be detected by the uninformed; they always are fair game for the slick operator.)

One good way to avoid being taken in by statistical arguments that suppress evidence is to ask yourself whether there isn't additional information needed to come to a sensible conclusion. Take the *Soviet Life*[1] article, "About Millionaires, Family Budgets and Private Business, Soviet Style," which implied that Soviet citizens can indeed become rich, even millionaires.

Can Soviet citizens accumulate considerable savings? Of course they can. Here are some figures to prove it:

Savings bank deposits

Item	1970	1976
Total accounts (in millions [of accounts])	80.1	113.1
Accounts in urban banks (in millions)	58.9	84.0
Accounts in rural banks (in millions)	21.2	29.1
Total deposits (in billions of rubles)	46.6	103.0

But taken alone, these figures don't prove much of anything. For example, simple calculation yields the information that the average deposit was about 910 rubles. But, first, how much is a ruble worth? (In Italy, 910 lira won't buy much more than a couple of cans of garbanzo beans at the local grocery.) It turns out that 910 rubles were worth about $1,400 in U.S. dollars in 1975. That'll buy a lot of borscht but hardly makes anyone rich. Second, how many people, if any, have savings of, say, 100,000 rubles? (That amount would at least make a person paper rich.) Third, what can be bought in the Soviet Union for 100,000 rubles? (Being paper rich without much to buy doesn't make a person actually rich.) Finally, does even one private person have a million rubles saved up? (The article wants very much for you to conclude that there are such persons in Russia, but it doesn't say that there are.) Until we get the answers to questions like these, suppressed by *Soviet Life*, we're in no position to evaluate their claims about all those rich people in Russia.

The foundations of magical belief and practice are not taken from the air, but are due to a number of experiences actually lived through, in which man receives the revelation of his power to attain the desired end. We must now ask: What is the relation between the promises contained

---

[1] April 1978. *Soviet Life* is a Soviet magazine published especially for American readers and distributed in the United States by an agreement between the U.S. and U.S.S.R.

in such experience and their fulfillment in real life? Plausible though the fallacious claims of magic might be to primitive man, how is it that they have remained so long unexposed?

The answer to this is that, first, *it is a well-known fact that in human memory the testimony of a positive case always overshadows the negative one. One gain easily outweighs several losses.* Thus the instances which affirm magic always loom far more conspicuously than those which deny it.

—Bronislaw Malinowski, *Magic, Science and Religion*

The battles surrounding the Massachusetts no-fault insurance law provide another case in which the average person should have known (but generally didn't) that information was being suppressed. One of these battles centered on attempts to lower auto insurance premiums by 15 percent. The response of the insurance industry was a vast campaign in which they claimed that bankruptcy was possible. Typical was the article in the *New Britain Herald* (12 October 1970, by David L. Walter) on the problems of the insurance industry, and their need to raise rates:

> Over the past ten years, the insurance industry has paid out $2 billion more in claims than it has collected in premiums, says a spokesman for the Insurance Information Institute. . . .

The impression given is that without a rate increase, insurance companies would soon be unable to pay insurance claims.

But this conclusion was not warranted by the facts, as the spokesman for the Insurance Information Institute and the writer of the article ought to have known. Insurance companies don't just put premiums in a vault; they *invest* them, and use investment profits along with premiums to meet insurance claims. So the pertinent figures were *total* income and total outgo, which yield total profits. During the ten years in question, the insurance industry took in comfortably more in premiums and investment profits than it paid out in claims and operating expenses.

Jeane Dixon, the world's most phenomenal seer, says a UFO carrying super-advanced humans from a hidden planet will land on Earth within a year—and will help us overcome all disease, starvation, and war. In a fantastic vision, the famed psychic saw aliens helping us by implanting vital secrets in the minds of Earth's scientists—and also landing to make face to face contact with us. Mrs. Dixon said the small, smooth-skinned beings spoke telepathically directly to her, explaining: "Your people have reached a stage of readiness to accept the concepts we are about to give you . . . I know that these aliens—who are really just better-

developed humans from a planet on the opposite side of the sun—will begin transmitting their secrets to us no later than August 1977. They will also land by then."
—*National Enquirer,* 14 September 1976

When you hear about some marvelous correct prediction made by Jeane Dixon or some other famous seer, don't commit the fallacy of suppressed evidence. Instead, remember their klinkers also, like this typical one of Jeane Dixon's.

2.   Unknowable Statistics

Statistics always seem precise and *authoritative*. But statistical facts can be just as unknowable as any others. Here is a letter received several years ago which contains examples of **unknowable statistics** that would be hard to top:

Dear Friend: In the past 5,000 years men have fought in 14,523 wars. One out of four persons living during this time have been war casualties. A nuclear war would add 1,245,000,000 men, women, and children to this tragic list.

It's ludicrous to present such precise figures as facts. No one knows (or could know) the exact number of wars fought up to the present time, to say nothing of the number of war casualties. As for the number of casualties in some future nuclear war, it would depend on what kind of war, and in any event is a matter on which even so-called experts can only speculate.

The average American child by age eighteen has watched 22,000 hours of television. This same average viewer has watched thousands of hours of inane situation comedy, fantasy, and soap opera and an average of 4,286 separate acts of violence.
—D. Stanley Eitzen in *Social Structure and Social Problems in America* (Boston: Allyn & Bacon, 1975)

Statistics—*knowable, or unknowable? And if knowable roughly, what about that precise figure of 4,286?*

3.   Questionable Statistics

But it is not just *unknowable statistics* that should be challenged. Some kinds of statistics are knowable in theory but not always in fact. Business statistics, a case in point, often are questionable. Or at least there are those who think so.

Take the statistics published by the federal government on business conditions in the United States. Oskar Morgenstern is one expert who argues that these statistics are very questionable indeed.[2]

One of the major problems with government statistics is that their margin of error (not usually reported) is often greater than the "significant" differences they report. We read in the newspapers that the economy grew in a given month at a rate amounting to 5 percent a year, perhaps an increase of 1 percent over the previous year. Everyone is pleased at this increase in the growth rate of the economy. But the *margin of error* on government growth rate statistics very likely is much greater than 1 percent, as Morgenstern indicated, citing one of the government's own revisions:

> If the rate for the change [in growth] from 1947 to 1948 was determined in February, 1949, when the first figures became available, it was 10.8 percent. In July, 1950, using officially corrected figures, it became 12.5 percent; in July, 1956, it fell to 11.8 percent—a full percentage point. All this for the growth rate from 1947 to 1948!

Add to this the fact that even the officially corrected figures cannot take account of the deliberately misleading or false figures businessmen sometimes provide the government (to cover their tracks or to mislead rival companies) and it becomes clear that the margin of error on figures for the gross national product has to be fairly large.

If they had an IBM, a Merck, a Burroughs, or a Smith Kline in there, I think the [Dow Jones industrial stock] index would be substantially higher than 830–850. If IBM was in there over the last fifteen years, the Dow might be closer to 1,200 than 850.
—Jack Egan, *New York* magazine (21 May 1979)

The Dow Jones Industrial Average is followed religiously by all sorts of investors and quoted daily in newspapers and on radio and television. Yet what it says about the stock market depends on which stocks are included in the Dow average. There is little reason today to think that the Dow accurately reflects the market as a whole, although, of course, it does give some indication of how stocks are doing.

In addition, there is the problem arising from the need to use a base year (because of price fluctuations):

> If a year with a high (or low) gross national product is chosen as base year, this will depress (or raise) the growth rate of subsequent years. . . .

---

[2] Oskar Morgenstern, *Qui Numerare Incipit Errare Incipit* (roughly, "He who begins to count begins to err"), *Fortune*, October 1963.

An unscrupulous or politically oriented [!] writer will choose that base year which produces the sequence of (alleged) growth rates best suited to his aims and programs. . . . These are, of course, standard tricks, used, undoubtedly, ever since index numbers were invented.

In other words, if you want to show that a given year had a high rate of growth, choose a low base year, and vice versa for a low growth rate. Meanwhile, the true rate of growth remains unknown, except for broad, long-term trends.

Statistics on Illegal Commerce

Statistics on employment and the gross national product are subject to another (little noticed) problem, namely, that a good deal of employment and industry in the United States is illegal (racketeering, gambling, drugs, prostitution, migrant farm labor) so that figures on these activities must be either guesswork or based on tangential evidence (for instance, legal sales of gambling and marijuana equipment, or records of convictions for prostitution).

This brings to mind a problem in interpreting statistics on gambling, legal or illegal. Take the statement in a recent article[3] that ". . . somewhere between $15 billion and $30 billion a year is being wagered illegally" in the United States every year. Does this literally mean that the total amount of all illegal bets placed in a year is about $15–$30 billion? If so, the figure is uninteresting because the amount is very small. Or does it mean that that much money *changed hands?* If so, the figure is very interesting indeed. (How they know is another matter.)

To see the importance of this distinction, suppose four friends play poker every week, and let's say that on a given evening they play about 100 hands at ten bucks a pot. (Not exactly big-time gambling.) That's a thousand dollars an evening—or $52,000 a year, which does sound like heavy action. But if the players are anywhere near even in ability, less than a hundred dollars may actually change hands by the end of an ordinary evening of play. And over the course of a whole year, given that winners on some evenings are losers on others, as little as $500–$1000 may end up in different hands. So while the amount actually wagered is very large, perhaps around $50,000, the amount that actually changes hands (the figure that counts) is probably very small. By analogy, imagine for a moment that in ordinary shopping at a department store, goods were bought and sold back and forth several times before any goods changed hands permanently. Obviously, total sales would constitute a worthless figure—what would count is the dollar value of goods that permanently changed hands. It's the analogous figure for gambling—the amount of "goods" (money) that permanently changes hands—that is crucial. Are those alarming statistics on gambling, legal or illegal, estimates of the amounts wagered or the amounts that changed hands over a period of time? Does anyone have good statistics on the amount that permanently changes hands in illegal gambling?

---

[3]*[MORE]*, January 1978, p. 12.

A cute trick of some "experts" is to "predict" the future simply by continuing current trends into the future. Population trends are a good example. Take this item from *Parade* magazine, "Intelligence Report," by Lloyd Shearer (March 1979):

Women in West Germany are limiting their families to an average of only 1.4 children. If that rate continues, the current population of West Germany (57.2 million) will decline to about 49 million by the end of this century, to 22 million 100 years from today. [The article implied that it will continue if West Germany doesn't do something about it."]

But is that rate likely to continue? Who knows? We do know that some factors are likely to change, the death rate being an important example (if the death rate in West Germany continues to decline from now until the year 2000, West Germany's population will have increased, even if the 1.4 average continues—and there isn't any firm reason to think either that it will or that it won't). Imagine being alive in, say, 1880, and trying to predict the population of the United States in 1980 simply on the basis of the 1880 birth and death rates. The result wouldn't be anywhere near the true figure. (This is a case where background knowledge should lead us to suspect the results of low-level induction.)

Biased Polls

Government statistics may report confidently on things that are not known with such precision, but at least they bear some resemblance to the truth. Many statistics, however, don't even have that virtue. An example is the statistical evidence obtained from surveys that ask "loaded" or biased questions. In general, the technique is to ask a question in such a way that you are more likely to get the desired answer.

Evangelist Billy James Hargis conducted a poll of 200,000 names of "subscribers to various publications . . . a sampling of 200,000 average Americans," and reported the results in a letter to the *Houston Post* (April 1979). Here are a few of the questions and the responses:

3. Are you in favor of the diplomatic death of Taiwan as the price of recognizing Red China? 111 said yes; 16,889 said no.

4. Do you favor retaining loud-mouthed, pro-terrorist, racial agitator Andrew Young as a U.S. ambassador to the United Nations? 564 said yes; 16,436 said no.

5. Are you willing to pull U.S. troops out of Korea and risk surrendering the country to the Communists after our boys bled and died on the Korean battlefield? 503 said yes; 16,497 said no.

9. Are you ready to surrender our way of life in order to "accommodate" left-wing forces here in America? 52 said yes; 16,780 said no.

While the extremely lopsided results are almost certainly due in part to a biased sample (biased samples are discussed below), in part it results from the loaded nature of the questions. It takes some nerve to favor retaining a "loudmouthed, pro-terrorist, racial agitator" or to be "ready to surrender our way of life in order to accommodate left-wing forces here in America."

Reprinted by permission of *National Review*, 150 East 35 Street, New York, NY 10016

Polls also are used to determine consumer preferences and habits. Of course, statistics compiled from such surveys need not be worthless; it is possible to construct reliable surveys, although it's generally expensive and takes trained personnel. But all too frequently, surveys of this kind are worthless.

Here is another example, taken from a *TV Guide* article (9–15 June 1979):

Our recent poll of viewer attitudes toward television programming (May 12, 1979) produced some findings that beg for discussion.
    For instance, half of those we polled—49 percent—claimed they were watching less television than they did a couple of years ago. A similar finding had been reported some weeks earlier in a poll by the Washington *Post*.
    What's baffling is that those who make it their business to monitor actual viewing habits and TV-set usage—such companies as Nielson and The Roper Organization—say viewing is *up*, not down.

An article in *Parade*, "Keeping Up with Youth" (11 March 1979), contained the following nifty:

Census takers point out that the percentage of those [in census surveys] who say they voted is considerably higher than the official count.

Or what about this one (paraphrased from the *Columbia Journalism Review*, July/August 1978):

> One year the Toronto *Sun* included the name of a nonexistent columnist in a poll of feature popularity. He received a 7 percent readership rating.

There is a moral here: Even when they don't lie, respondents don't necessarily tell the truth—one reason being that they often don't know the truth, as in this last case.

Well, will people tell the truth when they know it? Yes, when they have no reason not to, but *no*, when they have such a reason—as this bit from *Scientific American* (August 1978) illustrates:

> The University of Arizona . . . project is an effort to get quantitatively reliable data on household food input and output. Some of the earlier results are striking. Poor people interviewed in Tucson [Arizona] say they never buy beer, but their garbage gives them away. The point is that beer cannot be lawfully acquired with food stamps.

In a test of beer drinkers:

Drinking from a six-pack without labels, beer lovers decided the quality of the beer was not very good and showed no particular preference for one bottle over another—even though their favorite brand was included as one of the unlabeled bottles. Later, given the same six packs, this time with the proper brand labels, the taste rating improved immeasurably and drinkers showed a definite preference for their own brand.

—Jeffrey Schrank, *Snap, Crackle, and Popular Taste* (New York: Delacorte, 1977)

In assessing poll results, we have to bear in mind the various peculiarities of human nature which lead respondents to stray from the truth. Since most popular brands of beer of a given type (for example, regular, as compared to low calorie) taste pretty much the same, factors such as snob appeal, pandered to by advertising ("Tonight, let it be Lowenbrau"—trading on the snob appeal of the name of a famous old, and excellent, German beer applied to an ordinary American beer) determine most beer preferences. But few beer drinkers are aware of being snobs—that's the sort of thing we tend to deceive ourselves about.

---

4. Hasty Conclusion

Statistics often seem more significant than they are, leading to commission of the fallacy of *hasty conclusion* in its statistical version. The *Saturday Review* (9 February 1974) ran an article stating that college entrance scholastic aptitude test scores are declining in America, indicating, according to the article, that students in the United States are not as bright (or well-educated) as they used to be.

But their conclusion was hasty. For it failed to take account of the fact (mentioned in the article) that the percentage of the total high school population taking these tests has increased—many more academically poor students now take them. (The fallacy *hasty conclusion* often goes hand in hand with that of *suppressed evidence,* as this example illustrates.)

Voters often judge their representatives by how they vote on a few supposedly key roll calls. But frequently these roll calls are just for show—for the voters back home—the issue already having been decided by committee votes or back-room dealing. To adequately assess the performance of representatives, even on a single important issue, without being guilty of *hasty conclusion,* we have to look behind the facade every elected body erects to make it appear the members are doing roughly the job they're supposed to do, whether they are or not. (Remember, the best elected officials need PR techniques just as much as the worst.)

Before Senate defeat of a bill providing a $290 million subsidy for the proposed U.S. supersonic transport plane (SST), backers of the bill tried to line up support for it by blunting one of the main objections to the SST, namely sonic boom. They did this by passing a motion banning supersonic flights over land in the United States. As a result, some senators who felt that sonic boom was a greatly overplayed issue found themselves voting *for* the bill banning supersonic land flights, even though they were against the content of the bill; they did so hoping that as a result the $290 million SST appropriation would be passed by the Senate the next day.

The SST vote also illustrates the difficulty of assessing failure to vote on a measure. Senator Magnuson attached an amendment to the overall transportation budget bill (of which the SST appropriation was a part) which stipulated that the Portland, Oregon, International Airport would get no funds until detailed and exhaustive environmental studies were completed. Oregon's Senator, Mark Hatfield, tried to get the amendment removed, but was told that Magnuson might be willing to strike his amendment *after* the SST vote was taken. Hatfield was thus in a bind. He was known to be opposed to the SST. Yet if he voted against the SST appropriation, Magnuson's amendment would not be withdrawn, and Portland would lose its airport funds. On the other hand, it would look bad to vote for the SST appropriation, since he was a well-known opponent of it. He did the only thing he could under the circumstances and announced he had a long-standing speaking engagement elsewhere. An Oregon voter who *merely* noted the missed vote simply failed to grasp the problem, and completely missed Hatfield's attempt to save Portland's airport money.[4]

---

[4]The SST story is even more complicated than that. In December 1970, the Senate voted against the $290 million appropriation for the SST. But the vote came late in the year and was followed by a beautiful squeeze play by the House. The House passed an amended Department of Transportation bill, which included three months' additional funding for the SST, and then adjourned for the year. A Senate vote against this bill would have cut off all funds for air traffic controllers (thus grounding all commercial planes) and for DOT employees. So the Senate voted

Courts and legislatures continually try to resuscitate the average person. But as we learn to appreciate the pluralistic nature of our society and the complexity of the human personality, the idea that there is a central point that adequately describes members of our society seems more and more ludicrous. . . . At least one state is resisting [the] trend to do away with the concept of the average person. The Tennessee Obscenity Act of 1978, which was signed into law last April, maintains that: "The phrase 'average person' means a hypothetical human being whose attitude represents a synthesis and composite of all the various attitudes of all individuals, irrespective of age, in Tennessee society at large, which attitude is the result of human experience, understanding, development, cultivation, and socialization in Tennessee, taking into account relevant factors which affect and contribute to that attitude, limited to that which is personally acceptable, as opposed to that which might merely be tolerated."

—From an article in *Human Nature* magazine (March 1979)

When we hear statistics about the average this or that, it's important to remember that some averages make sense while others do not. The average Tennesseean is a bit over 50 percent female, has about 1.9 children (if married), is mulatto (with a touch of oriental), and owns a home part of the year, renting the other part. In other words, the idea of an average Tennesseean is not just useless, it's ridiculous.

5. *Small Sample*

Statistics frequently are used to project from a sample to the "population" from which the sample was drawn. This is the basic technique behind all polling (as well as a good deal of inductive reasoning), from the Gallup Poll to the Nielsen television ratings. But if the sample is too small to be a reliable measure of the population, then to accept it is to commit the fallacy of the **small sample,** a variety of the fallacy of *hasty conclusion.*

This fallacy is committed frequently at election time, because a sufficiently large representative sample generally is quite expensive and difficult to obtain. There is a great deal of controversy about how large a sample has to be,[5] but there should be little argument about the following examples.

---

for the bill and thus to extend SST funding for three months more. So another "crucial" vote came up in March 1971. Citizens interested in the SST issue thus had to keep up with the topic for some time in order to determine how their representatives in Washington really affected the issue. (Senator Hatfield, incidentally, voted against continued funding for the SST in the March 1971 vote.)

[5] An extremely well-conceived poll, which takes care to obtain a truly representative sample, may be quite small and still be reliable. (How small depends on the nature of the sample.) The trouble with most small samples is that they're not selected with sufficient care because it's too expensive to do so. In real life, it may be cheaper to get a larger, less representative sample, or vice versa, but in any case getting a sample that combines the two often is too expensive to be practical.

An Evans and Novak column (October 1970) contained the following on the 1970 Connecticut Senatorial race: "In the blue-collar neighborhoods of this old factory town, the Rev. Joseph Duffey is losing—and losing badly—his audacious bid to weld a neo-Rooseveltian coalition." Their statement was based on a poll of sixty-seven Bridgeport voters in normally Democratic Italian-American working-class precincts, which showed Senator Thomas Dodd with 43 percent of the vote, Rep. Lowell Weicker with 27 percent, and Duffey with only 11 percent. This obviously was too small a sample on which to base more than tentative conclusions.[6]

The *Hartford Times* (13 September 1970), in a story on University of Connecticut "Hard Hats" (conservative faculty members), stated that "hardliners" tend to teach at the University of Connecticut in the physical sciences, while more liberal types tend to teach liberal arts. This conclusion was based on a study of the voting pattern on three resolutions concerning punishment for disruptive students. The trouble is that the three votes constitute too small a sample from which to draw more than a tentative conclusion.

An interesting variety of the *small sample* fallacy concerns statistical trends in small populations. An example is the newspaper headline stating that homicides increased by 20 percent in a certain locality over the previous year; which turned out to be based on an increase from ten to twelve.

6. Unrepresentative Sample

The Connecticut faculty survey referred to above also was defective in lacking what is called *instance variety*, thus constituting an **unrepresentative sample** of the population as a whole. In this case, the population was all relevant attitudes of University of Connecticut faculty members; the survey checked only attitudes on punishment for disruptive students. A faculty member who voted to punish disruptive students may not have been a "hardliner" on other issues.

An Evans and Novak column (*Toronto Star,* 19 July 1974) argued that "well-heeled" American suburbia had lost its faith in President Nixon, and wanted him out of office. Their conclusion was based on a survey of fifty-four registered voters in one district of Mamaroneck, New York, a Westchester County suburb of New York City.

But their conclusion was fallacious. In the first place, the sample size was much too small, even as a sample of the New York suburban area, much less of the nation as a whole. And second, the sample was not *representative*—we know after all that suburban areas in other parts of the country differ from West-

---

[6]Duffey did lose the election, and he lost primarily because he failed to pile up margins in cities like Bridgeport. But the election figures for Bridgeport show that Duffey lost there to *Weicker,* not Dodd. The figures were Duffey 18,273, Weicker 21,674, and Dodd only 5,909, a far cry from the sample cited by Evans and Novak. (Of course, the actual results are irrelevant to the charge of *small sample*. The sample would have been too small even if, luckily, it exactly mirrored the election results.)

chester County in their political makeup. Evans and Novak should have tried to make their sample representative of all suburban areas.

Scientists, of all people, aren't supposed to commit statistical fallacies. But they're human too. An interesting article on vocal responses during mating among different primate species (*Human Nature,* March 1979) turned out to be based on a sample of three human couples (each observed engaging in sex exactly once), a pair of gibbons, and one troop of chacma baboons.

7. *Questionable Cause*

And then there are the statistical variations on the fallacy *questionable cause.* A *New York Times* article on marijuana, which argued that marijuana is harmful to health, cited a report that twelve American soldiers in Vietnam had been reported to have smoked marijuana and to have had acute psychotic reactions. The implication was that marijuana-smoking *caused* the psychosis.

But the statistic cited is not significant by itself. We need to know at least the incidence of psychosis among U.S. soldiers in Vietnam who had not smoked marijuana. The horrors of war, after all, may well have been responsible for the psychosis, not marijuana. (There is also the question whether a sample of twelve was large enough to be representative in this case.)

Reprinted by permission of the Washington Star Syndicate, Inc.

It's not easy to determine what is the cause of what.

8. *Faulty Comparison*

Statistics have such an authoritative ring that it seems possible to do just about anything with them and get away with it. One trick is to juxtapose otherwise valid statistics in a way that *seems* to yield significant results, but actually does not, because the statistics are not of comparable types or because a more important comparison has been overlooked. Let's call this the fallacy of **faulty comparison.** (The chief variety, a relative of *questionable analogy,* is sometimes referred to as **comparing apples with oranges.)**

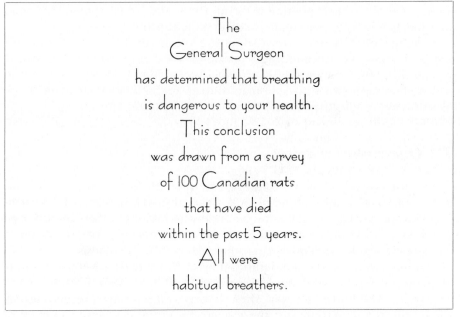

The
General Surgeon
has determined that breathing
is dangerous to your health.
This conclusion
was drawn from a survey
of 100 Canadian rats
that have died
within the past 5 years.
All were
habitual breathers.

Greeting-card humor illustrating some fallacy or other, no doubt.

The U.S. Chamber of Commerce magazine, *Nation's Business*, ran an article "Big Tax Reform Myth of 1972," which pointed out that although 107 millionaires paid no taxes in 1971, the remaining 15,323 having adjusted gross incomes over $200,000 did pay taxes—at a whopping 44.1 percent of adjusted gross income, much higher than ordinary taxpayers pay on their income.

The catch, which they suppressed, was that adjusted gross income is not total income—it's total income minus lots of things, such as one-half of capital gains (a very large item for millionaires). *Nation's Business* led its readers to commit the fallacy of *faulty comparison*—to compare the percentage of total income paid in income taxes by average taxpayers with the percentage of adjusted gross income paid in income taxes by millionaires.

In 1970, the Consolidated Edison Company of New York wanted to double the capacity of its power plant in Astoria (an area of Queens, a borough of New York City). Antipollutionists were against this expansion. In trying to combat the pollution charge, Con Ed's Jerry V. Halvorsen, Environmental Affairs Coordinator, argued that the expanded plant would actually produce less pollution.[7]

Let 5 stand for the existing capacity of the Astoria plant. Multiply by 1, the percentage of sulfur in the fuel we use now. And you get 5. Now let

---

[7] Quoted by Anna Mayo in the *Village Voice*, 18 August 1970. Incidentally, while *Time* magazine, *Newsweek*, and other mass media publications ill prepared their readers for the Three Mile Island nuclear near-disaster, Anna Mayo was informing *Village Voice* readers almost weekly of the poor safety record and the immense risks of current type nuclear energy plants.

10 stand for the proposed double capacity of the plant. Multiply by .37, the percentage of sulfur in the fuel we will use in the future. You get 3.7. And 3.7 is less than 5.

The conclusion he wanted the reader to draw was that pollution would be reduced even though power capacity would be doubled. But he obtained this result by *comparing apples with oranges*. (He also was guilty of a bit of *suppressed evidence*.) For if low-sulfur fuel was to be used in the new expanded plant, then it could be used in the plant already in existence. Doubling capacity would after all double pollution, as Anna Mayo was quick to point out.

Quality of Statistics Differs Widely

The fallacy of *faulty comparison* may also be committed when statistics from one time or place are compared with those from another. For the quality of such statistics often differs a great deal. Crime statistics are a good example. In many parts of the country, apparent increases in the crime rate can be achieved simply by changing the recording habits of police officers, for instance, by recording minor crimes by blacks against blacks, Chicanos against Chicanos, or Indians against Indians. In New York City, police can increase the crime total simply by walking down almost any main street and arresting hot dog, pretzel, or ice cream vendors; if a decrease is desired, they simply become blinder than usual to these everyday violations of the law. The same is true of prostitution, gambling, and homosexual activity, areas of crime in which the police generally have a special interest (a euphemistic way of indicating that police often get their "taste" of this kind of action). Police statistics simply do not accurately reflect the actual incidence of lawbreaking. Hence, if we compare figures on lawbreaking for one place or time with those for another, the result is apt to be ludicrous.

Equally silly are many of the statistical comparisons which fail to take account of inflation or (occasionally) deflation. Perhaps the classic inflation example is the one inadvertently furnished by Marvin Kitman in his book, *Washington's Expense Account* (New York: Simon & Schuster, 1970). Mr. Kitman was trying to prove that George Washington had lived relatively high on the hog during the Revolutionary War, which is true,[8] and also that he padded expense accounts, which is possible but not proved by Kitman's figures.

In a *Time* magazine article (Canadian edition, 28 July 1975, p. 40), rising food costs were attributed primarily to supermarkets not being as efficient as generally supposed. Statistics were used to justify the introduction of controversial new electronic systems: "[What we have at present is] a costly, cumbersome system that, for example, adds 24.3¢, *or 69%*, to the price of a pound of chicken between farm and checkout counter (see

---

[8] But you won't find this truth in many history textbooks, because it runs counter to an official myth.

chart).” In context, this made supermarkets look very inefficient indeed. But if *Time* had wished to make them look efficient, they could have used other figures from the same article to do so. For instance, they could have said instead that the 12.4 cents supermarkets themselves add to the retail price of a pound of chicken (a statistic on their chart) is only about 20 percent of the retail price, which is reasonably low, although not quite as low as a few years ago.

Washington’s accounts were kept primarily in Pennsylvania pounds. Mr. Kitman translated them into dollars via the Continental (Congress) dollar, equating twenty-six Continental dollars with one Pennsylvania pound. The trouble is that the value of the Continental dollar fluctuated widely, mostly downward, eventually becoming just about worthless (the origin of the phrase “not worth a Continental”).

Kitman listed Washington’s total expenses as $449,261.51 (note the aura of authority in that last 51¢!). An “expert” (who preferred to remain anonymous —perhaps because of the amount of guesswork involved) suggested $68,000 was a better figure.

In these examples, the comparisons themselves are faulty. Often, however, while the comparison is on the up and up, the *conclusion* is misleading. It is frequently stated that the American Indian has less to complain about than is usually supposed, and that we can’t have treated the Indian all that badly, since there are more Indians in the United States now than when Columbus “discovered” America. (This is disputed by some experts, who think the standard estimates on the Indian population in 1492 are too low. But in any event, the population then was probably not greatly different from what it is now.)

But even supposing the cited figures are correct, what do they prove? A more significant figure would be this (but still not terribly significant, given the immense amount of direct evidence that white men mistreated Indians). Take the number of whites and blacks in the United States in, say, 1783 (the end of the Revolutionary War), and compare that to the number of their descendants alive today (that is, don’t count later immigrants and their progeny—a good trick because of interbreeding, but not impossible to estimate). Now compare this increase with that of the American Indian. What we would no doubt find is that the white and black populations doubled many times over, while the Indians’ remained fairly stable.[9] If we had no direct evidence, then this comparison would be significant; but it would support the idea that the white man did, after all, mistreat the Indian.

9.   Ambiguity

Statistics would seem to be the last place to find the fallacy of *ambiguity;* numbers, after all, are so very precise. But what numbers are used to *count* may not be so precise.

---

[9] Actually, Indian population steadily declined until the Indians were completely conquered at the end of the nineteenth century. But in the past fifty years or so, their number has increased.

From a book review in *Human Nature* (August 1978) of Herman E. Daly's *Steady-State Economics* (San Francisco: W. H. Freeman, 1978):

Dissecting the notion that continuous growth in the gross national product is *per se* desirable, he emphasizes that the GNP is the sum of very different quantities. Those quantities include costs associated with economic "throughput," such as mining of ores and the cleaning up of polluted rivers; additions to capital stock, such as the production of automobiles; and services rendered by the capital stock, such as auto rental fees. ("Throughput," a word difficult to avoid in such discussions, refers to the flow of raw materials processed by the economic system.) "It makes no sense," Daly writes, "to add together costs, benefits, and changes in capital stock. It is as if a firm were to add up its receipts, its expenditures, and its change in net worth. What sense could any accountant make of such a sum?" And yet, in spite of numerous critiques of the value of the GNP as a measure, both from economists and others, one continually hears economists talking solemnly about how important it is for the GNP to grow. If its name were changed to the equally accurate gross national *cost* . . .

In 1970, Attorney General John Mitchell stated before the International Association of Chiefs of Police that the federal government placed only 133 taps during the first seven months of 1970. But (as pointed out in the *New Republic,* 24 October 1970) he must have had in mind only one kind of wiretap, for his figures did not include taps used in "internal security" cases, 48-hour "emergency" taps, or bugs, as opposed to wiretaps. The latter was especially deceptive, because Mr. Mitchell could expect police officers to know the difference between a wiretap and a bug, but not his wider audience (the general public) to which his statement ultimately was addressed. The public could be expected to assume that 133 was the total on electronic eavesdropping by the federal government. (Of course, if caught in the act, Mitchell could always have said he was speaking loosely, a defense that it is hard to counter, because life is short and in daily life we do tend to save time by speaking loosely.)

10. Statistical Fallacies in Context

It's harder to spot statistical fallacies in their usual context, jumbled all together with lots of other statistical arguments, than it is when they've been isolated as specimens in a textbook. So let's look at a batch of statistics thrown at us in one political column, and see if we can make sense of it.[10]

---

[10] The column is by John Cunniff. © 1970, the Associated Press. Reprinted by permission.

Inflation Notes

New York (AP)—The cost of a college education is going to be higher again this fall. Parents have become so accustomed to this statement that it no longer has any shock effect. But the figures, nevertheless, are rather numbing.

The median charges for tuition, fees, and room-board are expected to total about $2,502 in private coeducational colleges, up $200 from the 1969–1970 academic year.

Private women's colleges will be about $234 higher at $2,737, and private men's schools higher by $211 at $2,840. But those are the medians, meaning the figures half way between the highest and the lowest.

And what are the extremes? Well, at Bennington College in Vermont you must figure on total expenses of $4,325, which is $5 more than the price at Sarah Lawrence. Radcliffe, Tufts, Monterey Institute of Foreign Studies and several other schools will cost $4,000 or more. But students at public schools, such as the New York city colleges, may pay as little as $60.

The figures were compiled by the Life Insurance Agency Management Association to convince the public that they need to save well ahead to meet tuition costs—preferably through an insurance program.

At the rate prices are rising, however, the industry may find a good many families borrowing the cash value of their policies.

Once upon a time inflation was at the rate of only a couple of percentage points a year and most people hardly noticed it at all. But now it's 6 percent or more and few families can ignore it.

In an effort to show how damaging this can be if permitted to continue, the U.S. Savings and Loan League figured out that 30 years from now a man would have to earn $57,435 to equal his present $10,000 salary.

A $20 bag of groceries, 1970 style, would cost $114.87 in the year 2000. A $500 color television set would sell for $2,871, and a $3,000 automobile would carry a price tag of $17,230. A $25,000 home would be priced at $147,000.

Shocked? You should be. But don't forget either that these figures are not likely to be approached. Most economists would tell you that in all probability the economy would collapse long before 2000.

The statistics are interesting and informative. But the conclusions, stated or implied, are another matter. Let's start with the comparison between private school costs and those of public schools. In the first place, we are given the *average* for private schools, as well as two of the highest figures, but only the lowest figure for public schools. Thus, we are invited to commit the fallacy of *faulty comparison*.

But second, and more important, the figures for private schools cover room and board, while the $60 figure quoted for public schools does not —another example of comparing apples with oranges.

The column also quotes scare statistics on how damaging it would be if a 6 percent inflation rate continued into the future. A $25,000 home would cost $147,000, a $20 bag of groceries $114.87. But mere inflation proves nothing. The question is how *income* rises in comparison. If prices 30 years from now are six times higher than at present, then anyone making more than six times his present salary will be better off financially than now, and anyone making less than six times his present salary will be less well off.[11]

Statistics seem to baffle almost everyone. Here is a choice item from an article in *Human Behavior* (April 1977):

We once gave a test to 200 educators, asking what percent of children read at grade level or below. Only 22 percent answered correctly—50 percent of children.

Even teachers have a hard time keeping straight on the difference between comparative and absolute scales.

Another comparative rating that causes confusion is the IQ rating, since half of all who take the test must be rated below 100, given that 100 merely marks the halfway point in results.

Profit and loss statements make for dull reading, but sometimes studying them is the only way to uncover statistical sleight of hand. Take the following item from a story in *Ramparts* magazine.[12] American Telephone and Telegraph Co. (AT&T, the Bell Telephone system) is one of America's largest military contractors, its particular baby being the ABM. In one case, its subsidiary, Western Electric Company, took a profit of $113 million on an Army ABM contract of $1.6 billion. This amounts to "only" 7.9 percent, and those satisfied with outward appearances no doubt looked no further, satisfied that 7.9 percent was more or less in line with accepted practice.

But in fact, the profits to Western Electric, and thus to Bell Telephone, were immense and grossly out of line. The above figures served only to conceal suppressed data, which *Ramparts* magazine brought to the surface. For Western Electric itself did only $359 million of the work, including $82 million for administrative expenses. So its profits at the very least were 31.3 percent, a tremendously exorbitant profit rate.

---

[11] Of course, the effect of inflation on economic activity is another matter.

[12] *Ramparts*, November 1969. Notice that it is a *non*mass media magazine that ran this exposé.

Here is roughly how it worked, so that everyone profited but the federal government. Western Electric subcontracted $645 million of the contract to Douglas Aircraft, which took a profit of $46 million (7.6 percent). Douglas then subcontracted all but $103 million, so that its profit on actual work done was 44.3 percent. Of course, the sub-subcontractors, Consolidated Western (a division of U.S. Steel) and Fruehoff Trailer Corporation, also took their profits.

So the government ended up paying profits to Consolidated and Fruehoff, profits on profits to Douglas, and profits on profits on profits to Western Electric.

The details of a particularly flagrant overcharge on part of this contract illustrate the care that must be exhibited in handling profit and loss statements. Here is the *Ramparts* account of this detail:

> Probably the greateat chutzpah shown by Western, however, was in the scrupulous insistence on paying rent of $3 million to the government for the use of two surplus plants where much of the Nike production work was done. Ordinarily the government would have simply donated the use of the plants, but Western insisted on paying. Then again, Western has to make a buck too, so it added the $3 million to its "costs." The government had to turn around and give the rent money back as a reimbursement, plus $209,000 profit on it. Nothing excessive, just about seven percent. A reasonable profit.

Finally, it ought to be pointed out that military contracts are different from many others only in degree. Bell, for instance, uses the same profit on profit system in its purchases of telephones from—surprise—Western Electric. First, Western Electric takes a profit on the "sale" of the telephones to Bell, and then Bell takes a profit on the "cost" of telephones purchased from its own subsidiary, Western Electric.[13]

Summary of Fallacies Discussed in Chapter Five

Statistical fallacies are fallacies in which statistics play a significant part. The varieties discussed in Chapter Five are:

1. *Suppressed evidence.*

   Example: Suppression of the fact that insurance companies *invest* premiums, and thus have income in addition to the premiums themselves with which to pay claims.

2. *Unknowable statistics.*

   Example: The letter stating there have been 14,523 wars in the past 5,000 years.

---

[13] For more on AT&T numerology and other machinations, see "Getting a Handle on AT&T" by Marjorie Boyd, *Washington Monthly*, January 1979, and the AT&T reply in a letter to the editor, February 1979 (which would make a good exercise item).

3. *Questionable statistics.*

Example: Government business statistics calculated down to tenths of a percent. (It was pointed out that we should be careful in considering the results of polls, for polls often are improperly conducted, in particular by asking loaded questions, but also by polling too small or unrepresentative samples.)

4. *Hasty conclusion.*

Example: Concluding that students are not as bright (or well educated) today as they used to be on the grounds that college entrance scholastic aptitude test scores are declining.

5. *Small sample.*

Example: The Evans and Novak use of a sample of sixty-seven Bridgeport voters to prove Duffey would lose in his race for the Senate.

6. *Unrepresentative sample.*

Example: The Evans and Novak use of a sample from one district of Mamaroneck, New York, to prove that upper middle class suburbia in America overwhelmingly wanted Nixon out of office.

7. *Questionable cause.*

Example: The implication that marijuana caused American soldiers in Vietnam to have acute psychotic reactions.

8. *Faulty comparison.*

Example: Uncritically comparing crime statistics from one time or place with those from another.

9. *Ambiguity.*

Example: Attorney General Mitchell's use of the word "wiretap" to mean only one kind of electronic eavesdropping (not covering so-called bugs, for instance) in reporting statistics on government surveillance, correctly assuming that most people would construe the term more widely to include all electronic surveillance.

Exercise I for Chapter Five

Explain what (if anything) is wrong with the uses of statistical evidence in the following items. Be specific. For instance, if you say the fallacy is *questionable statistics*, state which statistics are questionable and explain why you think so.

1. An Evans and Novak political column rated the chances of State Senator Sander Levin, Democratic nominee for governor of Michigan, as poor, on the basis of a poll of sixty-four blue-collar suburban workers of Warren, Michigan. The poll showed 36 percent for Levin's opponent, 42

percent for Levin, and 22 percent undecided, in a normally very heavily Democratic stronghold. Later evidence showed that the poll correctly predicted the outcome of the election.

2. In 1978, the National Highway Traffic Safety Administration placed a value on human life, for purposes of assessing the costs to society of an accidental death, of $287,175.

3. *Article in University of Maryland Baltimore County* Retriever, *(19 September 1977), which used the following figures to argue that the "crime wave" on campus was decreasing:* Aggravated assaults decreased by 50 percent. There were two in 1975, one in 1976. . . . Car thefts decreased slightly in 1976, with four cars stolen as compared to five in 1975.

*4. Smoking marijuana definitely leads to heroin use. A report by the U.S. Commissioner of Narcotics on a study of 2,213 hardcore narcotic addicts in the Lexington, Kentucky, Federal Hospital shows that 70.4 percent smoked marijuana *before* taking heroin.

5. U.S. Customs officials justify their method of solving the heroin problem (catching drug smugglers) by citing the fact that heroin seizures are up sharply, from 210 pounds seized in 1969 to 346.8 pounds in 1970, to a staggering 1,308.85 pounds in 1971.

*6. *Column by James J. Kilpatrick, August 1970, in which he argued for more action on the drug problem:* J. Edgar Hoover released his 1969 Crime Report a week ago. Last year, for the first time, there were more arrests in the U.S. for violations of drug laws than for violation of liquor laws— 223,000 drug offenses against 213,000 liquor offenses.

7. *From Dr. Joyce Brothers's column in the* Houston Post *(3 October 1976):*
Question: You should be more fearful of rape at home because rapes occur more frequently in private homes than in back alleys.
Answer: TRUE. Studies indicate that more rapes are committed in the victim's home than in any other place. Almost half took place in either the victim's home or the assailant's; one fourth occurred in open spaces; one fifth in automobiles; one twelfth in other indoor locations.

8. *From article claiming to prove a causal link between junk food diets and antisocial behavior (*Moneysworth, *November 1977):* If you project a curve showing the increase in behavioral disturbances and learning disabilities over the past 25 years, you will find that it parallels the increase in the dollar value of food additives over that time . . .

9. *Reported by Dan Nimmo in his book* The Political Persuaders *(Englewood Cliffs, N.J.: Prentice-Hall, 1970).Mr. Nimmo presented this view and then argued against it:* . . . Students of politics . . . point out that factors shaping voting choices are affected only marginally by campaign appeals. The principal factor consistently related to voting decisions is the party loyalty of the voter. . . . So long as a substantial portion of the electorate is committed to a party (and studies indicate that proportion to be four out of five voters), campaigns will have little effect on voting patterns.

10. *Ford campaign worker, Fall 1976:* When you hear all those scare statistics about our economy and unemployment, just remember this: More Americans now have jobs than at any time in our history prior to Mr. Ford taking office.

*11. *From campaign literature of anti-abortion candidate, Ellen McCormack, in 1976 presidential race:* When pollster Louis Harris dismissed Mrs. McCormack's overall showing of better than 3 percent as insignificant, the candidate fired back: "The fact that 3 percent is insignificant will certainly be news to Ronald Reagan, who lost New Hampshire to Gerald Ford by less than 3 percent—or to George Wallace, who lost Florida to Jimmy Carter by that figure—or to Morris Udall, who lost Wisconsin by 1 percent—or to dozens of Congressional candidates in 1974 who lost by 3 percent or less. The presidential elections of 1960 and 1968 were also decided by less than 3 percent."

12. *Article in* Boston Globe, *26 June 1974, on youth, drugs, and alcohol:* "We're seeing a tremendous switch back to alcohol." Dr. Chafetz (of National Institute on Alcohol Abuse) cited a recent national survey of 15,000 boys and girls, aged 11 to 18, in which 92% reported alcohol use but only 38% said they smoked marijuana.

13. *W. Allen Wallis and Harry V. Roberts in* Statistics: A New Approach: It is three times as dangerous to be a pedestrian while intoxicated as to be a driver. This is shown by the fact that last year 13,943 intoxicated pedestrians were injured and only 4,399 intoxicated drivers.

14. *Item in* Parade *magazine, July 1974: Women and Film.* Hollywood is currently producing a plethora of films about unending car chases, murders, Watergate-type detective stories and relationships between men, as in the Oscar-winning *The Sting,* for instance. What's happened to the simple, good old male-female pictures? Are they passe? Part of the answer lies in numbers. Of the 3,068 members in the Producers Guild of America, only eight are women. The Directors Guild represents 2,343 men and 23 women; and the Writers Guilt has 2,828 male and 148 female members.

*15. Vancouver *(British Columbia)* Sun, *10 July 1975:* Britain has a strong socialist tradition more preoccupied with the distribution than the production of wealth. But distributionist preoccupations are a luxury for rich nations, which Britain no longer is. Since 1945, while world living standards tripled and productivity increased more than it did in the preceding 10,000 years, Britain went from being the second richest nation in northwest Europe (behind Sweden) to being the second poorest (behind Ireland).

16. *Article in Baltimore* Sun, *"Crime Rate Dips in City During 1978":* During the first quarter of this year, 902 fewer "major" crimes were reported in Baltimore than in the same period last year, according to city police. The 6.2 per cent drop occurred despite the fact that the city force was about

150 below authorized strength. . . . Since 1970 an annual rise in crime has been reported in only one year—1974.

Dennis S. Hill, a police spokesman, . . . suggested that innovative programs of the department in recent years are beginning to bear fruit. "After all, we are operating with less police officers now than we were a year ago," he said. "Our clearance rate is higher than the national average in every category. That means that the police officers are becoming more productive."

*17. New York *magazine, 12 September 1972, article on alcoholism:* A genetic biochemical deficiency could be the reason some persons become alcoholics while others don't. Dr. Stanley Gitlow, President of the American Medical Society on Alcoholism, [stated] that more than 80 percent of the alcoholics he has seen had a blood relative who also was an alcoholic.

18. *Richard C. Gerstenberg, General Motors Board Chairman, arguing against more stringent auto exhaust emission standards, stated that the Clean Air Act passed by Congress would force auto makers to put out a car which:* . . . would emit fewer hydrocarbons per day than would evaporate from two ounces of enamel you might use to paint your shutters.

19. Newsweek, *31 July 1972, article on a government program to give rent money directly to the poor to find their own housing:* Financially, the program is a definite success, because the cost to the government has averaged out at only $1,500 a year per family—a hugely favorable comparison with the $25,000 per unit cost of new low-income housing.

20. *Item from* Detroit Free Press *by Ronald Kotulak, entitled "When Doctors Struck, Death Rate Fell":* If surgeons performed fewer operations more people would still be alive.

This controversial conclusion, by a public health expert from the University of California at Los Angeles, is the latest and perhaps most serious attack on the surgical field. . . .

The newest charge was made by Dr. Milton I. Roemer, professor of health-care administration at UCLA, after studying the effects of a five-week doctor strike in Los Angeles in 1976.

Roemer and Dr. Jerome L. Schwartz from the California State Department of Health found that the death rate in Los Angeles County declined significantly during the strike.

They said that fewer people had non-emergency surgery, so there was less risk of dying.

"These findings . . . lend support to the mounting evidence that people might benefit if less elective (non-emergency) surgery were performed in the United States," said Roemer. "It would appear, therefore, that greater restraint in the performance of elective surgical operations may well improve U.S. life expectancy."

*21. It's a well-known and much pondered over fact that every United States president elected at twenty-year intervals died in office, starting with

William Henry Harrison, elected in 1840, and continuing with Lincoln in 1860, Garfield in 1880, McKinley in 1900, Harding in 1920, Roosevelt in 1940, and John Kennedy in 1960. Only one other president, Zachary Taylor, has ever died in office. So the odds are pretty bad for anyone foolish enough to run in 1980 and unlucky enough to win election.

22. *Jane B. Lancaster, in "Carrying and Sharing in Human Evolution,"* Human Nature *(February 1978), in which she argued that some other primates are much more vicious than homo sapiens:* During the five years of observing the habits of a community of chimpanzees at the Gombe Stream Reserve in Tanzania, researchers witnessed eight attacks between the community and neighboring groups. These fights resulted in the deaths of at least two elderly males, an adult female, and four infants, the equivalent of an annual murder rate of 1,400 per 100,000 chimpanzees. The murder rate in the United States, 88 per 100,000 people in 1976, becomes insignificant in comparison.

23. Baltimore *magazine, March 1979, article on the social costs of drug use in the state of Maryland:* Start with the understanding that a so-called "dime" ($10) bag of heroin . . . today sells for $50. Some addicts need six bags per day to keep from going into physical withdrawal. Cost: $300 daily. At 365 days a year, this amounts to $109,500 . . .

How do you support a $110,000-a-year habit? One 28 year old . . . prostitute with three children . . . explains:

"Normally, I'll turn anywhere from six to 12 tricks a day and shoplift at Hutzler's or any large department store. Other times we'll spend the day over in Rockville at White Flint Mall boosting [shoplifting] at Bloomingdales and Lord and Taylor's. Once a month we'll try and pull a con game . . . and at least once a week I'll pull a stick-up either around the Block or down off Park Avenue."

Suppose every addict supports his or her habit by stealing every day. Multiply, then, the $110,000 it costs the heroin addict to support his yearly habit by the 32,625 known narcotic addicts in the state and you get a figure of over 3.5 billion dollars a year.

24. *Excerpted from a letter from Calhoun's Collectors Society, Inc.:* Back in April, 1971, I bought my first "collector's plate" for $25. . . . I made the mistake of mentioning to my husband that one day it might be worth a lot more than I paid for it. He laughed and suggested . . . he could recommend a good stock broker.

Well, getting to the "last laugh" department—that $25 plate now lists for $580. That's an increase of 2,300 percent in just six years. The Dow-Jones in that same time has actually gone down from 950.82 as of April 28, 1971 to 769.92 on January 31, 1978. . . .

I'm now working for a company that's in the very thick of collectibles, and everyone here is excited about a new series of plates by the artist Yiannis Koutsis called "The Creation." This series is yours at a huge discount if you join Calhoun's Plate Collectors Club. The experts tell me this may be the most important plate series of the past ten years. But I don't want you to think I'm an expert. I'm still just a collector, but I've learned this lesson very well: Some plates, like some stocks, shoot up in value quickly. But even if they don't, collector's plates are works of art that you can enjoy as objects of beauty.

Exercise II for Chapter Five

Here are some excerpts from an article in the *Washington Post* (similar articles appeared in newspapers and magazines around the country, all drawing on the same figures), which gave the general impression that the rich pay an unfairly large amount of federal income taxes.[14] Analyze this article, showing: (1) what claims are made; (2) what arguments (if any) are given for each claim; (3) whether or not the main point of the article (that the rich pay an unfairly large amount of federal income taxes) is justified by the evidence and reasons presented; (4) any fallacies committed in the article (being sure to explain carefully why they are fallacies); and (5) what relevant information, if any, has been omitted (explain how this extra information affects the arguments presented):

Richer Half of U.S. Pays 94% of All Income Taxes . . .
Upper-Income Brackets Shouldering Disproportionate
Share of Tax Burden

The richest one-fourth of American households—those with incomes of $17,000 a year or higher—took home half the income in this country in 1976 and paid more than 70 percent of all personal income taxes. By contrast, those in the poorest one-fourth—wage earners making less than $5,000 a year—received less than 5 percent of the nation's income that year and paid a miniscule 0.1 percent of the income-tax tab. Those in the richest 5 percent of the country—taxpayers with incomes of $30,000 or more—earned 22 percent of the income in 1976 and paid 39.2 percent of all income taxes. By contrast, the poorer half of all persons filing tax returns earned 19 percent of all income and paid 6 percent of the personal income taxes in 1976, while the richer half paid 94 percent.

Those figures, compiled by the Treasury Department from estimates based on 1976 income levels, show a stark fact about the way the tax burden is distributed in this country: While it's true, as some studies show, that wealthier persons enjoy the biggest tax breaks and deduc-

---

[14] Art Pine, "Richer Half of U.S. Pays 94% of All Income Taxes," *Washington Post*, 13 March 1978. © 1978 by The Washington Post. Reprinted by permission. For some clues helpful in dealing with this passage, see Nicholas von Hoffman's syndicated column, "The Rich Taxed Unfairly?", which appeared (among many other places) in the Baltimore *News-American*, 27 March 1978.

tions, they also shoulder a disproportionate share of the tax burden—far beyond what is perceived generally. . . .

While the proportion of Americans' personal income eaten up by the income tax has remained relatively constant over the past few years, at about 13 percent, the burden of that tax load has shifted to higher income brackets. For example, figures compiled by the Tax Foundation show that the richest 25 percent of the nation's taxpayers paid 68.3 percent of all taxes in 1970. By 1975, that had risen to 72 percent. Those in the richer 50 percent paid 89.7 percent of the total tax in 1970. By 1975, that had increased to 92.9 percent. All taxpayers in the richer 50 percent bracket saw their share of the total tax tab rise.

At the same time, those in the poorer half enjoyed a shrinking tax burden during the period. The taxes paid by the lower half fell from 19.3 percent in 1970 to 7.1 percent in 1975. For the poorest 25 percent of all taxpayers, the proportion of the total tax bill fell to 0.4 percent in 1975, from 0.9 percent in 1970. . . .

With the combination of inflation and higher tax rates in the upper brackets, the wealthiest of the nation's taxpayers pay disproportionately high shares of the total tax burden—even including their shelters and deductions. For example, the richest 1.4 percent of the nation's citizens —some 985,000 whose incomes total $50,000 or more a year—take home 10.7 percent of the income, but pay 23 percent of the taxes. The wealthiest 0.3 percent—those in the $100,000-and-up category—receive 4.5 percent of the total income, but pay 10.5 percent of the tax burden. (The poorest 0.3 percent escape taxes altogether.)

The breakdown portrayed by these figures pertains only to personal income taxes. With Social Security payroll taxes included, the pattern is different but the point remains the same. The figures used in the computations include income from capital gains—profits from the sale of stocks or other assets—only half of which are subject to tax. The totals for tax liability include writeoffs and deductions. But the fact remains that, for all the complaining about wealthy taxpayers, those in the richer half of the nation's income brackets are paying 94 percent of the personal income taxes. The other half is paying the rest.

Exercise III for Chapter Five

Find examples of the statistical fallacies discussed in this chapter from items in the media (newspapers, television, magazines, radio), and explain what makes you think they are fallacious.

It makes a great deal of difference what we call something. Political cartoonist Jules Feiffer suggests that military bureaucrats know this just as much as do any other bureaucrats.

Chapter Six

Language

> An important art of politicians is to find new names for institutions which under old names have become odious to the public.
> —Tallyrand

> Find out who controls the definitions, and you have a pretty good clue who controls everything else.
> —Ellen Willis in *Rolling Stone*

1. Cognitive and Emotive Meaning

If the purpose of a sentence is to inform, or to state a fact, some of its words must refer to things, events, or properties. Some of its words thus must have what is commonly called **cognitive meaning.** The sentences made up of them also may be said to have cognitive meaning—provided, of course, that they conform to grammatical rules.

But words also may have **emotive meaning**—that is, they also may have positive or negative overtones. The emotive charges of some words are obvious. Think of the terms "nigger," "wop," "kike," "queer," and "fag." Or think of four-letter sex words, which even in this permissive age rarely appear in textbooks.

The emotively charged words just listed have negative emotive meanings. But lots of words have positive emotive overtones. Examples are "freedom," "love," "democracy," "springtime," and "peace." On the other hand, many words have either neutral or mixed emotive meanings. "Pencil," "run," and "river" tend to be neutral words. "Socialism," "politician," and "whiskey" tend to have mixed emotive meanings.

In fact, almost any word that is emotively positive (or negative) to some may be just the opposite to others, perhaps because one person's meat is another's poison. "God," for instance, has quite different emotive overtones for a sincere believer and for an atheist. Similarly, "dictatorship," a negative word for most Americans, in some contexts has positive overtones in the Soviet Union.

Terms that on first glance appear neutral often turn out to be emotively charged, sometimes because the charge is fairly small. But even when the charge is quite large, we may fail to notice it. The words "bureaucrat," "government official," and "public servant," for instance, all refer to roughly the same group of people, and thus have roughly the same cognitive meaning. But their emotive meanings are quite different. Of the three, only "government official" is close to being neutral.

Emotive Meaning Is Not the Enemy

It is sometimes claimed that emotive meaning gets in the way of rational "objective" thought. According to this view, serious intellectual uses of lan-

guage should be stripped of their emotive content so that we can deal rationally with their cognitive content. Thus, newspapers, textbooks, political rhetoric,
even advertisements, on this view should be written in emotively neutral language.[1]

But it isn't at all clear that this view is correct. For one thing, the emotive
meanings of terms differ from person to person, so that an expression neutral
for one person frequently will be emotively charged for another. Further, it is
extremely difficult, perhaps impossible, to write, say, history books, news
articles, or political speeches using only emotively neutral terms. And finally,
it is debatable whether such writing can be read easily or with profit, in
particular because it is so dull (think for instance of public school history texts,
which tend to be written in a dull, emotionally flat, drone). The point of
becoming familiar with the emotive side of language is not to be better able to
discount its emotive force, but rather to become aware of how this otherwise
useful feature of language can be used to con us into accepting fallacious
arguments. The point is to understand this language tool—a tool that, like
most others, can be, and is, used for both good and evil purposes.

2.   Emotive Meaning and Con Artistry

Con artists take advantage of the emotive side of language in two very
important ways: First, they use emotive meaning to mask cognitive meaning
—to whip up emotions so that *reason* gets overlooked; and second, they use
emotively neutral terms, or euphemisms (less offensive terms used in place of
more offensive ones), to dull the force of what they say and thus make acceptable what otherwise might not be.

Until very recently, *New York Daily News* editorials were famous for their use
of emotively charged expressions. A relatively mild *Sunday News* editorial (8
September 1974) on a campaign reform bill started with the title "A Snare and
a Delusion" (compare that with the emotively less charged "An Unsatisfactory
Bill," or even "A Misguided Bill"). It then referred to the bill's "*ogreish* feature" and the idea of "*saddling* the taxpayers with the cost of campaigns"
(compare: "assessing the taxpayers . . ."), finding the saddling "*obnoxious*" (not
just "ill advised" or "wrong"). Some other emotively charged expressions it
used were "well-disciplined *band of zealots*," "*grab* control," "*ridiculous*," and
"increase the clout." (See the exercise in Chapter Seven for another *Daily News*
editorial using lots of colorful language.)

Doublespeak, Jargon, Bureaucratese, Newspeak . . .

Government officials and other politicians tend to be masters of emotive
con games. In fact, they have invented a whole new vocabulary of emotively
dull or misleading terms and expressions.

---

[1] Proponents of this view often associate all evaluative language with emotive meaning, including that of ethics and aesthetics. This assumes that evaluative terms such as "right" and "good" as
used in sentences such as "Killing is sometimes morally right" and "That is a good painting" are
basically emotive terms, a conclusion many would deny.

Take their language of war, remembering that war, the real thing, is unvarnished hell. During the Vietnam War, we used particularly nasty weapons (for example, fragmentation bombs and napalm) in areas where they were certain to kill thousands of civilians. We dropped far more bombs on that small nation than on Germany and Japan combined in World War II. To make all this palatable, a "doublespeak" language was developed. Here are a few examples (with translations):

Pacification center	Concentration camp
Incursion	Invasion (as in the "Cambodian incursion")
Protective reaction strike	Bombing
Surgical strike	Precision bombing
Incontinent ordinance	Off-target bombs (usually used when they kill civilians)
Friendly fire	Shelling friendly village or troops by mistake
Specified strike zone	Area where soldiers can fire at anything—replaced "free fire zone" when that became notorious
Interdiction	Bombing
Strategic withdrawal	Retreat (when our side does it)
Advisor	Military officer (before we admitted "involvement" in Vietnam) or CIA agent
Termination	Killing
Infiltrators	Enemy troops moving into the battle area
Reinforcements	Friendly troops moving into the battle area
Selective ordinance	Napalm (also "selective" explosives)

Watergate-ese reached its peak with Nixon's press secretary Ron Zeigler, who was responsible for the famous "all previous White House statements about the Watergate case are inoperative." Here is his reply when asked whether some Watergate tapes were still intact:

> I would feel that most of the conversations that took place in those areas of the White House that did have the recording system would in almost their entirety be in existence but the special prosecutor, the court, and I think, the American people are sufficiently familiar with the recording system to know where the recording devices existed and to know the situation in terms of the recording process but I feel, although the process has not been undertaken yet in the preparation of the material to abide by the court decision, really, what the answer to the question is.
>
> Zeigler's remark so impressed the Committee on Public Doublespeak of the National Council of Teachers of English that they gave him their first annual Gobbledygook award for his effort. They also gave Colonel David Opfer, USAF press officer in Cambodia, an award for this gem:
>
> You always write it's bombing, bombing, bombing. It's *not* bombing! It's air support.

The doublespeak introduced during the Vietnam War was a good example of military jargon, which is itself a species of *bureaucratese*. The point of bureaucratese, of course, is to numb the reader into submission by replacing succinct, pungent locutions with long-winded or dull ones. Thus, bureaucrats speak of *undocumented workers*, not illegal aliens; of *termination with prejudice*, rather than assassination (CIA lingo); of *end use allocation*, instead of rationing; and of *diversion*, rather than theft (as in "200 pounds of highly enriched uranium diverted by Israel"). They speak of *plausible deniability* (as in "Once the White House tapes became known, Nixon lost his *plausible deniability* on the Watergate coverup"—the tapes were said to be a *smoking gun*). They write of being *selected out*, not fired (as in "Foreign Service Officer Smith was again passed over for promotion, and is therefore to be selected out").

And then, in a class by itself, the crowning achievement of Nazi phraseology, purified of the stench and horror of extermination camps: *The Final Solution*.

> The name of the dreaded murder squad in Uganda during the reign of Idi Amin Dada was "Public Safety Unit" (PSU).

Here are more examples of doublespeak in action: The first law in Japan regulating prostitution and establishing red light districts was called "Regulation on Earning a Living by Renting Rooms."[2]

---

[2] Lloyd Shearer, "Intelligence Report," *Parade* magazine, 6 September 1976.

Nearsighted: See poorly far away.
Farsighted: See poorly close up.

Example of poorly chosen terminology (or nomenclature). Even people who wear glasses don't know how to explain the term(s) naming their own afflictions.

The American Telephone and Telegraph Company (AT&T) pushed a bill through Congress designed to "choke off its competitors"[3] labeled, naturally, "Consumer Communications Reform Act."

Herman Kahn, off in his think tank somewhere, speaks of "response to post-attack blackmail" when he wants to refer to (can you guess?) *surrender* (in an all-out nuclear war). He also speaks of "crisis resolution," "conflict termination," or "deescalation" when he means surrender. The word "surrender" is practically forbidden in government circles, one reason being that a 1958 law forbids money to be spent on possible surrenderings, even if a nuclear attack has effectively defeated us.[4]

You can consistently win debates if you consistently use two words: "baby" and "kill."

—Dr. J. C. Willke, Vice President, National Right to Life Committee, at a pro-life (which means anti-abortion) convention, teaching others to teach the pro-life position (St. Louis, 1978)

Choosing words and phrases with just the right emotive force is a vital part of the art of rhetoric.

Here is a trivia item (or is it?): We're all familiar with "Hail to the Chief," traditionally played at the appearance of the president of the United States. During World War II some of us were dismayed when we realized that this translates into German as "Heil, Der Fuhrer."

---

[3] *New York Review of Books,* 3 February 1977.
[4] See Ron Rosenbaum, "The Subterranean World of the Bomb," *Harper's,* March 1978.

Here is an example of critic doubletalk, a distinct dialect (from a Harriet Johnson review in the *New York Post*):

The Brahms sang with detachment as if the music were a coat-of-arms which he hung on the wall while he took the frame and exhibited it.

Possible translation: The Brahms sang. (Metaphors do have content. We do know roughly what it means to say the Brahms sang; what all that business about a coat-of-arms hung on the wall means is anybody's guess.)

Here's an item which prompted a nomination for the 1978 Gobbledygook award (from *Dollars and Sense,* July/August 1978):

National Airlines reported that it picked up an extra $1.5 million in after-tax profits last May, thanks to the "recent involuntary conversion of a 727 aircraft." An airline spokesperson admitted under questioning that the "involuntary conversion" was actually a crash in Florida in which three passengers died. The spokesperson defended the company's use of the euphemism by saying it was "a widely used accounting term."

Sometimes people get the notion the purpose of EST is to make you better. It is not. I happen to think that you are perfect exactly the way you are. . . . The problem is that people get stuck acting the way they were instead of being the way they are.
—Werner Erhard, Erhard Seminars Training (est), quoted in *Harper's,* October 1975.

Mumbo-jumbo con artistry used to get you to overlook the ambiguity in the phrase "the way you are." If you're "stuck acting the way you were," *well, then, sorry, Charlie, but that's the way you* are.

Apropos Al Smith's famous remark that law school is where you learn to call a bribe a fee, here is an item from *New Times,* on illegal bribes by big business:

Asked by a *New York Times* reporter about the recent bribery disclosures, a professor of management and business at the University of California replied, "At a high level of abstraction, it's clear that American companies should not engage in wholesale bribery abroad, but I can't pass judgment until I get down to the operating details and ask when a bribe is a tip or a commission."

Much legal maneuvering is just to make sure that, legally, a certain name gets put onto something—for instance, the name "subcontractor" onto the person paid to help complete a job, instead of some other, bad, name, say "employee." "Employee" is bad because an employee must be paid according to the minimum wage law, while a subcontractor is not legally being paid a salary and thus is not subject to the minimum wage law—a subcontractor thus can be paid whatever desperation may make acceptable. Yes, United States law does so operate this way.

Of course, it operates pretty much the same way in most other places, too. In Moslem Saudi Arabia, the commandment not to make graven images is taken quite seriously; until recently photography was therefore forbidden. But aerial photography is such a boon to oil exploration that something had to be done. So:[5]

> King Ibn Saud convened the Ulema [a group of Moslem theologians who have great power over public morals] and eventually prevailed over them with the argument that photography was actually good because it was not an image, but a combination of light and shadow that depicted Allah's creations without violating them.

Any large organization is going to twist words for profit if it can get away with it. A certain large corporation defended the judgment of one of its employees whose mistake caused a great deal of trouble by arguing that the person was a "trained employee," the implication being that a "trained employee" ought to know the right thing to do, so the company was not negligent. But as they were using the expression, "trained employee" meant just "employee put through a company training program." Whether the program was any good, or whether the employee actually learned what was being taught, is another matter.

In 1979, Washington, D.C., striking public school teachers defended their demands to remain just about the best treated and best paid grade school teachers in the country (in the face of objections that indicated that they also were among the worst teachers, measured by how much students learn) by pointing out that all full-time D.C. teachers have teaching certificates indicating that they are trained grade school teachers. Again, what this really means is just that they all have completed a training program for grade school teachers—whether they are trained in the sense that they know how to teach small children is something else.

---

[5] Peter A. Iseman, "The Arabian Ethos," *Harper's*, February 1978.

> I never flatly said something that I thought was incorrect. I gave political answers. I gave answers that circumvented the questions, which were political.
> —Ron Ziegler, Nixon's presidential press secretary, in 1978, after admitting he told untruths to the press, but never knowingly.

Next it's Joseph D. Duffey, Assistant Secretary of State for Educational and Cultural Affairs (Washington is a wonderland of titles) in 1978, concerning work of the Bureau of Educational and Cultural Affairs:

> At such a time, the stimulation of transformational linkages necessary for meaningful two-way communication must supersede propagandistic and chauvinistic functions which in the past constituted too large a share of our activities.

The *Washington Star* has a regular "Gobbledygook" item in every issue. Here was their "Gobbledygook" for 22 September 1978:

> From a proposed Department of Energy rule, Federal Register, July 10, 1978: "Base period means the month corresponding to the current month in the 12-month period ending in the second full month prior to the month in which the Administrator issues an order effectuating the special rule, or such other 12-month period as the Administrator should consider appropriate."

What gives this quote zing is the key word "effectuating."

Let's examine one more political example to illustrate the sneakiness of "denatured" language. Here is Admiral Isaac C. Kidd, Chief of Navy Materiel, explaining a Navy memo urging contractors to spend another $400 million to keep Congress from cutting Navy appropriations:[6]

> We have gone with teams of competent contract people from Washington to outlying field activities to look over their books with them . . . to see in what areas there is susceptibility to improved capability to commit funds.

In other words, the Navy asked contractors to try to increase costs so the Navy could spend more money. Doublespeak masks the true import of language behind the dull mush of emotively neutral circumlocutions.

---

[6]*Washington Monthly*, May 1972.

D. C. REDEVELOPMENT LAND AGENCY

M E M O R A N D U M   May 4, 1972

TO : SEE ATTACHED DISTRIBUTION LIST

FROM: Harold D. Scott

SUBJ: Intra-Agency Communication

      In order to avoid negative re-
flections as a result of dysfunctional
internal communications, and in order to
enhance the possibilies of coordinated
balances I am strongly urging that any
item having a direct or indirect affect
on the NW#1 Project Area be made known
to me before, rather than after it's oc-
curence, when possible.

      Your cooperation in achieving a
better communication channel relative to
NW#1 would be greatly appreciated.

Attachment

Government memos often use jargon to hide (relative) triviality—to make communications seem more important than they really are (in addition to protecting the writer by getting a document "on the record"). The above memo, translated into plain English, seems to say simply this: Please let me know when something is going to happen which concerns NW#1 Project Area before it happens rather than after, when it's too late. *But it all sounds so much more important and professional in doublespeak.* This was a "Memo of the Month" in the *Washington Monthly.*

Legislation by Redefinition

One way to get around a law is to change the meanings of key terms or expressions. The law in many places requires that no interest be paid on checking accounts. To get around this, a few banks have instituted a system whereby depositors have two accounts, one savings and one checking (with no minimum balance). By switching funds from one account to another at the proper moment—when the depositor's "check" must be made good—the bank makes sure there is always enough money in a checking account to cover checks drawn but never any money not drawing interest. The effect is that you have a checking account, labeled a savings account, into which you deposit money, and a phantom "checking account," labeled a checking account, into which you need deposit nothing. You thus get interest on a checking account mislabeled a savings account. Clear?

The U.S. Constitution grants Congress the sole right to declare war. So a president who wants to engage in a military venture without getting the consent of Congress (perhaps it could be obtained at best only with great effort and political expense) will be inclined to *rename* his military venture. U.S. military forces have fought in several places since World War II, our last declared war—the most prominent being Korea, Vietnam, and Cambodia.

Rosalynn Carter wanted to be head of a new twenty-member presidential commission on mental health. But the law says she can't be given that post, because she is a relative of someone in a high government position. So she became "honorary chairperson" instead, with all the powers usually associated with being chairperson. Marriage to the president of the United States has its privileges, and the right to call a thing something else so the law will deal differently with that thing—to fool around with names to get what you want —is (sometimes) one of them.

Academese

Now for a bit of *academese,* which has a sleep-inducing quality all its own. First, a tiny snippet from Zellig Harris's well-known text "Structural Linguistics," to give a feel for the genre:

> Another consideration is the availability of simultaneity, in addition to successivity as a relation among linguistic elements.

Which may, or may not, mean simply that we can simultaneously do things like wink an eye and talk and we also can say words one after another. You didn't know that, did you?

In his book *The Dragons of Eden,* Carl Sagan explains a bit of academese:

> With this evidence, paleontologists [titles in the professions rival those in government] have deduced that "bipedalism preceded encephalization" by which they mean that our ancestors walked on two legs before they evolved big brains.

The *Washington Monthly* (February 1979) noticed that writer Tom Wolfe referred to what he perceived as a very self-centered generation in America as the "me" generation, but when social scientists picked up the idea, they translated it as "the culture of narcissism."

It might be naïvely supposed that academics who wrote in academese would as a consequence not be read, and thus have little influence in their fields. But that isn't the way it works. Here is a typical example of the writing of a very famous and extremely influential sociologist, Talcott Parsons:

> Skills constitute the manipulative techniques of human goal attainment and control in relation to the physical world, so far as artifacts for machines especially designed as tools do not yet supplement them. Truly human skills are guided by organized and codified *knowledge* of both the things to be manipulated and the human capacities that are used to manipulate them. Such knowledge is an aspect of cultural level symbolic processes, and . . . requires the capacities of the human central nervous system, particularly the brain. This organic system is clearly essential to all the symbolic processes . . .

This passage was cited by Stanislav Andreski,[7] who translated it into ". . . A developed brain, acquired skills, and knowledge are needed for attaining human goals." Which sounds about right.

From *Non-Being and Something-Ness*, by Woody Allen. Drawn by Stuart Hample. © 1978 by I. W. A. Enterprises, Inc. and Hackenbush Production, Inc. Reprinted by permission of Random House, Inc.

A common feature of academese, as of all jargon, is padding—adding significant sounding sentences here and there which in fact say little or nothing. Here is an example from a *Human Nature* article (August 1978) on psychological causes of illness: "Although the effects of mental attitudes on bodily disease should not be exaggerated, neither should they be minimized." True. And here's one from *Psychology Today* (July 1979): "As soon as there are behaviors you can't generate then there are responses you can't elicit." Yes.

[7] In *Social Science as Sorcery* (London: Andre Deutsch, 1972).

3.   *Sexism in Language*

In the last ten years or so, a minor language revolution has been taking place as a result of the demands of women's rights advocates and because of a quickly evolving consensus against sexist language. Perhaps the first sign of this consensus was the publication of "Guidelines for Equal Treatment of the Sexes . . ." by McGraw-Hill publishing company, guidelines that were quickly adopted by most publishers.[8] Here are some dos and don'ts listed in various places in the guidelines which show how far this part of the language revolution has gone:

NO	YES
mankind	humanity, human beings, human race, people
If a man drove 50 miles at 60 m.p.h.	If a person (or driver) drove 50 miles at 60 m.p.h.
the best man for the job	the best person (or candidate) for the job
manmade	artificial, synthetic, manufactured, constructed of human origin
manpower	human power, human energy, workers, workforce
grow to manhood	grow to adulthood, grow to manhood *or* womanhood

(1) Reword to eliminate unnecessary gender pronouns.

NO	YES
The average American drinks his coffee black.	The average American drinks black coffee.
(2) Recast into the plural.	Most Americans drink their coffee black.

(3) Replace the masculine pronoun with *one, he or she, her or his*, as appropriate. (Use *he or she* and its variations sparingly to avoid clumsy prose.)
(4) Alternate male and female expressions and examples.

NO	YES
I've often heard supervisors say, "He's not the right man for the job," or "He lacks the qualifications for success."	I've often heard supervisors say, "She's not right for the job," or "He lacks the qualifications for success."

---

[8] Reprinted by permission of the McGraw-Hill Book Co.

NO	YES
congressman	member of Congress, Representative (but Congress*man* Koch and Congress*woman* Holzman)
businessman	business executive, business manager
fireman	fire fighter
mailman	mail carrier; letter carrier
salesman	sales representative; salesperson; sales clerk
insurance man	insurance agent
statesman	leader; public servant
chairman	the person presiding at (or chairing) a meeting; the presiding officer; the chair; head, leader, coordinator, moderator
cameraman	camera operator
foreman	supervisor

NO	YES
the men and the ladies	the men and the women; the ladies and the gentlemen; the girls and the boys
man and wife	husband and wife
Bobby Riggs and Billie Jean	Bobby Riggs and Billie Jean King
Billie Jean and Riggs	Billie Jean and Bobby
Mrs. King and Riggs	King and Riggs or Ms. King (because she prefers Ms.) and Mr. Riggs
Mrs. Meir and Moshe Dayan	Golda Meir and Moshe Dayan or Mrs. Meir and Mr. Dayan

NO	YES
the fair sex; the weaker sex	women
the distaff side	the female side or line
the girls or the ladies (when adult females are meant)	the women
girl, as in: I'll have my *girl* check that.	I'll have my *secretary* (or my *assistant*) check that. (Or use the person's name.)

lady, used as a modifier, in *lady* lawyer	lawyer (A woman may be identified simply through the choice of pronouns, as in: The *lawyer* made her summation to the jury. Try to avoid gender modifiers altogether. When you must modify, use woman or female, as in: a course on women writers.)
NO	**YES**
Pioneers moved West, taking their wives and children with them.	Pioneer families moved West. Or Pioneer men and women (or pioneer couples) moved West, taking their children with them.

A *Wilmington Comment* on Governor Tribbitt's appointment of Irene Shadoan of the Associated Press as his press secretary at $20,000 a year: "If he wants to pay $10,000 a mammary, that's his business."
From *Delaware State News*, reprinted in *Ms.* magazine

Can you imagine a similar remark about paying a man $10,000 a testicle?

On the other hand, things can be carried too far. It would be silly, for instance, for Germans to stop referring to their homeland as *The Fatherland,* or Englishmen, that is, ah, citizens of England, to their "mother tongue." Nor does there seem to be anything wrong with the predominantly male members of a ship referring to their particular tug as *she.* And what, if anything, was gained by having the second, fourth, and sixth Atlantic hurricane of 1979 called "Bob," "David," and "Frederic" rather than, say, "Betsy," "Dolores," and "Florence"?

Summary of Chapter Six

1. Most words have emotive meanings (in addition to cognitive meanings). Words like "oppression," "kike," and "bitch" have more or less negative (con) emotive overtones; words like "spring," "free," and "satisfaction" positive (pro) emotive overtones; and words like "socialism," "marijuana," and "God" mixed emotive overtones.

   Words that have roughly the same cognitive meaning often have radically different emotive meanings: "Bureaucrat," "government official," and "public servant," illustrate this.

   The point of becoming aware of the emotive side of language is not to learn to avoid such language—the emotive element gives language much of its charm, interest, and importance. Emotively neutral language is dull. The point is to learn to use the emotive side of language effectively and not to be taken in by its misuses.

Con artists use the emotive side of language (1) to mask cognitive meaning by whipping up emotions so that reason is overlooked; and (2) to dull the force of language so as to make acceptable what otherwise might not be. The latter often is accomplished by means of euphemisms (less offensive expressions used in place of more offensive ones) or a kind of doublespeak that lulls the unwary into acceptance.

It also should be noted that the meanings of words and expressions sometimes are changed so as either to get around or to take advantage of laws, rules, or customs. Calling Mrs. Carter "Honorary Chairperson" when she was really chairperson (contrary to the law) is an example.

2. The English language contains features that mirror sexist attitudes of our past. The McGraw-Hill guidelines have been adopted by most publishers to rid written English of these locutions. For example, they require us to replace the word "manpower" by, say, "human power."

Exercises for Chapter Six

1. Critically evaluate this short *New York Daily* editorial (5 April 1972), paying special attention to its use of emotive language.

Any Old Jobs for Homos?

Herewith, a cheer for the U.S. Supreme Court's ruling Monday (with Justice W. O. Douglas dissenting—but you knew that) that states governments have a right to refuse employment to homosexuals.

Fairies, nances, swishes, fags, lezzes—call 'em what you please—should of course be permitted to earn honest livings in nonsensitive jobs.

But government, from federal on down, should have full freedom to bar them from jobs in which their peculiarities would make them security or other risks. It is to be hoped that this Supreme Court decision will stand for the foreseeable future.

    a. List the heavily emotive words or expressions you feel are used unfairly, explaining *why* in each case.

    b. Rewrite the editorial so that its cognitive import is the same, but the language used is as emotively neutral as possible. Compare your version with the original editorial for persuasive power.

2. What do you think (and why, of course) of Robert J. Ringer's explanation (in his book *Looking Out for Number One*) of President Kennedy's famous statement, "And so, my fellow Americans, ask not what your country can do for you; ask what you can do for your country"?

Ask what you can do for your *country*? Does this mean asking each of the more than 200 million individuals what you can do for him? No, individuals are not what Kennedy or any other politician has ever had in mind when using the word *country*. A country is an abstract entity, but in

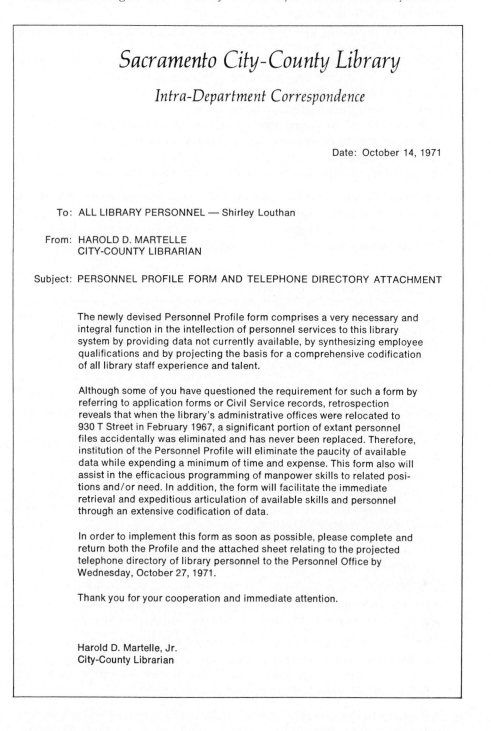

Sacramento City-County Library

Intra-Department Correspondence

Date: October 14, 1971

To: ALL LIBRARY PERSONNEL — Shirley Louthan

From: HAROLD D. MARTELLE
CITY-COUNTY LIBRARIAN

Subject: PERSONNEL PROFILE FORM AND TELEPHONE DIRECTORY ATTACHMENT

The newly devised Personnel Profile form comprises a very necessary and integral function in the intellection of personnel services to this library system by providing data not currently available, by synthesizing employee qualifications and by projecting the basis for a comprehensive codification of all library staff experience and talent.

Although some of you have questioned the requirement for such a form by referring to application forms or Civil Service records, retrospection reveals that when the library's administrative offices were relocated to 930 T Street in February 1967, a significant portion of extant personnel files accidentally was eliminated and has never been replaced. Therefore, institution of the Personnel Profile will eliminate the paucity of available data while expending a minimum of time and expense. This form also will assist in the efficacious programming of manpower skills to related positions and/or need. In addition, the form will facilitate the immediate retrieval and expeditious articulation of available skills and personnel through an extensive codification of data.

In order to implement this form as soon as possible, please complete and return both the Profile and the attached sheet relating to the projected telephone directory of library personnel to the Personnel Office by Wednesday, October 27, 1971.

Thank you for your cooperation and immediate attention.

Harold D. Martelle, Jr.
City-County Librarian

politicalese, it translates into "those in power." Restated in translated form, then, it becomes: Ask not what those in power can do for you; ask what you can do for those in power.

3. On the opposite page is another memo used by the *Washington Monthly* as a Memo of the Month. Translate the body of the memo into plain English, coming as close to the original meaning (so far as it can be determined) as you can.

*4. Translate the following excerpt (from *Usable Knowledge: Social Science and Social Problem Solving,* by Charles E. Lindblom and David K. Cohen— mentioned in a book review in the *Washington Monthly*):

By social problem solving, we mean processes that are to eventuate in outcomes that by some standard are an improvement on the previously existing situation, or are presumed to so eventuate, or are conceived of as offering some possibility to so eventuate.

5. Here is a passage from a United States history textbook, *America: Its People and Values* (by Leonard C. Wood, Ralph H. Gabriel, and Edward L. Biller):

A friendly Indian named Squanto helped the colonists. He showed them how to plant corn and how to live in the wilderness. A soldier, Captain Miles Standish, taught the Pilgrims how to defend themselves against unfriendly Indians.

How is emotive language used to slant this account? In what other ways is it slanted?

6. Try to find some examples of inappropriate names being applied to things so that the law, custom, or whatever will deal with these things differently (as, for instance, the law allowing Rosalynn Carter to be the chairperson by calling her the "Honorary Chairperson"), and explain the chicanery.

7. Check the media (newspapers, magazines, television, radio, books) and find several examples of doublespeak or jargon, and translate into plain English.

8. Check the media for sexist uses of language, and translate so as to remove the sexist connotations.

9. Check your automobile insurance policy (or somebody's insurance policy). If it isn't written in the new clear style, rewrite the first 250 words or so to say the same thing in plain English. (Lots of luck.)

"If the coach and horses and the footmen and the beautiful clothes all turned back into the pumpkin and the mice and the rags, then how come the glass slipper didn't turn back, too?"

Two important factors in critical or creative thinking are (1) the ability to bring relevant background information to bear on a problem; and (2) the ability to carry through the relevant implications of an argument or position to determine whether they hang together. The above cartoon illustrates the latter. The child carries through the reasoning in the Cinderella story and finds it wanting. A child who brings relevant background information to bear on the Santa Claus story (for instance, a child who realizes there are millions of chimneys for Santa to get down in one night and wonders how he could manage to do so in time) illustrates the former.

Chapter Seven

Analyzing Extended Arguments

*The prejudice against careful analytic
procedure is part of the human impatience
with technique which arises from the fact
that men are interested in results and
would like to attain them without the
painful toil which is the essence of our
moral finitude.*
—Morris R. Cohen

*There is no expedient to which a man will
not resort to avoid the real labor of
thinking.*
—Sir Joshua Reynolds

So far we have considered relatively short arguments and these mainly to illustrate fallacious reasoning. But in daily life we usually encounter longer passages, containing several connected arguments. It takes more than just the ability to spot fallacies to deal with such extended passages.

There are many methods for analyzing extended passages; what is best for one person may not be for another. The margin note-summary method introduced in this chapter is a method many people find congenial as an ideal to be approached more or less in daily life as time permits and interest dictates.

The margin note-summary method is based on the idea that a summary is more easily digested than the original material and therefore more accurately evaluated. (Of course, the summary must be accurate to begin with.) There are four basic steps in the margin note-summary method:

1. Read the material to be evaluated.

2. Read it through again, this time marking the important passages, perhaps with an indication of content written in the margin (taking advantage of what was learned from the first reading).

3. Use the margin notes to construct a summary of the passage.

4. Evaluate the original material by evaluating the summary, checking the original to be sure there are no differences between the two which are relevant to the evaluation.

1. Editorials

Newspaper, magazine, radio, and television editorials constitute an important and interesting part of the political scene. Let's examine an editorial from the *New York Times*, often said to be the best and most influential newspaper in the United States. The flavor of their editorials reflects their august position (in other words, their editorials tend to be stuffy). Here is the *Times* editorial[1] with margin notes attached.

Astoria Compromise

As an interim answer to a difficult problem requiring immediate resolution, Mayor Lindsay's compromise decision on the proposed generating plant in Astoria has much to recommend it. Consolidated Edison has won permission to go ahead and build what it regards as urgently needed capacity to meet this community's electricity needs. But those who opposed the project because of understandable fear of additional pollution can console themselves that the expansion will be only half that originally requested.

(1) Conclusion: Lindsay compromise is good.

(2) Permits Con Ed what it thinks is needed capacity.

(3) But it's a true compromise: Con Ed permitted only one-half the requested increase.

Unfortunately, before the Mayor settled the issue, he fostered a bitter public debate that not only pitted some of his key subordinates against each other, but also inflamed the passions and fears of many. The angry reactions of some Astoria residents to the Lindsay compromise raise the unhappy possibility that the dispute has not ended, and that new and difficult roadblocks may appear to hamper those trying to build even the smaller generating plant the Mayor has approved.

[Paragraph skipped because anecdotal; not relevant to the main drift of the editorial.]

The future may show, however, that the real importance of Mayor Lindsay's decision was its enunciation of an important principle fundamental to a rational antipollution policy. In effect, Mr. Lindsay has recognized that the city's supply of clean air is a limited resource whose availability must be protected by a comprehensive policy that takes account of all sources of pollution, rather than merely dealing with individual sources in isolation. "If some pollution is inevitable and the choice is between sufficient electrical power or streets congested with automobiles," the Mayor said, "I would choose electrical power."

(4) Real import of L's decision: it voices idea that air is limited & all pollution sources must be considered.

(5) He advocates electric power over auto pollution when choice required.

Having articulated his correct understanding that tradeoffs must be calculated and choices made, Mayor Lindsay has already appointed a five-member committee to work out a plan for limiting motor vehicle pollution here. The organization called Citizens for Clean Air has gone a step further and asked the Mayor to ban

(6) Believing tradeoffs necessary, he's appointed committee to plan.

(7) Lindsay asked to ban private cars from

---

[1] "Astoria Compromise," © 1970 by The New York Times Company. Reprinted by permission.

private automobile traffic from Manhattan south of 59th Street during business hours. This is the direction in which the city must move to protect its most precious possession, the air its citizens breathe.

And here is an itemized summary of what one person takes to be the main points of the editorial:

1. Mayor Lindsay's compromise on Con Ed's Astoria plant expansion has much to recommend it.

2. It permits them to build what they believe is urgently needed capacity.

3. But it compromises with the other side, since Con Ed is permitted only half of the increase it asked for.

4. The real import of Lindsay's decision may rest in his voicing of the rational antipollution idea that clean air is limited and must be protected by policies that consider all sources of pollution.

5. Lindsay (rightly?) advocates choosing electric power over auto pollution when a choice is required.

6. Understanding that "tradeoffs must be calculated" and "choices made," Lindsay has appointed a committee to plan for limited auto pollution in New York.

7. Citizens for Clean Air has asked Lindsay to ban private autos from parts of Manhattan during business hours.

8. This is the direction New York must move in to obtain clean air.

Two things need to be said about using the margin note-summary method. First, when we skip part of a passage, we make a value judgment that the skipped material is relatively unimportant. It takes practice and skill to know what to include and what to omit, and "experts" will differ on such matters. And, second, margin notes and summaries are shorthand devices, and should be briefer than the passage analyzed. But any shortening runs the risk of falsification. When using margin notes or summaries to aid in reasoning, remember that we don't want to draw conclusions from the shortened version that would not be valid for the original.

Notice that the *Times* editorial contains very few, if any, unnecessary emotive or value-tinged terms, and was constructed in a fairly orderly way. (Compare this with the *Daily News* editorial used as an exercise at the end of the chapter.) Nevertheless, it is not a paragon of rationality. Let's take the important statements in the editorial one by one, and then append a general comment.

Assertion 1 simply presents the claim to be defended in the editorial—that Lindsay's compromise was, on the whole, good. Assertion 2 tells us that Con Ed believed the increase was needed. Was Con Ed right? A very technical question; we are forced to bow to Con Ed's view unless someone presents pertinent evidence to the contrary (or unless we already have relevant back-ground information). Expert testimony of this kind frequently is refuted by other evidence. But in this case, apparently, it was not; Con Ed did seem to need increased capacity to cover increases that were likely if unrestrained use of power continued to be permitted. (Whether they needed to double the Astoria plant capacity is another matter.)

Assertion 3 in effect comes close to saying that Lindsay's Solomon-like decision was right *because* it was a fifty-fifty compromise. The *Times* editorial thus seems to have committed what is often called the fallacy of the *golden mean,* since it nowhere defends Lindsay's decision *qua* its being a halfway measure. For instance, it doesn't argue that granting only one-quarter the requested increase would not be sufficient, or that granting it all would be too much. Assertion 4 is noncontroversial. Almost everyone pays lip service to it. (Living up to it is another matter.)

Assertion 5, while controversial, was not at issue between antipollutionists, Con Ed, and the mayor. We have here a genuine value judgment of great importance concerning which all of us must make up our minds. If the need to reduce air pollution forces us to choose, say, between restricting private auto travel or restricting electric power use (for example, of air conditioners), which should we prefer? There are facts pertinent to the choice, such as the possibility of alternative modes of transportation. But they don't automatically determine the choice. It is human beings, using these facts, who must decide. Notice that the *Times* editorial neither presents these facts nor reasons from them. It simply presents Lindsay's conclusion.

But assertion 6 is the crux. (Let's skip 7 and 8 to shorten the discussion.) There are two important comments to make about 6: First, some opponents of Mayor Lindsay claimed that for a while at least, we could have both less power plant pollution and less auto pollution without restricting the use of either, by (1) putting new power plants out of town in low-pollution areas; (2) requiring electric power producers such as Con Ed to use more expensive but also more efficient antipollution devices,[2] and (3) requiring more expensive but also more efficient auto pollution devices, ultimately requiring replacement of internal-combustion engines by something else, such as the gas-turbine en-gine.

And, second, talk of "tradeoffs" and "compromises" masks the fact that while Con Ed was granted something tangible by Lindsay's decision (an in-crease in productive capacity), the other side was given talk and promises (a commission set up to *plan* for limiting pollution).

In other words, as opponents of Mayor Lindsay argued with some justifica-tion, he granted an increase to Con Ed, which inevitably would increase air pollution, but only paid lip service to one of the antipollutionist arguments (that ultimately we must choose between power and autos, and power should on the whole win). In addition, Lindsay ignored the other major antipollution-ist proposals to expand power facilities out of town and to require more expensive but also more efficient emission devices and equipment.

---

[2] For more on this, see article by Anna Mayo in the *Village Voice,* 13 August 1970.

The *New York Times,* it should be pointed out, seems to have been guilty along with Mayor Lindsay. In particular, the *Times* was guilty of suppressing evidence contrary to the conclusion it wanted to draw. This is one of the *Times*'s chief devices for making its editorials seem plausible to its readers. Its position of prestige and authority does not permit open appeals to emotion or prejudice of the kind many other newspapers employ. Omissions are much less obvious than the use of emotively charged phrases. They also are probably more effective with an intelligent but inadequately informed audience.

2.   Speeches and Debates

Political speeches and debates are generally listened to rather than read. This makes critical analysis much more difficult (because the arguments zing by too quickly for proper assessment), and margin notes become impossible (except on written versions).

One way to handle spoken rhetoric is to write down the point or points at issue and then, as they are presented, write down the reasons given pro and con for each point. The result will contain the essence of what has been said, which we then can analyze when there is more time.

But another way to deal with spoken rhetoric is to get a written copy of the text. Written copies are usually quite easy to get by writing to the speaker (for instance, writing to the White House for a copy of a presidential speech), and often are printed in newspapers and magazines. Similarly, television debates and issue programs, becoming more and more important, can be obtained by writing to the network or other originator of the material. When the issue is serious enough, it's worth the effort to obtain a written version of what was said.

Let's now look at some excerpts from the CBS "Sixty Minutes" program of 5 November 1978.[3] ("Sixty Minutes" has for some time been the most influential news program on television—there have been weeks when it has won the highest Nielsen listener rating of any program.) The topic this time was the Scottsdale, Arizona, private-enterprise, nonunion fire department. Here is the first excerpt, with margin notes attached:

Mike Wallace: In other cities Scottsdale's size, there are at least a hundred full-time fire fighters on the payroll. Scottsdale does it with forty-five career professionals, who work longer hours and make more than their counterparts in the area, and the twenty-six auxiliaries, who can earn an extra $200 a month above their regular city pay. The price tag for this manpower? It costs the taxpayers of Scottsdale a bargain $700,000 a year, compared to the national average of $2 million a year for cities Scottsdale's size.

(1) Wallace: *Scottsdale's private nonunion fire department employs 45 full-time & 26 part-time fire fighters, far fewer & at much less cost than the average for its size.*

---

[3] © CBS Inc. 1978. All rights reserved. Originally broadcast 5 November 1978 over the CBS Television Network as part of the "60 Minutes" program series.

William Howard McClennan: But Scottsdale is a glorified volunteer fire department.

Wallace: William Howard McClennan, president of the strong and militant International Association of Fire Fighters—175,000 members. He despises Fire Chief Lou Witzeman's fire department. His union back in 1971 went out to Scottsdale, took a look, and then filed a report on Witzeman's nonunion outfit. It was not favorable.

He's been lucky you say. His fire defenses are all glitter and veneer, with no substance. The citizens are not properly protected. The stations are too far apart, the runs too long, the time factor too great, et cetera. . . . That was seven years ago. I would think that Scottsdale would be lying in ruins by now.

McClennan: Every one of those things you've just read off, Mike, the same is true. Hasn't changed any. He's been lucky. . . .

Wallace: And you think that some day their luck is going to run out?

McClennan: That's right.

Wallace: And that's when they're going to need—

McClennan: A real fire department.

> *(2)* McClennan: *But it's a glorified volunteer dept.*
>
> *(3)* Wallace: *Have they just been lucky not to have had a fire catastrophe?*
>
> *(4)* McClennan: *They've just been lucky. Their luck will change some day, & they'll need a "real fire department."*

So far, the stage has just been set for the major exchanges. Wallace clearly is going to try to uphold the idea that the Scottsdale nongovernment, nonunion fire department does a good job at much less cost. McClennan is going to argue that their success so far has just been luck and that the department is not providing adequate fire protection, particularly because it is nonunion. But even at this point, McClennan has hit below the belt in calling Scottsdale's professional, paid fire department a "volunteer" fire department. It is nonunion, not volunteer; it has some part-time employees, not volunteer employees.

Now here is the next exchange:

Wallace: But other experts heartily disagree with McClennan. They found that Witzeman's Rural-Metro does provide effective fire protection, and economically. In fact, at a far lower cost than surrounding Arizona communities pay.

McClennan: You'd have to analyze that, and then take a city of the same size, with the same conditions, with a . . . paid fire department, and see what the difference is in . . . dollars and cents loss . . . by fire. . . .

Wallace: The very thing that you've suggested, President McClennan, has been done by the Institute for Local Self-Government. It's been done by this outfit out in Berkeley, California. And I've got to tell you, Scottsdale comes up with very, very good marks on every point that you raise. . . .

> *(5)* Wallace: *Other experts disagree with McClennan. They think Scottsdale's department provides effective protection at a lower cost than surrounding cities.*
>
> *(6)* McClennan: *You have to take a city of the same size, with similar conditions, with a paid fire department, & compare money losses from fires.*
>
> *(7)* Wallace: *That was done by the Institute for Local Self-Government in Berkeley, & Scottsdale does well.*

McClennan: They couldn't put a match out, Mike, if there was a fire.

Wallace: But putting a match out was not what the Institute had in mind. Their job was to rate the fire departments in Scottsdale and in three neighboring communities. And their professional survey concluded that Scottsdale's nonunion fire department performed just as efficiently and for far less taxpayer money than the other three union fire departments. That is what bothers President McClennan. For you see, McClennan's IAFF had tried but failed to unionize Scottsdale's Rural-Metro. And he has charged that because there is no union, Witzeman can cut his fire-fighting force to dangerous, unsafe levels.

McClennan: We feel, as members of a union, that our interests should be looking out for the guy that rides on the back step, and we should be fighting—they have the proper number of men there at all times. It takes X number of men to do this and to get that line of hose and to get that water operating on the fire.

(8) McClennan: *The IFLSG couldn't put a match out in a fire.*

(9) Wallace: *That wasn't their job. They compared Scottsdale with three nearby communities, & found their nonunion department just as effective at far less cost, apparently without being understaffed, as McClennan charged, because there is no union.*

(10) McClennan: *As union members, we should look out for the fire fighter's interests, & should want the proper number of fire fighters on trucks at all times.*

In this exchange, McClennan is guilty of an interesting irrelevancy: that the IFLSG couldn't put a match out in a fire, since, as Wallace pointed out, their job was to evaluate fire departments, not put out fires. This irrelevant comment was intended as an attack on the credibility of an expert witness, the IFLSG, and thus indirectly but no less falsely charged Wallace with committing the fallacy of *appeal to authority.*

McClennan then attacked Wallace's claim that the Scottsdale department is doing a satisfactory job by arguing that they sometimes go to fires with fewer fire fighters than needed, that is, fewer than union rules require. And that certainly gets to the nub of one of the key issues in this as well as many other disputes concerning union and nonunion labor: whether union rules require *featherbedding* (that is, require more labor than is really needed, the classic example being the fireman required on diesel trains that have no fires to stoke).

So far, Wallace has argued that experience shows Scottsdale's department doesn't seem to need more men on fire trucks, indicating that union requirements do indeed constitute featherbedding. McClennan says they're just lucky. This means that the issue comes down to a question concerning statistics. Witzeman's private company has been fighting fires in Scottsdale for thirty years; is that enough time to get a representative sample of fire-fighting problems in the city of Scottsdale? Common sense says *yes.*

(In the next exchange, omitted here to shorten matters, fire chief Witzeman also argued that union rules aim at having sufficient numbers of fire fighters at the biggest fires, while his rules require just the number needed for each fire. Witzeman also argued that rigid fire inspections and, as in the case of Scottsdale, a strict fire sprinkler code, save a great deal on fire protection. This points the way to reducing fire damage without having a lot of fire fighters on each truck.)

Wallace: Are the taxpayers of Scottsdale really getting shortchanged . . . by having Witzeman's penny-pinching department protect them? One way to find out how good a fire department is is to check on that town's fire insurance rating. We did, with the Arizona Insurance Service Office. They told us that Scottsdale's insurance premiums for homeowners are no higher than those in surrounding towns. So a Scottsdale resident has got to say, . . . "Look, I'm getting good fire protection. My insurance premiums are the same. And I'm paying half the price they're paying next door. . . ."

(11) Wallace: *Scottsdale's fire insurance premiums are no higher than for surrounding towns, evidence that insurance companies believe the risk is no higher.*

McClennan: My answer is simple. If . . . it's all that you paint it to be, Mike, . . . how come there's only one in the whole United States?

(12) McClennan: *Then why is this the only one in the whole United States?*

Wallace: You're a very powerful organization. . . . You support politicians. It's going to be very difficult for a . . . town to turn their back on the IAFF, and you know it.

(13) Wallace: *It's hard politically for a town to defeat an entrenched fire fighters' union.*

McClellan: Public employees were always good at that, Mike. That's why they survived.

(14) McClennan: *Public employees survive because they have been good at that.*

McClennan's first task was to counter Wallace's evidence concerning insurance premiums. He had to show that the insurance companies were wrong in this case. He tried to do this by appealing to the authority of a *common practice* —namely, the practice of having union fire departments. Wallace countered this by arguing in effect that insurance companies are better authorities than those who have unionized a fire department, pointing out that unionization often depends on political rather than just economic or safety factors. Is he right? For what it's worth, this writer's background information supports Mike Wallace; until quite recently, it would have been very hard for a city to oust a government employees union. So the expert opinion of insurance companies, who stand to lose a great deal of money if they're wrong, should weigh more heavily. Of course, cities that hire too many fire fighters also lose (waste) a great deal of money—but that's public money, nobody's in particular, and experience shows that that is another matter entirely.

Wallace: McClennan said his union would revisit Scottsdale to see what has happened there in the seven years since his union's last report.

McClennan: We're going to give it another look, no question about it. . . .

Wallace: Why?

McClennan: Because I want to see if some of these things that you've brought out here today are actually so.

(15) McClennan: *We're going to reevaluate the Scottsdale fire department performance to see if anything you said about it is true.*

Wallace: In other words, you're keeping an open mind?

(16) Wallace: *You're keeping an open mind?*

> *McClennan:* Yeah, sure, I'm keeping an open mind.
> *Wallace:* You mean it's possible . . . that you're going to come down on the side of Scottsdale—
> *McClennan:* No way! No way, Mike.

(17) McClennan: No way.

McClennan thus intended to keep an open mind while being sure all along that Scottsdale's department would receive low marks. Mike Wallace had neatly trapped him into being *inconsistent* while admitting the truth that he didn't have an open mind on the merits of Scottsdale's privately owned, cheap (but effective) fire-fighting company.

So thanks to Mike Wallace, CBS, and "Sixty Minutes" for a pretty carefully researched and reasoned performance, quite unusual for the mass media.

3. Political Columns and Articles

Political columns and articles are two other kinds of extended arguments ripe for analysis. Here is a political column by the syndicated columnist Patrick J. Buchanan,[4] with margin notes.

U.S. Blacks Would Fight in Africa

Washington. Of all the inane remarks our "point man" at the U.N. has made, none is more disturbing than the statement 10 days ago.

(1) Our U.S. Ambassador, Andrew Young, makes inane and very disturbing (false?) statements.

In the event of an East-West showdown in Africa, says Andy Young: "I see no situation in which we would have to come in on the side of the South Africans . . . You'd have civil war at home. Maybe I ought not to say that, but I really believe it. An armed force that is 30 percent black isn't going to fight on the side of the South Africans."

This is not some hotheaded young leader of SNCC talking. This is the United States ambassador to the U.N., who holds Cabinet rank. And he has warned publicly that if his president and Congress declare that America's vital interests require the use of military force guerrillas in southern Africa, black American soldiers will mutiny. And black American civilians will rise up in insurrection.

(2) In particular, he said; (a) no situation will arise forcing U.S. troops to fight against blacks in southern Africa; (b) civil war would result here; & (c) a 30 percent black army won't fight against blacks on the side of the South Africans.

One wonders if Young—babbling away into every open microphone—is remotely aware of the slander he has leveled at the patriotism of black America.

(3) Young has slandered the patriotism of black Americans.

---

[4] Patrick J. Buchanan, *New York Times*, 26 March 1977. Reprinted by permission of The Chicago Tribune–New York News Syndicate. (The last two paragraphs, which add nothing new, have been omitted.)

When the United States entered World War I, Irish-Americans died in the trenches alongside British soldiers whose fellow units were, even then, snuffing out the flames of Irish freedom. In that same war German-Americans fought and killed their own cousins fighting for imperial Germany and the Kaiser.

(4) In the past, ethnics fought loyally, even when fighting against soldiers from the ethnic groups of their origin: for example, Irish & Germans in WWI & Germans, Italians, & Japanese in WWII.

During World War II, German-Americans, Italian-Americans, Japanese-Americans fought loyally against Nazi Germany, Fascist Italy, Imperial Japan.

They all put loyalty to America above any residual loyalty to the homeland of their fathers and grandfathers. What Young is saying is that black Americans —who have been here centuries, not just decades—do not have that kind of loyalty to the United States. In a crunch, he is saying, black America will stand with their racial kinsmen in Marxist Angola and Mozambique— rather than with their white countrymen in the United States.

(5) (a) Those groups put American loyalty above all else; (b) Young says black Americans instead will stand with racial kin in southern Africa.

What makes Young's flippancy fairly chilling is that he has just confided to the editors of *Newsweek,* "I get the feeling that Jimmy Carter wants me to take charge of Africa. . . .

Anti-white racism already seems to have become the determining factor in U.S. policy toward that continent.

(6) Anti-white racism has become the determining U.S. African policy.

Up at the U.N., Jimmy Carter, grinning away at the muted mouthpieces of some of the rankest, blood-stained ogres in history, announced that the United States had just rejoined the world conspiracy to strangle Rhodesia to death. Because Southern Rhodesia does not have "majority rule," we too will no longer buy Rhodesian exports. [This was before majority rule was won in Rhodesia.]

(7) Pres. Carter told the U.S. we won't buy (chrome) from Rhodesia because they don't have majority rule. Yet we'll buy from totalitarian Russia, controlled by communist party of less than 6 percent of population.

We will buy chrome instead from Soviet Russia, a hostile, totalitarian empire ruled by an elite party which claims the membership of less than 6 percent of the Soviet population.

How many countries in Africa, how many in the world, have majority rules with minority rights guaranteed?

Idi Amin comes from a small, dominantly Moslem tribe in Uganda which is mercilessly persecuting members of larger Christian tribes. Yet the United States, which now considers it illegal and immoral to buy Rhodesian chrome, is delighted to buy Idi Amin's coffee.

(8) Idi Amin's Uganda is ruled by small Moslem tribe persecuting larger tribes, yet we buy their coffee.

The most virulent strain of racism in the world today is not anti-black, anti-yellow, or anti-red; it is anti-white.

(9) Worst form of racism in world now is anti-white.

Reflect a moment: What makes the ruling tribes in Rhodesia and southern Africa so hated? Are they the most barbaric, repressive, dictatorial in Africa, and the world? Hardly! What makes them evil, unacceptable— what mandates their destruction—is that the skin of these particular ruling tribes is not black, but white. . . .

(10) Southern Africa is hated so much because whites rule there, not blacks.

One reason for making such an exhaustive summary is to be sure we understand the material being analyzed, which means at least being sure we have zeroed in correctly on its main conclusions, and accurately lined up its supporting arguments—we don't want our critical analysis to be of a *straw man.* In everyday life, time is too short for us to analyze even a fraction of what we read. Shortcuts therefore are in order. How short the cuts should be depends on time and the importance of the material. We're going to give a modestly full analysis of Buchanan's column; the reader may see shortcuts that would be useful in a real life analysis of this column. But first, note how much less convincing the summary is stripped of emotively charged words and expressions like "flippancy," "chilling," "babbling," "grinning away," and "blood-stained ogres."

It should be clear that Buchanan has several fish to fry in this column. He wants to argue, first, against Andrew Young as U.N. Ambassador, on grounds of his having a big, inaccurate, intemperate mouth—point (1) in the summary; second, against U.S. policy toward southern Africa, which in effect means toward Rhodesia and the Union of South Africa, on grounds that it is inconsistent with the rest of what we do—points (7) and (8) in the summary; third, that U.S. policy is anti-white—points (6) and (9) in the summary, as well as, indirectly, (7) and (8); and, finally, that Young was wrong to doubt black patriotism—point (3) in the summary. Bearing this in mind, let's look at each of the eleven points in the margin note-summary:

(1). The first point just sets the tone for the article, charging that Young is an irresponsible blabbermouth. He did do a lot of talking; the question is whether it was the wrong kind. Anyone who doesn't already believe it was wrong should be looking for Buchanan's reasons for making that judgment.

(2). The second point gives part of the relevant quote from a Young speech. It certainly supports the view that he uttered rather contentious remarks for an ambassador. The question is whether his remarks, in particular the one Buchanan quoted from, were "inane," "disturbing," or some such.

(3). The third point in the summary is that Young's remarks slandered the patriotism of black Americans, who would and ought to fight where told to. If true, it lends support to the charge made in (1) that Young said things he shouldn't have.

(4) and (5). Buchanan then argues for point (3) by analogy: white ethnic Americans fought against their ethnic kin in past wars, so black Americans ought to be prepared to fight against their racial kin in southern Africa, and will in fact fight against black southern Africans if required to do so (which is why Young's remark was a bad one—it was just plain false).

But Buchanan's analogy is not a good one, because the cases compared are not relevantly similar. His analogy is thus *questionable.* Take the German-

Americans who fought in World War II against their ethnic kin in Nazi Germany. This was a case where the security and even survival of the United States was believed to be at stake—a Nazi victory could have meant the end of the United States as we know it. That is definitely not the case with southern Africa.

Further, although the Nazis persecuted some (non-Jewish) Germans, on the whole it was non-Germans (Poles, Russians, and others) who were their targets. But when Young made his comment, southern Africa was ruled by white minorities who enslaved black majorities. Having black American soldiers fight in support of such white minorities thus would be more like having had Christian Americans (white or black) fight in Uganda on the side of Idi Amin's government against persecuted Christian religious kin (black or white). Suppose in that circumstance a Christian ambassador to the U.N. said: "I see no situation in which we would have to come in on the side of Amin [meaning, as Young meant in the case of Rhodesia and South Africa, on the side of the enslaving ruling minority]. You'd have civil war at home. An armed force that is 80 percent Christian isn't going to fight on the side of a Ugandan minority persecuting our fellow Christians who are its majority." (Buchanan passed over the fact that Young was talking about siding with an enslaving small minority against an enslaved large majority struggling for freedom.) Would Buchanan have argued that such a comment slandered the patriotism of Christian Americans? Or that it was "inane" and "disturbing"?

This last brings us to another problem with his column. There are at least two complaints Buchanan can be making: first, that Young is too outspoken to make a good ambassador; and second, that what he says is far from the truth. The first is a claim for which he provides evidence; let's grant it, although there are arguments on the other side (for instance, that Young's outbursts were good for relations with black-ruled African countries). The second (that Young strayed far from the truth) Buchanan backs up by his analogy with other ethnic Americans, an analogy we argued above was not cogent. This means he has not successfully defended his claim that Young's remarks were false, or "inane," or whatever.

(6) and (9). The second half of Buchanan's column argues for the conclusion that American policy in southern Africa is anti-white (the implication being that that's why we had talkative Young as U.N. Ambassador). Point (6) merely states this conclusion; point (9) restates it.

(7) and (8). This is Buchanan's defense of point (6), that our policy is anti-white. He argues that support of majority rule cannot be the real reason for our not buying chrome from Rhodesia, contrary to President Carter's claim, because we buy chrome from Russia and coffee from Uganda where no majority rule exists. So it must be that we're anti-white in our policies.

But this argument is poor. In effect its form is this: either it is our African policy to support majority rule or else our policy is anti-white. It can't be that our policy is to support majority rule, because we don't do so in general (think of Uganda and Russia). Therefore, our policy must be anti-white.

The argument has the form *disjunctive syllogism*, introduced in Chapter One, and is deductively valid. But are its premises warranted? No, they aren't.

Its first premise is unwarranted, because there are many other policies we might have toward southern Africa (for instance, to support anti-communist governments, or to support stable or reliable governments), thus setting us up for a *false dilemma.* And its second premise is at least questionable. Buchanan does show that our policy cannot be *merely* to support majority rule, since we support minority governments elsewhere. But he doesn't show that our policy is not, say, to support majority rule when we can afford to. It could have been, and in fact seemed to have been the case, at least with respect to Rhodesia and the chrome-buying problem, that support of majority rule fitted nicely with other policy objectives, while in the case certainly of the Soviet Union and plausibly of Uganda, supporting majority rule would have meant sacrificing all sorts of other objectives.

General conclusion. Buchanan manages to provide good evidence for at best only one of his conclusions—that Young was too talkative and contentious to be a good ambassador. He didn't prove that Young's remarks were inane or that they should be disturbing (he didn't even prove they were false or give reason to doubt them). He didn't show that Young had slandered black Americans, since he never showed that what Young said was false. *(Slander:* a false report maliciously uttered, tending to injure reputation.) And finally, he didn't show that American policy toward Africa (or anywhere) is anti-white. (Without mountains of evidence to support such a charge, the ironic idea that U.S. policy is or ever has been anti-white is ridiculous.) A typical political column?

Summary of Chapter Seven

Chapter Seven dealt with the analysis of lengthier arguments—an editorial, a television "debate," and a political column. The margin note-summary method was introduced for use in analyzing extended passages. This method consists of making notes (in the margins or elsewhere) as an aid in the construction of an itemized summary of the main points in the passage to be analyzed. The passage then is analyzed through an analysis of the summary. In constructing a summary, care should be taken not to misrepresent the passage. The point of the chapter was both to introduce the margin note-summary method *and* to get a little practice using it (or a similar method you find more congenial).

Exercises for Chapter Seven

1. Here is an editorial from the *New York Daily News*.[5] Read and reread the column, the second time writing down margin notes (or whatever your method calls for), using the results to construct a clear, accurate summary. Then critically evaluate the summary, being sure to mention somewhere

---

[5] © 1970 by the *New York Daily News.* Reprinted by permission.

along the way (1) misleading uses of language; (2) what you take to be the conclusion(s) the author intended us to draw, and why you think so; (3) which of these conclusions are supported within the column, and which are not, along with your evaluation of the support (showing how the support either does or doesn't do the job); and (4) which of these conclusions you accept and which you don't, with explanations. In doing all of this, use whatever parts of your world view and background knowledge you can show to be relevant. To put the instructions in a nutshell, evaluate each column, bringing to bear whatever parts of your world view or background information you can show to be relevant. *Or,* to put it in a peanut shell: show what's right and what's wrong with each column. (Feel free to use any shortcuts you can show to be reasonable.)

The "White Flag Amendment"

—which masquerades as the "amendment to end the war" comes before the Senate tomorrow for a showdown vote.

This bugout scheme is co-sponsored by Sens. George McGovern (D-S.D.) and Mark Hatfield (R-Ore.). And despite some last-minute chopping and changing to sucker fence-sitting senators, the proposal remains what it has always been, a blueprint for a U.S. surrender in Vietnam.

It would force a pell-mell pullout of American forces there by cutting off all funds for the Vietnam war as of Dec. 31, 1971. It represents the kind of simple—and simple-minded—solution to Vietnam for which arch-doves and pacifists (as well as the defeatists and Reds who lurk behind them) have long clamored.

This amendment wears the phony tag of a "peace" plan. More accurately, it constitutes a first step toward whittling Uncle Sam down to pygmy size in the world power scales; it would fill our enemies with glee and our friends with dismay.

McGovern-Hatfield might appear a cheap out from Vietnam. But we would pay for it dearly in other challenges and confrontations as the Communists probe, as they inevitably do at any sign of weakness, to determine the exact jelly content of America's spine.

The McGoverns, Hatfields, Fulbrights, Goodells and their ilk would have the nation believe that its only choice lies between their skedaddle scheme and an endless war. That is a lie.

President Richard M. Nixon has a program for ending America's commitment in Vietnam, and it is now underway. It involves an orderly cutback in U.S. forces.

The White House method assures the South Vietnamese at least a fighting chance to stand on their own feet and determine their own future after we leave.

Equally important, it tells the world the U.S. is not about to pull the covers over its head and duck out on its responsibilities as leader of the free world.

We urge the Senate to slap down the McGovern-Hatfield amendment, and scuttle with it any notion that America is willing to buy off noisy dissidents at the price of its honor.

*2. Apply the instructions given in question 1 to the following political column by Jeffrey St. John, which appeared in the *Columbus* (Ohio) *Dispatch* (9 May 1972).[6]

Could Swamp Courts

Women's Lib Amendment Not Simple Legal Formula

By Jeffrey St. John

(Copley News Service)—"The legal position of women," observed the late Supreme Court Justice Felix Frankfurter, "cannot be stated in a simple formula, especially under a constitutional system, because her life cannot be expressed in a single simple relation." A procession of contemporary legal scholars made much the same argument prior to congressional passage of the Women's Equal Rights Amendment now before various state legislatures for ratification.

Political pressures in this presidential year have given a militant minority of women powerful leverage for enactment. However, the respective state of the Union may come to regret ratification, if the two-thirds majority approves.

North Carolina Democratic Senator Sam Ervin has argued, along with legal scholars from the University of Chicago, Yale, and Harvard, that while the amendment would have no effect upon discrimination, it would "nullify every existing federal and state law making any distinction whatever between men and women, no matter how reasonable the distinction may be, and rob Congress and the 50 states of the legislative power to enact any future laws making any distinction between men and women, no matter how reasonable the distinction may be."

In the wake of any ratification, moreover, a legal avalanche would be unleashed that is likely to overwhelm the already overcrowded courts of the country.

In reality, the aim of a minority of militant women's liberationists is to bring about just such a state of legal and social anarchy. Like the disciples of Lenin in the early part of the century, Women's Lib seeks to use the law to destroy both existing law and the social structure.

In abolishing a legal distinction between men and women, the way is paved for sociological anarchy which militants can exploit for their own purposes of achieving political power.

---

[6] © 1971 by Copley News Service. Reprinted by permission.

The profound effect the Equal Rights Amendment would have on marriage contracts, the home and children is precisely what Women's Lib wants; to sweep such established social units away as a prelude to pushing the country headlong into a life-style not unlike that now practiced in hippie communes.

Philosophically, at the root of the women's liberation movement is an attempt to destroy the family structure as a means of bringing down the whole of society.

The form of "discrimination" upon which the Women's Lib movement bases much of its false, misleading, and dangerous campaign is less in law than in custom and social attitudes, especially in the fields of career and employment.

Like the civil rights movement, Women's Lib is seeking, by using the power of the state, to forbid individual discrimination as opposed to discrimination legally enforced.

This crucial distinction has not been made by most in Congress who approved the Equal Rights Amendment for Women. Nor has it been made by the few state houses that have already ratified the amendment.

One can predict the same chaos will follow passage of this amendment as that which followed the 1964 Civil Rights Act.

Legal scholars like the late dean of the Harvard Law School, Roscoe Pound, have argued that the guarantee of "due process" in the Fifth Amendment and "equal protection" clause in the 14th Amendment provide the necessary legal instruments for reform now demanded by women's liberationists.

But like some elements of the civil rights movement, militant feminists are not really interested in reform, but rather in revolution and destruction of the existing social fabric of the society.

3. Apply the instructions given for question 1 to this political column by Michael Novak in the *Chicago Daily News* (25 June 1977).[7]

According to *Time* magazine, there are a reported 150,000 homosexuals in Miami. Still, only 90,000 votes came out for the lavender against the orange in Miami's thirty-day war. On June 7, Miamians voted down a "human rights ordinance" for homosexuals by a 70–30 margin. The political question was decisively resolved in Miami, but a philosophical question remains. In a democracy, does anything go? Must citizens cease making moral discriminations? Does homosexuality make a moral claim on the Republic equal to that of heterosexuality?

By all means, the state should not intrude on the private life of citizens. But there is an entity more important than the state—call it the people, the culture, the society. The state ought not to spy upon private

---

[7] Novak, copyright, 1977, Universal Press Syndicate. All rights reserved.

sexual life. In the private sphere, large tolerance ought to be promoted. But society—as distinct from the state—has not only the right, but also the duty to make moral distinctions.

One great advantage to homosexuality is referred to constantly by homosexuals. Homsexual apologetics are full of "loving relationships," "warmth," "tenderness," and "loving touches." Married men and women rarely speak that way.

Two basic deficiencies in the homosexual way of life lead many persons not to wish it for themselves or their children, and to regard it as a flawed way of life. The first is the narcissism of one's own sex. Heterosexuality is not just "an alternative life-style." It is rooted in the cycle of the generations, that long prosaic realism of familial responsibilities that is the inner rhythm of the human race.

The second deficiency follows from the first. The relationship between two males, or two females, may be loving, tender, and satisfying. It is quite likely—far more so than among married men and women—to be transient. There is a restlessness in homosexual life that is not accidental or fortuituous, but structural.

The future of the human race does not depend on homosexuals as it does upon the married union of men and women, with all the skills and necessities acquired in such unions. Although the state need not interfere in homosexual unions, it has a critical stake in heterosexual unions. These unions are difficult. To help them to succeed is of indispensable priority.

At an early stage, all humans are polymorphous. Each of us could become homosexual as well as heterosexual. In a world as sexually confused as ours, it would be surprising if the number of homosexuals failed to grow. The young today are in a more unsettled sexual state than in many other eras. The strong patterns of socialization that lead to heterosexuality have been enormously weakened.

A strange argument is advanced by homosexuals. We cannot, they say, influence your children to follow our example. But this claim flies in the face of social constraints in other moral matters. The individual homosexual may not influence a child, but public approval will. Does sex-role stereotyping make a difference? Does it make any difference which role models are set before the young? If not, then talk about women and blacks in textbooks, and violence in TV films, is beside the point.

The state should not legislate about private sexual life. But neither should it prevent society from withholding moral and public disapproval of what they regard as an undesirable form of living. Citizens should not be coerced into approving—in school courses upholding homosexuality, for example—what they do not approve.

Like war and the poor, homosexuals we shall always have with us. No matter what the socialization toward heterosexuality, on some it will fail to take. We cannot eliminate homosexuality. What we can do is to diminish the numbers it affects, and the suffering it entails.

What society teaches about homosexuality makes a difference. To teach that it is a matter of preference is different from teaching that it is morally wrong. Homosexuals have a right to live what some people regard as a deficient life, if they so wish. A free society may permit decadence, on the grounds that efforts to eliminate it would cause more harm than good.

Only a repressive society would try to punish homosexuals. Only a decadent society would grant them status. A wise society would try to provide conditions under which the talents of individual homosexuals could flourish, without holding up their condition for equal emulation.

4. Now apply the instruction for question 1 to this (much abridged) column by William F. Buckley, Jr.[8]

The Victory of Cesar Chavez

The Cesar Chavez people appear to have won their fight to unionize the grape-pickers in Southern California, and it is worth a moment to meditate on the means through which they succeeded in winning, and the consequences of their victory.

1. It is easy enough to say simply that it cannot be other than glad tidings that the grape-pickers in Southern California will be earning 20 percent more than they earned before. But of course there are those who will remind themselves that economics doesn't work that way, else —for instance—we would send Cesar Chavez to India, to call for a general strike because, over there, the hourly pay of a Ph.D. is less than the hourly pay of a grape-picker in Southern California.

The emotional difficulty with any discussion in this area is obvious. If it is established that the hourly pay of the grape-picker in Southern California is, say, $1.67, the temptation is to say that so insufficient a wage ought not to be condoned.

But the free market does not dispose of moral judgments. The question has been whether (a) you permit migrant workers, many of whom come in from Mexico, to continue to work at a price which is acceptable to employer and employees; or (b) you simply forbid said workers to come in to work at wages we consider to be too low.

The trouble with siding automatically with the apparently benevolent side of this argument is simply this: if the price of labor is raised, by political pressures, say, by 50 percent, then of course the extra cost is passed along to the grape buyers. Since the desire for grapes is not inflexible, it follows that there will be those who reject the new price; and their rejection will mean, according to the terms of the economic argument, very simply: fewer grapes sold, fewer migratory workers hired. . . .

Will Mr. Chavez now rest? Or will he move on to unionize farm workers in general. . . ?

---

[8] *On the Right,* © 1970, Washington Star Syndicate, Inc. Reprinted by permission.

5. This final exercise is for the mentally energetic. Here are four items on the "energy crisis," focusing on the causes of the long lines at gas pumps in several parts of the country in 1979. Read them carefully, use whatever method fits you best, and evaluate the whole mess, giving us the truth as each writer sees it, and your critical evaluation of that "truth."

The first appeared in *Time* magazine (14 May 1979) during that spring's gasoline shortage and long lines at the pumps:[9]

Pulling into a service station is beginning to seem like entering a combat zone. With more and more of the nation's 171,000 gas stations closing on weekends, shortening hours during the week, and cutting sales to $5 per customer to stretch supplies, frazzled and angry drivers are starting to boil over. . . .

Tempers will flare even more in the weeks ahead. Tight supplies have already forced nearly all oil companies to allocate deliveries to their retail outlets on a monthly basis, usually 90% or 95% of what the stations sold during the same month of 1978. Last week Texaco, Sun oil, Union and Exxon tightened their allocations still further, in the case of Exxon to 80% of the 1978 level. Thus, as summer progresses, drivers will find it increasingly difficult to buy gas toward the end of each month as service stations run dry.

Warnings of a gasoline squeeze have been voiced repeatedly since last winter by everyone from oil executives to Jimmy Carter and Energy Secretary James Schlesinger, all of whom have urged the public to curb its driving and start conserving fuel. No one has paid much attention, and people seem instead to grow more convinced by the day that the shortages are part of a price-gouging hoax perpetrated by Big Oil.

The real and immediate reason why supplies are tight is that overall output by the 13-nation OPEC cartel, which produces nearly half the world's oil, has been cut by between 7% and 10% since December, when shipments from Iran first stopped. Now that Iran is back to exporting, at two-thirds normal capacity, Saudi Arabia, Libya, Kuwait and other oil states are reducing their own deliveries to keep the market tight.

Supplies are also being crimped because demand for petroleum continues to grow. Last year's momentary surplus brought on by increased output from the North Sea and Alaska has been more than wiped out by rising consumption as well as OPEC's cutbacks. Steadily growing consumption of gasoline is causing most of the demand problem. Nearly 40% of all oil used in the U.S. goes for gasoline, and even though the price has almost doubled since 1973, the nation's 142 million motorists are burning it in record amounts. Not only have over 20 million new drivers streamed onto highways since 1973, but so have 24 million additional cars, trucks, campers, vans, Jeeps, dune buggies and other such toys for grownups.

Of the 154 million registered vehicles in the U.S., only passenger cars and light trucks must meet federal mileage standards. In the case of cars,

---

[9] Reprinted by permission from *Time*, The Weekly Newsmagazine; copyright Time Inc. 1979.

the standards require each automaker's fleet to average 27.5 miles per gallon by 1985. So far, the phasing in of new, more fuel-efficient autos has boosted the average mileage of the nation's total fleet of 98 million passenger cars by a scant half a mile per gallon, to 14.35 m.p.g. But the size of the fleet itself continues to grow, so consumption goes up, not down. Officials at the Department of Energy and oil company planners contend that consumption will level out and begin to decline by 1982, but no one knows for sure.

Federal clean-air standards are making the squeeze worse, because they require that U.S. cars from 1975 onward must use unleaded gas. That fuel now accounts for four out of every ten gallons sold and is in the shortest supply of all. A refinery needs up to 10% more crude to make a gallon of unleaded than leaded gas, and demand for the product has far outstripped the industry's ability to keep pace by expanding refinery capacity to make it.

As consumption climbs, oil companies are having to dip deeper into their gasoline inventories, which have dropped by just over 10% since last spring. Home heating-oil stocks have declined by an even sharper 16%, and DOE officials are calling in company executives one by one and telling them bluntly to start rebuilding their heating-oil stocks immediately by a full 140 million bbl. in the next five months in order to prevent the Squeeze of 1979 from turning into the Freeze of 1980. The switchover is essential but could reduce gasoline production by as much as 8% between now and October. . . .

Next, James J. Kilpatrick (*Washington Star*, 17 May 1979).[10]

Measles, chicken pox, whooping cough, mumps—take your pick of contagious diseases. None of them spreads as swiftly as the contagion of panic. This week the gasoline panic promises to reach epidemic levels, and it makes no sense at all.

Why are we in this fix? What accounts for the mile-long lines at service stations? Are the oil companies engaged in some vile conspiracy to withhold gasoline in order to drive the price up? From various sources in industry and government, clear and convincing answers can be found.

There is no evidence of conspiracy. The petroleum industry is monitored more strictly than any other industry in America. The oil companies live under the thumb of the Department of Energy, the Interior Department, the Securities and Exchange Commission, and a dozen other agencies. It is beyond belief that the companies collectively could conceal millions of gallons of gasoline, and it would be profitless and pointless for them to do so.

The current unhappiness results from three immediate causes and one historic cause.

(1) At a time of insatiably rising demand, the supply of crude is trending down. March imports of 8.3 million barrels per day were less than 1

---

[10] Kilpatrick, copyright, 1979, Universal Press Syndicate. All rights reserved.

percent above March of last year. The Iranian crunch is being felt. Refineries are uncertain about supplies. Inventories of total oil stocks are uncomfortably low and must be replenished.

(2) In order to build up inventories of heating oil for next winter, refineries have been producing less gasoline. The government has asked the companies to provide a reserve of 240 million barrels by October 1. This is a prudent step, but it results in less gasoline for the time being.

(3) Motorists as a breed have surrendered to panic. Roughtly 145 million trucks, buses, and passenger cars are registered in the United States. If we surmise that their gas tanks normally average half full, we can get a quick picture of what happens when owners struggle to get their tanks all the way full. There is no way under moon or sun that a billion gallons of gasoline suddenly can be supplied to meet this extraordinary demand.

The long-range cause is known to all of us. When it comes to energy consumption, we are the most profligate, wasteful, extravagant people on earth. We have yet to take conservation seriously. Other Western nations long ago looked facts in the face and accommodated to them. You don't see these mile-long lines in France or Germany or Japan. You see small cars; you see people walking or riding bicycles; you see gasoline at $2 to $3 a gallon.

What will it take to make Americans comprehend the truth? The era of cheap energy has passed. Barring some wholly unexpected stroke of technological genius, that era will not come again. There is no escape from reality in accusing the companies of conspiracy or blaming it all on Jimmy Carter and the Congress.

Industry and government spokesmen are not threatening us with a return to the Stone Age. The situation can be handled without serious hardship if each of us will make this much of an effort: Cut consumption by 5 percent. It is absurd to complain that such a reduction cannot be achieved. Every one of us who drives, say, 200 miles a week can think of ways to drive 190 miles instead.

Want an example? Look at the parking lots of suburban high schools. They stretch out for acres and acres. Is it seriously contended that every one of those student vehicles is necessary? Every one? Or what of the 180,000 privately owned airplanes that serve the convenience of corporate executives, sportsmen, and others? Is it too much to ask them to cut their flying hours by 5 percent?

If we will stop blathering about nonexistent conspiracies, and begin conscientiously to conserve, we can recover from the current epidemic. The first step is to call a halt to petulant blame-fixing. The fault is not in the companies or the Congress or the Arab nations.

The fault, dear fellow guzzlers, is in ourselves.

Now here are Michael Kramer and Dave Marash in "Birth of the Gas Pump Blues" (*New York* magazine, 4 June 1979):[11]

---

[11] Copyright © 1979 by News Group Publications, Inc. Reprinted with the permission of *New York* magazine.

Celebrating a Blessed Event

If you're one of those people who think Jimmy Carter is whistling "Dixie" when he moans about the oil crisis, take heart. You're right: We've been screwed. The Great Oil and Gas Shortage of 1979 is a bastard child, the product of government bungling and industry greed.

You don't have to be a Nobel laureate in economics to follow the story. Simply accept this premise: The oil business is in business to make money.

• *Supply:* The next time an oil-company heavyweight blasts the ayatollah, consider this—the Iranian revolution has been a godsend for the oil industry, the best thing to happen since the embargo of five years ago. Just as the embargo turned out to be an excuse for the last big jump in oil prices, so this time is the Iranian uprising.

Behind every scam are accommodating statistics, so perhaps it should come as no surprise that the oil-industry data trotted out by government and company spokesmen alike all come from one source: the oil industry itself. What may come as a surprise, however, is the fact that those very same statistics, when carefully examined, exonerate Iran and implicate the industry and the American government.

For every single month since the Iranians turned off the spigot, America has actually imported *more* oil than during the comparable month in 1978. That's right. *More.*

This past December, when Iranian oil flowed smoothly, United States petroleum imports stood at 8.9 million barrels a day. In January, without Iran's contribution, imports fell to 8.5 million barrels a day. But this was still 450,000 barrels a day *more* than had been imported during the same month a year earlier. On a quarterly basis, America took in 40 billion barrels of oil more during the first quarter of this year than was imported during the same period a year ago.

Where did all this oil come from? From the rest of the oil-producing world, which did, in fact, increase its production.

• *Demand:* The reason for our current crisis, says the government, is insatiable demand—even increased imports can't quench our thirst.

True enough—January demand was up 8 percent over a year ago, and February showed a 5 percent jump. But then the graph lines even out. In March, American demand for gasoline was just 1.5 percent higher than in March of 1978. In April, when the trees and meadows turn green and driving becomes a pleasure, gasoline demand actually fell to a level equal to that of April 1978 and a full 2 percent below the April 1977 consumption, a year the industry considers normal.

Given these supply-and-demand numbers, how do we explain the present pump panic? One answer comes from John O'Leary, the deputy secretary of energy. He calls the oil industry's performance "prudent" management. Four decisions help define O'Leary's version of "prudent" management. Two were made in the boardrooms of Big Oil, two at the White House.

• Nineteen seventy-eight was a year of stable oil supplies and slightly depressed prices. As described by Exxon board chairman Clifton Garvin, "Last year and the year before, there was a surplus in production capability around the world of about 10 percent, and those in the media came to refer to this as a glut. It's not a glut." Okay. When does 10 percent overproduction not lead to a glut—and the natural corollary, cheaper oil and gas? When you keep the stuff off the market.

Rather than take advantage of the increased supplies and bargain-basement prices, American oil refineries did just the reverse: They spent the year of 1978 running down their stocks of crude oil and gasoline. Imports were held below the levels considered normal, and crude reserves were taken from the storage tank, converted into gasoline, and sold. When prices are cheap and supplies seem stable, there's no profit in holding on to a commodity. So, in 1978, American oil men didn't.

Since the oil business never misses a chance to carp about the instability of its supply sources, one wonders why the industry operates on just a two-week inventory. The answer *seems* to be that a low margin of supply provides greater opportunity for market manipulations—like the contrived panic that peaked at the lead-free pumps in California this month.

As the industry ran down its stocks of crude oil in 1978, the supplies of motor gas were run down even further. By August of 1978, crude had been depleted to 7 percent below the levels of a year earlier, but gasoline had run down a whopping 18 percent. This pattern continued throughout the year—well before the Iranian cutoff.

Since the beginning of this year (after the Iranian shutdown), American crude oil stocks have been rebuilt, from 297 million barrels on hand in January to 322 million barrels in April. Meanwhile, gasoline supplies have gotten shallower. In other words, since January, supplies of crude oil have been building up in American storage tanks faster than the industry has been willing to turn them into gasoline for our cars. Or, as John O'Leary so mildly put it to a congressional hearing: "Refiners appear to have been somewhat conservative in their use of available crude oil and gas stocks."

It's not our fault, says the industry. "We just don't have enough equipment in place to supply the demand," says John Simmons, president of ARCO petroleum products. "Our refineries are producing at their maximum," echoes board chairman Fred Hartley of Union Oil of California. "Actually," adds Exxon's Garvin, "in the first four months of this year, the refineries in this country were operating 3 or 4 percent above what they were a year ago." Actually, the industry's own data say otherwise: For the first four months of this year, according to the American Petroleum Institute's figures, the nation's refineries worked at just 85 percent of capacity, about the same rate as in 1978, at which time, the industry itself has admitted, the policy was to underproduce in order to reduce inventories. Is it any wonder that demand—and prices—soar?

Into this situation—low crude supplies due to industry sell-offs and a demonstrated reluctance to convert what crude there is into gasoline

—comes the Carter administration with two apparently important moves.

The first federal step to "correct" the problem involved the reallocation of gasoline supplies to retail dealers scheduled for May 1. Says Samuel Van Vactor, Oregon's chief energy planner: "The Energy Department screwed up. . . . The new regulations encourage companies to cut back" on their allocations, so again a product of quickly rising value stayed in the storage tank—and became more valuable. Of course the industry calls this "prudence." "We had no idea how the new federal allocations would work," says one industry source, "so we felt we had to reduce our May shipments to dealers just to let things sort themselves out." In effect, things sorted themselves out in motorists' panic.

Since more and more drivers need the lead-free stuff, the panic was worse there, and again the Carter administration seems to have helped the worst to happen.

As the Iranian situation began to affect the price, but not the supply, of crude oil, the administration advised the oil companies to help moderate the OPEC price rise by avoiding the lighter-weight, higher-priced kinds of crude. The industry cooperated—but it did not leave the market entirely. American purchasers bought the less expensive, heavier crude, leaving the lighter-weight oil to the Europeans and Japanese. The net effect of the administration's recommended "boycott" was no real boycott at all, and the price of all types of oil fell not one cent. Worse still, American gasoline consumers were severely penalized by this action since the unleaded gasoline we are required to use in our cars in order to comply with governmental regulations is made mostly from the very same lightweight crude our government was telling our oil companies not to buy.

A Chevron spokesman sums up the situation best: "Had we the same [lighter-weight] crude available this year as we had last year, we could make 3 percent more gas right now and 7 percent more for the summer." Which would obliterate the shortage.

The future? The administration is finally encouraging the oil companies to buy lightweight crude, so supplies of lead-free gasoline should be plentiful before long. The prices will be higher, undoubtedly—but not, as the evidence suggests, inevitably.

Finally, here is economist Eliot Janeway (*Atlantic Monthly*, November 1979):[11]

GASOHOL: Solution to the Gas Shortage

Alcohol is back in the news again, . . . [It] is readily mixable with gasoline. Blended in the ratio of one part alcohol to nine parts unleaded gasoline, gasohol can free the United States from reliance on the OPEC

---

countries and provide a painless alternative to the ultimatum President Carter has delivered: Use less and pay more for automobile fuel.

Hair shirts of the sort the President prescribes do not fit the country's style or its frame. The country runs on its carburetors; the economy will stall if people can't drive. But practical conservation at the point of fuel production, which is what gasohol offers, would keep the economy moving.

Working people have more sense than policy- and opinion-makers do, and they're onto the pocketbook promise of alcohol—not merely as consumers with a vested interest in their lifestyles, but as income-earners who need to stay on wheels to stay ahead of their creditors. That is why gasohol is becoming the hottest liquid product since bathtub gin.

If gasohol becomes the boon it could and should become, little credit will go to the Administration or to the oil industry. . . .

[President] Carter's Administration . . . has joined with the oil companies and with the farm college economists, the most reactionary element among the economic fraternity, in denigrating gasohol. Nevertheless, gasohol has managed to bludgeon its way back into the picture, courtesy of the Corn Belt states and the pressure brought to bear in Congress by the farm lobby. Over White House resistance, farm and sugar state senators forced on the Administration a four-cents-a-gallon exemption on the federal excise tax on alcohol produced from agricultural products. This cut was not enough to make gasohol competitive in price with unleaded gasoline until Governor Robert Ray stepped in with an additional eight-cents-a-gallon exemption on Iowa's excise tax, thus enabling gasohol to sell as premium gas within pennies of the price of gasoline in Iowa. . . .

. . . The agricultural tax exemption is a must for now, and so is its extension to plant-made alcohol to make possible a far greater flow of crude-oil-conserving gasohol into the nation's gas pumps. The oil companies already have on hand an abundance of the necessary raw material. The basic gaseous by-product in all oil refining and petrochemical operations is ethylene. Hydrated (a simple reaction with water), it produces ethyl alcohol ready for mixing with unleaded gasoline: four pounds of ethylene can be converted into one gallon of alcohol, or ethanol. The United States has ethylene to burn. In fact, that is exactly what we are doing: wasting it in many ways in the refineries when it could be converted into ethanol. The Stanford Research Institute, professing entire innocence of the consequences of its findings, reported last year that the oil industry was still flaring off 10 billion pounds of ethylene a year into the smog above its fractionating towers.

The 2.5 billion gallons of alcohol gone with the wind as a result of the oil industry's addiction to waste in its refineries could contribute more than half the alcohol we need to close the gasoline gap, a gap whose size is readily calculated. On a business-as-usual basis we burn more than 100 billion gallons of gasoline a year, 40 percent of it unleaded (the proportion of unleaded production may run as high as 45 percent by next summer, even though the Environmental Protection Agency has delayed its unleading deadline for one year to increase gasoline production). A 10 percent mix of alcohol with unleaded calls for a little less than 4 billion gallons of alcohol a year. The evangelical peddling of conservation at the gas pumps, where it will hurt the working consumer, is distracting the energy debate from the overdue need for conservation at the point of production, where it will help.

Nor is this all. The country's chemical industry—including the petrochemical operations of the oil industry—admits to a conservatively rated ethylene capacity of 37 billion pounds a year. But thanks to the gas crisis, 8 billion pounds—not less than 21 percent of our ethylene production capacity—have been knocked out of action by the combination of falling sales and rising costs. Moreover, another 6.5 billion pounds are scheduled to come on line by 1981. The capacity now idle could produce another 2 billion gallons of alcohol a year, and the ethylene due by 1981 could add another 1.6 billion gallons. That makes a total of 6.1 billion gallons of alcohol a year to be derived chemically—enough to keep the country comfortably ahead of the gasoline shortfall.

Other expedients are crying out for use, too. To take just one example, the oil refineries routinely burn by-product ethylene as refinery fuel. Switching to fuel oil, which they sell for much less than ethylene, would actually widen their margins and win them gratitude. Fuel oil sells for about fifty cents a gallon, or seven cents a pound. Ethylene, with about the same heat value, hydrated into ethanol for gasohol use and sold at fifty-two cents a gallon, would bring thirteen cents a pound—the present price for ethylene which continues to waver and weaken by the month. In fact, the ethylene glut is so large, it is holding prices at 1976 levels despite paranoiac claims by the industry that demand is outstripping supply. Some oil and chemical industry analysts are now privately admitting that the ethylene glut could be with us through 1985.

Any poll of representative opinion would come up with a bare 5 percent recognition factor of the reality that the world oil surplus and the domestic gasoline squeeze have been developing independently of each other. There is no longer any denying the world oil surplus. The Washington *Post* reports that even the CIA, which is not exactly swift in its perceptions, estimates 1979 world oil production as running 5.8 percent ahead of last year, when supply was glutted and demand was booming, despite the curtailment in Iran, the cutbacks by the cartel, and the shutdown of rigs in the U.S. due to decontrol hopes and tax fears. The wires are crackling from Rotterdam and London to every point in the world offering tanker loads at deepening price concessions, subject to slow pay. These offers to dump crude are eliciting more laughs than sales. No one is hurting for lack of crude oil imports into the U.S., as the Washington *Post* coverage makes clear. The major oil companies are embarrassed because of the ease with which they stepped up their oil imports even after crude oil flows from Iran were shut off, while in the United States, gas lines were making headlines.

The product of the relationship between the Carter Administration and the oil companies is the myth that U.S. gasoline supplies ease or tighten according to crude oil imports. The recent pinch at the pumps goes all the way back to the [1930's] three-way alliance of Standard Oil of New Jersey, Du Pont, and General Motors, which Ford failed to break up and which committed the country to lead additives. By a fateful coincidence, the environmentalists won their fight to take lead out of the refining process at the same time that OPEC declared war against the U.S. However, while the environmentalists were concentrating on their anti-lead crusade, they were not alert to the need to substitute an alternative additive, or to the availability of alcohol for the role. The oil companies, after their fashion, were intent on going along with the mandate to take the lead out of gasoline since they had lost their fight: Normal oil refining practice had come of age relying on lead additives to raise the octane rating and, at the same time, maximize the yield of gasoline recovered from each barrel of crude. But as the lead continues to go out of the refinery, the gasoline yield from crude oil continues to come down.

Technical ignorance, even about such a rudimentary matter, is normal for the government. It is also standard operating practice for the bookkeepers who now run the auto industry. As for the engineers who run the oil companies, they have bruises and blood to show for their confrontations in the public domain; and so they had an alibi for having kept their silence until the environmentalists were caught gumming up the works. Yet not a peep was heard from Motor City. . . .

The bottom line is that after five years of entirely nonpartisan bureaucratic momentum, we are getting 14 percent less gasoline out of a given amount of crude oil flowing through the refineries. For the previous fifty years, an average dose of lead additive (a few grams per gallon) had been relied on to raise the base octane rating of gasoline by 8 points. Consequently, refineries were able to produce a base gasoline of only 80 octane and still market an 88-octane gasoline. The lead additive made it possible for oil companies to use less oil and make more gasoline. By contrast, unleaded requires more intensive processing and yields lower octanes. For years the gasoline yield from crude oil stood at 54 percent and had reached a record high of 54.5 percent in 1974 before the unleading requirement. But taking the lead out of 40 percent of all the gasoline we consume has lowered the overall yield (regular and unleaded) to 47 percent; the yield of unleaded alone from crude is now estimated to be down to about 42.5 percent.

It is not as if lead were the only octane booster conceivable or available in the refining process. It happens that alcohol has a 100-octane rating. It creates no emission problems and provides a powerful weapon for outgunning OPEC without shooting ourselves. The environmentalists would have been on unassailable ground today if they had done their technical homework and had promoted the substitution of alcohol for lead additives.

The simple expedient of providing the incentives to convert ethylene into ethyl alcohol would insure against further gas crunches without reverting to pollution, and it would also slash imports of crude oil. Just 4 billion gallons would displace 28 billion gallons, or 667 million barrels, of crude oil per year. Each gallon of ethanol produced from oil and gas and mixed with 9 gallons of unleaded will displace no less than 7 gallons of crude oil.

(For the benefit of those interested in the calculation, here's how it works. Each gallon of alcohol would replace 2.35 gallons of crude oil which would otherwise be needed to produce unleaded gasoline. In addition, because alcohol improves the yield of unleaded gasoline from crude oil by raising its octane rating, only 1.83 gallons of crude oil instead of 2.35 would be needed to make a gallon of gas. Since alcohol improves the gasoline yield by a factor of .52 gallons of crude per gallon [2.35 − 1.83 = .52], one gallon of alcohol added to 9 gallons of unleaded fuel would save an additional 9 × .52, or 4.68 gallons of crude oil; 4.68 added to 2.35 equals 7.03 gallons of crude oil saved for every gallon of alcohol added to 9 gallons of unleaded to make gasohol. Four billion gallons of alcohol could, therefore, effect a 28-billion-gallon yearly reduction in crude oil consumption.)

At $22 a barrel, OPEC's present contract price, a 28-billion-gallon reduction of imports would knock $14.67 billion off the nation's annual oil import bill—roughly half the yearly trade deficit. It would also cut consumption of OPEC crude by 25 to 30 percent. . . .

The technology, the raw materials, and the incentives are all at hand, but a nation in which the chemists and engineers are making the economic decisions while the Ph.D.'s in human relations are making the technical decisions seems strangely unable to exploit them. Gasohol offers a way to avoid a ludicrous eventuality: a government-sponsored gasoline shortage in the face of a worldwide crude oil price collapse. The rest of the world is already anticipating the latter. If anything is surer than OPEC opportunism and American confusion, it is that alcohol can be produced more cheaply from the chemical by-products of oil and gas than from fermented corn, provided the tax is right. At $2.80 a bushel, the raw material cost for making a gallon of alcohol from corn is about $1.10, while the cost of a gallon of alcohol from ethylene is only about fifty-two cents. Chemically derived alcohol is cheaper and more energy-efficient than agriculturally derived alcohol, as every country experimenting with both already knows. If corn alcohol is a sell-out in Iowa, chemical alcohol is bound to be a bargain in New Jersey, given the same excise tax relief. If the government officials and technological intelligentsia insist on disputing the potential of gasohol, let them tell us why.

In politics, the image often is the message.

Chapter Eight

Advertising: Selling the Product

Would you persuade, speak of interest, not of reason.

—Ben Franklin

Advertising persuades people to buy things they don't need with money they ain't got.

—Will Rogers

Advertising is the most exciting, the most arduous literary form of all, the most difficult to master, the most pregnant with curious possibilities.

—Aldous Huxley

Advertising is so obviously useful that it's surprising it has such a bad name. Ads tell us what is new, what is available, where, when, and for how much. They tell us about a product's (alleged) quality and specifications, and sometimes even show us the product itself (on television or in pictures). All for free, except for the effort of reading, or paying attention.

Yet there are legitimate gripes about advertising. Most ads exaggerate or are otherwise misleading; some even lie. Surely that's not what we want. And since some products are advertised more heavily or more effectively than others, ads lead us to choose what we otherwise would not, to choose what if we were completely rational we would not choose. And that too is undesirable.[1]

But let's pass over these issues and move to the more pressing problem —how we can best use advertising without getting used.

One solution to that problem is to become familiar with the devices and gimmicks used in advertising to con the unwary, or more politely, to appeal to our emotions, weaknesses, or prejudices. It should come as no surprise that these devices are pretty much the same as those used in most persuasive rhetoric (except that ad experts are the acknowledged masters).

1. Ads Don't Say What's Wrong with the Product

No product is perfect. Hence the completely informative ad would mention at least some drawbacks of the product. But no one has yet seen an ad that

---

[1] A third common charge against advertising is that it increases sales costs and thus increases retail prices. But this charge is false. It's true that advertising costs a great deal of money, but not true that it raises prices. That would be true only if things could be sold more cheaply by some other selling method, and quite clearly there is no such other method. It's no accident that virtually all businesses advertise—they don't know a cheaper way to sell their products. (For a fourth, less common but more accurate charge, see the box starting on page 178.) Those who argue that advertising raises prices forget that if a company does not advertise it will have to increase other selling costs (for instance, sales commissions).

deliberately says anything negative about a product.[2] As David Ogilvy stated in his best seller, *Confessions of an Advertising Man* (New York: Atheneum, 1963, p. 158), "Surely it is asking too much to expect the advertiser to describe the shortcomings of his product." And that's exactly the point, for this means that practically every ad is guilty of the fallacy of *suppressed evidence* by concealing negative information about the product.

Movie and theater ads routinely quote the few nice words in a negative review, while omitting all the critical ones. Here is a quote from an ad for a porno flick, *Sometime Sweet Susan,* which appeared in the *New York Post* (21 February 1975):

> Shawn Harris is pretty . . . the lusty doings, of course, get the most screen time.—Judith Crist, *New York* magazine

And here's the entire Judith Crist review:[3]

> *Sometime Sweet Susan*'s press agent boasts that it is "the *first* hard-core film *ever* made with Screen Actors Guild approval." Lord knows there's little else to boast about in this dreary little film that tries to rise above its genre with superior performances, auspices, and production values. It succeeds only in being less ugly than some and as boring as most. Co-produced by Craig Baumgarten and Joel Scott, with a screenplay by Scott and Fred Donaldson, who directed and edited the film, it's a two-thirds rip-off of *The Three Faces of Eve,* with Susan a schizophrenic as a result of her inability to reconcile her lusty doings with her moral upbringing. It's *the lusty doings, of course,* that *get the most screen time,* with all the porn rituals (hetero- and homosexual twosomes, threesomes, and a dash of sadism) observed.
>
> Union membership does not guarantee quality of performance. As Susan, *Shawn Harris is pretty* and uninteresting, and Harry Reems, the biggie of *Deep Throat* and *The Devil in Miss Jones,* proves, as Susan's psychiatrist and sex-fantasy lover, that acting with clothes on is not his forte. Neil Flanagan, a professional nonporn actor, tries unsuccessfully to beat his low-comedy dialogue as the head of the mental hospital. And Baumgarten, an ex-Lindsay aide, shows small promise as an actor in his role as Susan's first lover, although a male critic thought he "makes a rather impressive debut as a hard-core performer." To each his impressions.

---

[2] Except when employing "reverse twist," that is, trying to make a virtue out of an apparent defect. The Avis Rent-A-Car campaign—"We try harder (because we're only number two)"—is an example. Another is the Volkswagen "think small" ad campaign.

[3] *New York* Magazine, 24 February 1975, p. 66. Copyright Judith Crist. Reprinted by permission.

All of us come from someplace else.

Just once, you should walk down the same street your great-grandfather walked.

Picture this if you will.

A man who's spent all his life in the United States gets on a plane, crosses a great ocean, lands.

He walks the same streets his family walked centuries ago.

He sees his name, which is rare in America, filling three pages in a phone book.

He speaks haltingly the language he wishes he had learned better as a child.

As America's airline to the world, Pan Am does a lot of things.

We help business travelers make meetings on the other side of the world. Our planes take goods to and from six continents. We take vacationers just about anywhere they want to go.

But nothing we do seems to have as much meaning as when we help somebody discover the second heritage that every American has.

America's airline to the world.

See your travel agent.

A few ads generate "needs" that didn't exist before, and probably still don't (ads for vaginal deodorant sprays are the classic case). Some generate needs for things which satisfy us somehow, but on the whole aren't good for us, a prime example being cigarettes. But most appeal to already existing genuine needs, desires, and fears. Ads that trade on our fear of offending are an example (mouthwashes, deodorants). The evil in this last (innocent-looking) type of advertising is mainly that it makes us spend more time, effort, and money on heavily advertised products that satisfy only marginal desires and fears, while spending less on things that might make our lives much more satisfying. In other words, this kind of advertising—in fact, advertising as a whole—skews our values so that we tend to favor those needs that advertisers can make more money developing over our other, often more pressing ones. Occasionally, however, an ad comes along that reminds us of what (for most of us) are much more important values, even though we tend to forget them in the hustle and bustle of everyday life. This Pan Am ad is one of those rare ads that tend to push us in the right direction. Yes! If we can afford it (and more of us could if we spent less on lesser needs), just once, we should walk down the same street our great-grandfather walked.

I'm a salesman. Salesmen don't tell you things that will cause you not to buy a product. If you are buying a used car, the salesman won't tell you what is wrong with the car.

—U.S. Army recruiter, Dallas, Texas, answering charges that military recruiters mislead potential recruits (*Moneysworth*, May 1979)

Anyone thinking of enlisting in the military should realize that military recruiters are sales representatives who get paid to sell their product and that they will not necessarily tell you the fine print that sometimes makes all the difference.

2.   Ads Play to Emotions Much More Than to Reason

One would suppose that the best ads would make rational appeals to selfish interests. A few successful ads do just that. Still, the chief appeal in most successful ads is emotional—the appeal is to desires and fears, not reason.

Consider the successful Schlitz ads that shouted at listeners to grab all the gusto in life they could, because "you only go around once" in life. The appeal was selfish (imagine them saying instead that you only go around once in life, so do all the good things that you can do for others—give Schlitz to poor beer-drinking friends now.). But it also was an emotional appeal, empty of reasons for drinking Schlitz rather than a competing brand.

One fear most of us have when we go shopping is that what we want will cost too much. We should expect then that ads will try to allay that fear, say, by quoting prices for low-end merchandise—the bait—so that they can get us into the store and sell us better quality higher-priced goods—the "switch" in the "bait and switch" gambit.

Another fear we have when shopping is that we're going to make the trip for nothing because they won't have what we want. That's why one of Montgomery Ward's more effective ad campaigns was centered around the simple statement, "I got what I wanted, at Ward's." The point was to reassure us that we needn't fear wasting our time when we shop at Ward's.

One of the classics of advertising history is built around a headline that for a time became a part of the language:

> *They laughed when I sat Down at the Piano*
> *But when I Started to Play!* . . .

The appeal of this ad was to the desire to shine at parties. In the fine print, having put the prospective customer in the proper emotional frame, the ad promises to teach piano playing quickly and with "no laborious scales—no heartless exercises—no tiresome practicing." Reason would caution the reader. How, after all, is it possible to learn to play the piano without lots of practicing? But no matter; emotions sufficiently aroused will override rationality—in a sufficient number of cases. This famous ad was a tremendous money maker.[4]

Somewhere West of Laramie

SOMEWHERE west of Laramie there's a broncho-busting, steer-roping girl who knows what I'm talking about.

She can tell what a sassy pony, that's a cross between greased lightning and the place where it hits, can do with eleven hundred pounds of steel and action when he's going high, wide and handsome.

The truth is—the Playboy was built for her.

Built for the lass whose face is brown with the sun when the day is done of revel and romp and race.

She loves the cross of the wild and the tame.

There's a savor of links about that car—of laughter and lilt and light—a hint of old loves—and saddle and quirt. It's a brawny thing—yet a graceful thing for the sweep o' the Avenue.

Step into the Playboy when the hour grows dull with things gone dead and stale.

Then start for the land of real living with the spirit of the lass who rides, lean and rangy, into the red horizon of a Wyoming twilight.

JORDAN MOTOR CAR COMPANY, *Inc. Cleveland. Ohio*

Appeals to emotion sell products. Reason gets left behind. See They Laughed When I Sat Down *for more on this ad, important in the history of advertising for its play on emotions.*

---

[4] The headline on the ad became so well known, and remained so, that Frank Rowsome, Jr., used its opening phrase as the title of his delightful book on advertising, *They Laughed When I Sat Down* (New York: Bonanza Books, 1959). Some of the other examples used in this chapter also appear in Rowsome's book.

3.   Ads Often Are Deceptive or Misleading

Among the three or four widely used deceptive or misleading devices, *false implication*—stating something that is (usually) true while implying something else that is false—is perhaps the most insidious.

London Fog commercials frequently are set in London, suggesting that London Fog raincoats and jackets are made in England. In fact, they're made in Baltimore, Maryland, U.S.A. The ads never say they're made in England, but some people are bound to think so, which is why the commercial makers went to the trouble of showing models standing in front of Big Ben.

The Armour Star frank ads, which correctly stated that one pound of Armour franks and one pound of steak are equal in nourishment, implied that a hot dog meal is just as nourishing as a steak meal. But did you ever try eating ten Armour franks at one sitting?

A letter stating on the outside that it was "From the desk of Art Linkletter" (a bit of *appeal to authority*) also had this hook for the reader in bold type on the envelope: "Now you can save up to 50 percent and more on many famous brand items." The truth in that claim is that they'll sell you a very few standard items (not popular ones) for 50 percent off or close to it, but the bulk of what they're selling is at prices pretty much like those in ordinary discount stores. The catch is the weasel expression "up to."

Ads like this demonstrate the importance of having good background information. Most people haven't got the faintest idea what a standard markup is for the various kinds of retail goods, so they don't see 50 percent off on a popular item as an impossibility. They don't realize that retailers themselves typically have to pay more than 50 percent of the retail price for standard brand items, and therefore have to charge much more. (Some items, like cosmetics and jewelry, often do have markups as high as 50 percent, but even here the markup is not high enough to enable retail outlets to regularly sell standard brands for half price and make money.)

We Can't Tell a Lie About McDonald's Cherry Pie[5]

When is a cherry pie not quite a cherry pie? Apparently, when it's a *McDonald's Cherry Pie*. Recently, a CU subscriber wrote us complaining that she'd bought a McDonald's pie that contained only 1½ cherries. She felt cheated.

So we investigated We analyzed cherry pies from four McDonald's restaurants in the New York area. The pies contained an average of five cherries each—slim pickings when compared to the package photo, which shows more than 100 luscious-looking cherries.

---

[5] From *Consumer Reports*, April 1979, p. 190. Copyright 1979 by Consumers Union of United States, Inc., Mount Vernon, N.Y. 10550. Reprinted by permission from *Consumer Reports*, April 1979.

McDonald's Cherry Pies appear to flout U.S. Food and Drug Administration regulations in two ways. First, they contain only about 20 percent cherries; by FDA regulations, a frozen cherry pie must contain at least 25 percent cherries by weight. Second, the photo on the package misrepresents what's inside. The package also appears to be in violation of the Fair Packaging and Labeling Act, since it contains no list of ingredients, no distributor's address, and no net-weight statement.

We wonder how many fast-food restaurants indulge in similar small deceptions. And at what point do many small deceptions add up to one big deception?

Claude Hopkins (a great in the history of advertising), was the first one to understand and use a beautiful variation on the false implication gambit. Hopkins believed it was a waste of money to claim your product is the best, or pure, or anything so general. He tried to understand his product sufficiently to be able to provide more specific "reasons why" a person should buy that product. (This may sound as though his ads really did inform the public about the product, and Hopkins himself may have believed this. But it didn't work that way.)

One of Hopkins's early and famous ad campaigns illustrates this well. When he was put to work on Schlitz beer ads, he discovered that each Schlitz bottle was sterilized with live steam. So he built his campaign around headlines such as "Washed with Live Steam!" omitting the fact that all breweries used live steam. He knew that competitors could not then advertise that they too used live steam—that claim had been preempted for Schlitz. And he knew most readers would assume that *only* Schlitz washed their bottles with live steam. (Apparently, he was right; Schlitz sales went from fifth to first in short order.)

Most ads claiming a certain quality for their product without explicitly asserting its uniqueness to that product are designed to make you *assume* that only their product has that quality. If you make that assumption, you reason fallaciously.

Another misleading or deceptive device frequently employed in ads is *ambiguity*. Fleishmann's margarine says on the package, "Fleishmann's—made from 100 percent corn oil." But on the side we read in the fine print that it's made from "Liquid Corn Oil, Partially Hydrogenated Corn Oil, Water, nonfat dry milk, vegetable mono and diglicerides and lecithin, artificially flavored and colored (carotene), Vitamins A & D added."

Well, did the statement mean that Fleishmann's is made from 100 percent corn oil and nothing else, or did it mean that the oil that is the main ingredient in margarine is 100 percent corn oil (instead of, say, partly soybean oil, as in many other brands)? If challenged, Fleishmann's can say they meant the latter while being confident that some consumers will take them to mean the former.

Shoot-Out in Marlboro Country

by Adam Hochschild[6]

A gathering storm darkens the desert sky. Heroic movie music. The TV screen shows the stark, barren mountains of northern New Mexico, and in their shadow, a lone cowboy slowly herding his cattle home. We first see him riding in the distance behind the ambling herd. Then closer; his head is bowed beneath a sweaty, broad-brimmed oversized hat. The scene could be straight out of one of the old Marlboro commercials . . . until the cowboy comes close enough for us to see the oxygen tank strapped to his saddle. Tubes from it run up his nostrils. "New Mexico rancher John Holmes has emphysema," the crisp British voice of the narrator informs us, "brought on by years of heavy smoking."

This scene is from a TV documentary called *Death in the West*. It is one of the most powerful anti-smoking films ever made. You will never see it. . . .

Death in the West was filmed in 1976 by director Martin Smith, reporter Peter Taylor and a crew from *This Week*, a weekly show on Britain's independent Thames Television network. The show is roughly the British equivalent of *60 Minutes*. Taylor's searing half-hour film simply intercuts three kinds of footage. The first is old Marlboro commercials—cowboys lighting up around the chuck wagon, galloping across the plains at sunset, and so forth. The second is interviews with two Philip Morris executives who claim that nobody knows if cigarettes cause cancer. The third is interviews with six real cowboys in the American West who have lung cancer or, in one case, emphysema. And after each cowboy, the film shows the victim's doctor testifying that he believes his patient's condition was caused by heavy cigarette smoking.

After opening with a commercial showing Marlboro men around a campfire, the film cuts to another campfire, where narrator Taylor is interviewing cowboy Bob Julian. "For Bob," Taylor says, "the last round-up will soon be over."

"I started smoking when I was a kid following these broncobusters," says Julian. "I thought that to be a man you had to have a cigarette in your mouth. It took me years to discover that all I got out of it was lung cancer. I'm going to die a young man." (He lived only a few months after the interview.)

Emphysema victim John Holmes, the man with the oxygen tank on his horse, tells what it's like to periodically gasp for breath. "It's hard to describe . . . it feels as if someone has their fingers down in my chest."

---

[6] This condensed version of "Shoot-Out in Marlboro Country" is reprinted by permission of *Mother Jones* magazine, January 1979.

Another man interviewed, Harold Lee, had only a few months to live, and you can see it in his stubbled, emaciated face.

Death in the West was shown only once, from London, to an audience of some 12 million TV viewers, in September 1976. It was high noon for Philip Morris, and the company walked in with guns blazing. Philip Morris promptly sued Thames Television and then got a court order preventing the film from being shown until its suit could be heard.

. . . Before the injunction, the American Cancer Society was eager to use the smoking program, and *60 Minutes* was negotiating to buy it from Thames TV. Officials at *60 Minutes* had seen a print of the film and were enthusiastic about using part of it on the air. "But then," explains the show's senior producer, Palmer Williams, "the people from Philip Morris —and I don't know how—heard we were interested. They came over here right away and wanted to know why. The very next day, out came this Queen's Bench Warrant or whatever the hell it was, barring Thames TV from selling the film anywhere in the world. So we couldn't get it."

Today, the film remains locked in a London vault, headed off at the pass.

Compare this with the Marlboro ad on page 182.

It's bad enough that private companies mislead us in their advertisements. That our own government does so is a disgrace. The hype to get people to enlist in the military is perhaps the most notorious. (Recall the box on page 176.) Typical is the Army ad headlined, "In today's Army, you earn good money while learning a skill to make even more money." The ad pictured some of the Army career categories (bureaucratese for "job"), implying that those who qualified could pick their own top job choices, clinching the argument with a detachable guarantee:

GUARANTEE

If you qualify, you can enlist for one of hundreds of exciting Army skills. Or you can choose the initial area or unit you'd like to serve in, near home in the continental United States or someplace new. Your choice will be *guaranteed* in writing before you enlist [italics in original].

The true guarantee is that you *may* qualify (or you may flunk out in training camp and so not qualify—but you can't back out then) and there *may* be an opening (if it is consistent with Army personnel needs). But the ad doesn't say this; it *implies* that you can qualify before entering the military and be guaranteed at the time of entry that you'll get a certain job or job location.

Robert Glatzer, in The Great Ad Campaigns from Avis to Volkwagen *(New York: Citadel Press, 1970), called the Marlboro campaign the "campaign of the century." This is a typical ad from that campaign (generally credited with vaulting Marlboros from way back in the pack to number one selling cigarette, both in America and in the world as a whole). Notice that it gives no reason why anyone should smoke Marlboros rather than another filter cigarette of similar flavor. The warning note appearing in the lefthand corner is required by law and did not appear in earlier ads of the campaign.*

> Schoolchildren might examine . . . the meaning of *free gifts* offered by
> savings banks in return for new deposits. Strictly speaking, if a gift is not
> free, it is not a gift. The bank's gifts, however, are not really free: If the
> deposit is withdrawn before a minimum period, the gift, or an equivalent
> amount of money, is taken back. The free gift turns out to be a condi-
> tional gift all along.
> —Fred M. Heckinger, in *Saturday Review/World,* 9 March 1974

It's hard to say where ambiguous shiftiness turns into out-and-out falsehood. The front of the package of Aunt Jemima frozen Jumbo Blueberry
Waffles reads, in large type, "With Real Blueberry Buds and Other Natural
Flavors." On the side of the package, in small type, the following ingredients
are listed: "Blueberry Buds [sugar, vegetable stearine (a release agent),
blueberry solids with other natural flavors, salt, sodium carboxymethycellu-
lose (a thickening agent), silicon dioxide (a flow agent), citric acid, modified
soy protein, artificial flavor, artificial coloring, maltol]." If we think of
"Blueberry Buds" as the name of the "sugar, vegetable . . ." concoction described on the side of the box, then it's true that the box contains real Blueberry Buds (that is, a real "sugar, vegetable . . ." concoction). And it's also true
that it contains Other Natural Flavors (in the Blueberry Buds, along with some
artificial flavors—the box doesn't say it contains none of those). So it's true,
the box does contain "Real Blueberry Buds and Other Natural Flavors." Or
does it? (Quaker Oats was nominated for a 1978 doublespeak award for this
one.)

An interesting variation on the ambiguity theme is the *ambiguous comparison.* A Colgate fluoride toothpaste ad claimed that "Most Colgate kids got fewer
cavities," but failed to state fewer than who. Again, the hope was that readers
would take the ad to claim that Colgate kids got fewer cavities than those
using other flouride toothpastes, such as Crest, by far the best seller at that
time. But the *true* claim was that Colgate fluoride kids got fewer cavities on
the average than they did before using Colgate, when, of course, some of
them used a nonfluoride toothpaste, or perhaps didn't brush their teeth at all.

No account of advertising gimmickry would be complete without mentioning *exaggeration.*[7] Here are a few quite ordinary examples (all from ads for
Broadway plays), culled from just one section of one newspaper.[8]

"In Praise of Love is Magic" *(In Praise of Love)*
"A mind boggling bawdy romp" *(The Madhouse Co. of London)*
"I haven't laughed as often or as heartily in years. . . . Audiences will
howl with laughter for years . . ." *(The Ritz)*

---

[7] If you read this statement as saying (as opposed to implying) that the account in this book is
complete, read it again. False implication?
[8] *New York Times,* 26 January 1975.

"Yes, Yes, a thousand times yes!" *(Diamond Studs)*

"The most foot-stompin', hand clappin' fun musical . . . in a dog's age" *(Diamond Studs)*

"Irresistible"*(An Evening with H. L. Mencken)*

"Tremendous! Engrossing! Devastating! Fantastical!" *(Black Picture Show)*

"The best I have seen in the American Theatre in 25 years" *(Sizwe Banzi Is Dead)*

"A comic masterpiece" *(God's Favorite)*

"Best mini-musical in town" *(I'll Die If I Can't Live Forever)*

These are advertisements for Broadway productions all of which were box office flops.

Seven movie ads in the same paper claimed their film was either the best or one of the ten best movies of 1974. (In an average year, about fifty films will advertise in New York as one of the year's ten best.)

In the same newspaper there were hundreds, perhaps thousands, of ads for all sorts of products which contained gross exaggerations. Products were advertised as: "A touch of the past, at yesterday's prices"; ". . . the most unique darkroom offer ever made"; ". . . incredibly warm and glamorous"; "the king of comfort chairs"; "Fifteen very special tours for a very special year"; ". . . still one great big beautiful bargain"; "offers you one incomparable ship . . . [and] a rare exciting transatlantic crossing"; "Unrivaled for quality service"; "The sale nobody can afford to miss"; "The world's most appreciated home spa"; "The event that fur connoisseurs wait for"; "The most creative furniture ever made for kids."

All of these almost surely were exaggerated: there is no "king" of comfort chairs; who could know in January 1975 that 1975 would be a "very special year"; what is so rare about a "rare exciting transatlantic crossing"; hardly anyone's "quality service" is "unrivaled"; and there is no sale "nobody can afford to miss."

4.   Puffery Is Legal

Most of the ads we just classified as deceptive or misleading also fall into the category of *puffery*, or *puffing*, a category that has gained legal recognition. In his book *The Great American Blowup*, Ivan L. Preston[9] characterizes puffery this way:

By legal definition, puffery is advertising or other sales representations which praise the item to be sold with subjective opinions, superlatives, or exaggerations, vaguely and generally, stating no specific facts. It appears in various verbal and pictorial forms, the best known being slogans which are used repeatedly, sometimes for years, on behalf of a throng of na-

---

[9] Ivan L. Preston, *The Great American Blowup* (Madison: The University of Wisconsin Press; © 1975 by the Regents of the University of Wisconsin).

tionally advertised products and services. Perhaps the oldest of these still actively used is P. T. Barnum's "The Greatest Show on Earth." One might call it the king of them all, which would be puffing about puffing.

He then furnishes us with a lengthy list of one-line puffs, from which the following have been selected:

"The World's Greatest Newspaper" *(Chicago Tribune)*
"When you say Budweiser, you've said it all"
"King of beers" (Budweiser)
"When you're out of Schlitz, you're out of beer"
"You can be sure if it's Westinghouse"
"State Farm is all you need to know about insurance"
"We try harder" (Avis)
"Ford gives you better ideas"
"Chevrolet—building a better way to see the U.S.A."
"Toshiba—in touch with tomorrow"
"Old Grand Dad—head of the Bourbon family"
"You can't get any closer" (Norelco)
"Allied Van Lines—We move families, not just furniture"
"You can trust your car to the man who wears the star" (Texaco)
"With a name like Smucker's, it has to be good"
"Georgia, the unspoiled"
"Live better electrically" (Edison Electric Institute)
"Come to where the flavor is" (Marlboro)
"Breakfast of Champions" (Wheaties)
"The American breakfast, no mistake, starts with sugar, milk, and Kellogg's corn flakes"
"Every kid in America loves Jello brand gelatin"
"Prudential has the strength of Gibraltar."

Preston then goes on to list several examples of puffery consisting entirely of names, "Wonder Bread" and "Super Shell" being two examples.

The law allows puffery because of an interesting line of reasoning, plus a good deal of fudging. It might be supposed that the law should prohibit most puffery in a general prohibition against false statements. But this would be a mistake. Truth or falsity is not the issue. *Deceptiveness* is. We don't want to forbid all false claims or even allow all true ones, for two reasons. First, a literally true claim may imply a false one. For example, a Bayer aspirin commercial pictured an announcer holding a bottle of Bayer aspirin while stating the truth that doctors recommend aspirin for pain relief, thus implying the falsehood that doctors recommend Bayer's aspirin. And, second, a literally false statement is not *deceptive* if hardly anyone takes it to be true. Here is Preston's example:

The representation that you'll have a tiger in your tank when you use Esso (now Exxon) gasoline illustrates a kind of falsity which is not deceptive. There's no tiger, but regulators have never found anyone who expected a tiger. There was no disappointment and therefore no injurious deception, even though there was falsity.[10]

So regulators are supposed to work on the theory that it is *deceptive* advertising that should be forbidden, not false advertising. So far, so good. Now comes the fudging. It has been decided in general, as a result of actual cases, that most puffery is not illegal because it is not *deceptive* (although there have been a few cases of successful prosecution for puffery, perhaps the best known being against Geritol). But, of course, puffery *is* deceptive—that's the point of it. If it weren't, it wouldn't be effective in getting people to buy products; it wouldn't be one of the main ingredients in so many successful ads.

In addition to appealing in this way to the authority of ad experts and what they think has been proven to sell sell sell—*not* a fallacious appeal, incidentally—Preston supports the view that puffery deceives with the following results from a 1971 survey:

In 1971, R. H. Bruskin Associates asked a sample of citizens whether they felt various advertising claims were "completely true," "partly true," or "not true at all." Puffery was not identified by name, but a number of claims fell into the category and were rated as follows:

(1) "State Farm is all you need to know about life insurance" (22% said completely true, 36% said partly true);
(2) "The world's most experienced airline" (Pan Am) (23% and 47% respectively);
(3) "Ford has a better idea" (26% and 42%);
(4) "You can trust your car to the man who wears the star" (Texaco) (21% and 47%);
(5) "It's the real thing" (Coca Cola) (35% and 29%);
(6) "Perfect rice every time" (Minute Rice) (43% and 30%)

And the highest score in the survey went to Alcoa's claim:

"Today, aluminum is something else" (47% and 36%).

Puffery does work. Which means it must be deceptive, even if regulators have decided otherwise. The moral is that we can't count on the government to protect us from deceptive advertising—there isn't good reason to expect that to work in the near future—so we have to learn to protect ourselves.

Time Tries Puffery to Save Movie Channel

Seems that Home Box Office, the pay TV station owned by Time, Inc., is having a bit of trouble. Viewers just aren't happy with the movies, and

---

[10]But in some puffery, as in this example, there is a less apparent deception. By advertising about putting a tiger in your tank. Exxon implied that its gas is peppier, or somehow better than other brands, which is false and deceptive.

subscriptions are falling off. What to do? Well, thought Time, Inc., why not take *On Air,* the monthly HBO program guide, and jazz it up so the viewers think they're getting terrific stuff? Accordingly, *On Air* managing editor and publisher Stephen Marmon was told to hype the offerings —as in "*Mandingo,* which HBO is screening tonight, is one of the greatest movies ever. . . ." Marmon declined.

Time, Inc., is presently advertising for a replacement for Marmon, but this time around, the stated job title for the person who will assemble the magazine is [not managing editor and publisher, but] "promotion manager."

[*More*], November 1976.

It's surprising how many people are surprised to find out this is the way things work. But then, some people don't know that most background laughter on television is canned. (Woody Allen's flicks Annie Hall *and* Manhattan *both have great scenes—no puffery here—in which this is nicely illustrated.)*

5. Ads Often Use Meaningless Jargon or Deceptive Humor

As language is used with less and less precision, it comes closer and closer to being meaningless noise or jargon (jargon fools us because it often sounds so sensible). Ads, of course, contain lots of examples, in some of which there is a kernel of sense to mask their general mindlessness. On the whole, jargon is used more in ads for products that either don't do the job well at all (cosmetics, hair restorers, weight reducers), or don't do it better than competing products (cigarettes, detergents, beer). But what does it *mean,* really, to say that a brand of detergent gets clothes "whiter than white," or "beyond white"? What does an ad ask you to do when it advises you to "recreate yourself"? When should you go to Bermuda to enjoy their "rendezvous season"? What is the "spring elegance" of a Denice original? All of these use language more or less in a jargony, almost meaningless way, a way designed not to *inform* but to misdirect. (Notice that most of these jargon expressions are loaded with highly positive, emotionally charged words.)

In addition to jargon, ads often soften the pitch by using humor (especially plays on words—puns) to mask weak or ambiguous appeals. A full-page Eastern Airlines ad centered around the headline statement, "It is now within your means to live beyond your means. At least for a weekend." Stripped of ambiguity and humor, the ad's claim fizzles down to simply "Fly now—pay later."[11]

---

[11] In other words, Eastern will extend you credit—if you're a reasonable risk, of course. If it were really beyond your means, Eastern obviously wouldn't extend credit.

Here are a few more examples of humor in advertising designed to put you in the mood to spend money on the product:

"Have you ever done it the French way?"[12] (French Lines); "Like money in the bank: the shoe that takes you everywhere, building interest all the way" (Saks Fifth Avenue); "Why anyone would want to fly beyond us is beyond us" (Jamaica Tourist); "Everything you always wanted in a beer. . . . And less" (Schlitz Light Beer).

Of course, humor has a legitimate use in advertising—to present significant claims in a more enjoyable, more palatable manner. For over twenty years Volkswagen Beetle ads humorously pounded away at the fact that VW Bugs were much smaller than most American cars, and got better gas mileage with greater ease of handling and parking. This was a legitimate use of humor because these claims were true, and not deceptive.

The complexity of language, and the care needed to make sure it isn't used deceptively or ambiguously, is illustrated by what sometimes happens when advertising is translated into foreign languages. David Ricks and Jeffrey Arpan (in *International Business Blunders*) illustrate this with some nice examples:

In Belgium, General Motors' slogan "Body by Fisher" came out as "Corpse by Fisher." American Motors' Matador all too appropriately translates into "Killer" in Spanish. But the real killer is the Pepsi slogan "Come Alive with Pepsi," which actually ran for a short while in Germany translated into the German literal equivalent of "Come Alive Out of the Grave with Pepsi."

---

6. Ads Trade on Human Tendencies to Reason Fallaciously

In our discussion of advertising so far, only the major types of fallacious appeals have been mentioned *(false implication, exaggeration, ambiguity, suppressed evidence)*. But others are used too.

Scott Paper introduced a new, twice-as-expensive-per-sheet paper towel by showing that one of their towels could mop up a huge puddle of water on the floor which would take other paper towels more than half a dozen sheets to sop up. They claimed that this proved Scott's new towels are more economical than any others. But mopping up big puddles is not the sort of thing one buys paper towels for—a two-bit sponge does that better and can be used indefinitely. In normal use, even the sturdiest paper towels tend to get thrown away after each use—convenience is one reason why we buy them. So Scott's new

---

[12] Sexual double entendre is common.

towels turn out to be more expensive to use after all. Scott invited us to commit the fallacy of *faulty comparison.*

Another common fallacy advertisers think they can get away with is *inconsistency.* The following two ads for General Electric television sets (which both appeared in the same newspaper ad) illustrate this:

(1) The Black Matrix Advanced Spectra-Brite TV Picture Tube [jargon, jargon]—hundreds of thousands of time-colored dots are surrounded by a jet black background to give the crispest, brightest picture in GE history.
(2) Porta Color "In Line" Picture Tube System With Slotted Mask— Now. Rectangles instead of dots for the brightest sharpest color in GE history.

If having one brightest picture sells television sets, why not have two?

Now let's take a gander at this Baltimore radio commercial for the Maryland State Lottery:

Hi. Ol' number 5 here [Brooks Robinson, Baltimore Oriole baseball great] going to bat for the lottery. And speaking of 5, I never hit five home runs in a row, but the lottery has scored with five straight championship years.

There's no definitive way to sort out a mess like this, but one way would be to say that it gently leads us into committing the fallacy of *irrelevant reason* (what's all that 5 magic?) and *appeal to authority* (what does Brooks Robinson know about lotteries that the rest of us don't?).

Ad experts have honed *appeal to authority* down to a fine art—they know just how to appeal to each sort of consumer, so well in fact that such appeals sometimes become a temporary part of the language. For example, if you want to appeal to children, you don't show mom and pop happily eating their Life cereal; you show an appealing little kid doing so (splicing in a bit of humor), with the voice-over, "Try the cereal Mikey likes." The key to such appeals is *identification*—kids identifying with other kids (and, in this unusual case, parents identifying with a little kid).

Advertising is part of a modern package that is transforming human life, for good and evil. Two of the evils are reduced quality and reduced variety of certain kinds of goods. While prepared or fast foods are perhaps the most important case, beer may be the most revealing. Here are some excerpts from a well-researched, first-rate *Los Angeles Times* article (27 May 1979):[13]

---

[13] A. Kent MacDougall, "Market-Shelf Proliferation—Public Pays," *Los Angeles Times,* 27 May 1979. Copyright 1979, Los Angeles Times. Reprinted by permission.

Market segmentation, brand proliferation and advertising intensification—all part of the same marketing strategy aimed at increasing market share and profits—comprise the dominant form of competition in most consumer packaged goods categories. Price competition is passé. Manufacturers realize that if one producer cuts prices, competitors will be forced to follow, and this will hurt the profits of all without giving the initial price-cutter any lasting advantage. Producers seldom cut the price even of a failing brand, preferring to let it die and to replace it with a new full-priced brand.

New brands are seldom priced lower and often are higher than brands already on the market. For instance, most brands of light beer are priced at a premium even though they contain fewer ingredients than regular beer. . . .

Anheuser-Busch, Inc., which promotes the naturalness of its beers, brews Michelob Light the natural way—by watering regular Michelob.

Whereas other brewers use enzymes to cut the carbohydrates in their light beers, Anheuser-Busch simply dilutes regular Michelob with carbonated water to achieve a 20% reduction in calories. . . . Says Willard F. Mueller, a University of Wisconsin economist who has made a special study of the brewing industry: "Selling a product that costs less to make at a higher price is the ultimate achievement in advertising-created product differentiation. Light beer fills that bill. . . ."

Another new segment is made up of "image" beers such as Lowenbrau. These carry prestigious foreign names but are brewed in the United States. According to a complaint to the FTC filed by Anheuser-Busch, Miller brews Lowenbrau domestically by methods that would be unacceptable in Germany, using cheaper malt, artificial additives, and injections of carbon dioxide gas rather than natural carbonation. Miller won't discuss the charges, saying its brewing formulations are confidential. . . .

Premium priced brands date from the 1930s and 1940s when several Milwaukee and St. Louis brewers expanded their sales nationwide. In shipping low-value (95% water) products long distances from single plants, they incurred relatively high transportation costs. To cover these costs, the national brewers charged higher prices than regional beers, justifying them with advertised claims to premium quality.

Today, national brewers operate plants in many parts of the country and their transportation costs are generally no heavier than regional brewers'. Yet the price differential remains and helps defray heavier advertising costs.

Meanwhile, many dark, strongly flavored local brews that couldn't match the advertising blitz of the national brands have died out. And both regional and national brewers have altered their formulas to make their beers lighter and more bland in taste (and less alcoholic in content) to appeal to the lowest common denominator of beer drinkers.

"Beers are becoming more homogenous and bland in taste, and there is less difference than ever between brands," says Robert S. Weinberg, a former Anheuser-Busch vice president who now operates a market research firm in St. Louis.

The FTC's seven-year-old antitrust suit against the largest cereal producers, Kellogg, General Mills, and General Foods, charges that they have used the proliferation and heavy promotion of just such basically similar cereals to inflate prices and profits artificially. The cereal companies also are charged with discouraging new competition by making the pieces of the cereal market so small and costly to acquire that outsiders do not find entry attractive.

As some alarmed businessmen have pointed out, the FTC's test case against brand proliferation in breakfast cereals can be applied to nearly all consumer packaged goods, from cigarettes to chewing gum, from shampoo to soft drinks. In nearly every product category, the use of brand proliferation to maintain or increase market share has the effect, if not always the intent, of pushing up prices, increasing profits for those most adept at playing the game, discouraging competition, and in some cases even reducing meaningful product variety and innovation.

Although it has yet to run afoul of the FTC for proliferation, the generally acknowledged master at churning out essentially similar brands and using them to plug market holes and preempt shelf space is Procter & Gamble. Its multiple brand entries in dozens of food, toiletry and household products make it the market share leader or contender in just about every category it's in.

"Isn't free enterprise wonderful?" a Procter & Gamble public relations man says of the multiplicity. Yes, indeed. But while any enterprising individual is free to make soap—it can be done at home—trying to sell it nationally in competition with a marketing giant that spends half a billion dollars a year on U.S. advertising seems a freedom without meaning to all but a handful of similarly huge corporations.

Manufacturing efficiency, often reduced by the shorter production runs associated with multiple brands, is less important in giving Procter & Gamble and other large packaged goods manufacturers an edge over smaller competitors than economies of scale in marketing.

The main reason that consumer packaged goods industries are becoming more oligopolistic is that market fragmentation and the soaring costs of new product development and promotion are deterring new entrants. Most would-be entrants simply cannot afford the huge advertising outlays required to penetrate the existing noise level and break down loyalties to entrenched brands. Nor can they borrow the capital required, because lenders know they can't recover tangible assets from an unprofitable investment in advertising the way they can from an unprofitable investment in plant and machinery.

7.   *Political Candidates and Programs Are Sold Just Like Other Products*

By now, just about everyone knows that political candidates are marketed pretty much like breakfast foods or laundry detergents. And that might be all right if the appeals in breakfast food and detergent advertising were rational. But they aren't, a fact we have been taking pains to illustrate.

Campaigns Focus on Television

Radio and, in particular, television have transformed the political process in recent years. A candidate standing in front of a camera can influence more voters in a one-minute spot commercial than candidates used to reach in a whole campaign. The result is a decline in the use of billboards, lawn signs, posters, newspaper ads, Fourth of July hoopla, and whistle stop campaigns. (But not in direct mail appeals.) Television wins or loses most political campaigns, which is why, for instance, publicity and campaign expert Gerald Rafshoon was a key member of the Carter administration White House staff. (But for some candidates, direct mail appeals raise most of the money. The trick in national campaigns in recent years has been to get a few "fat cats" to put up early "seed money" to finance direct mail appeals for the money needed to pay for the extremely expensive television exposure that wins or loses.)

In the 1970 New York race for governor (which he won quite handily), Nelson Rockefeller used by far the most massive television campaign in New York history—in fact, in any nonnational election in history. (Rockefeller, like some other rich candidates, had an advantage in having his own seed money. The expense of television campaigns has tended to make personal wealth the entry fee required to run for high office.) And yet, there is extremely little that is informative in television ads for political candidates.

The chief political ad device on television is the spot commercial, which generally runs from thirty to sixty seconds. It is almost impossible to say anything that is truly informative on any controversial topic in sixty seconds or less. Senator Philip Hart of Michigan, who used television ads in his successful 1970 campaign, put it this way: "How the hell can you describe in thirty seconds why you think a volunteer army is necessary?"[14]

The first presidential campaign in which television ads played an important role was the 1952 Eisenhower-Stevenson campaign. In that campaign, Gener-

---

[14] Quoted in *Time*, 21 September 1970.

al Eisenhower would read from letters received from "citizens" asking questions that Eisenhower then "answered." Here is an example:

> *Citizen:* Mr. Eisenhower, what about the high cost of living?
> *General Eisenhower:* My wife Mamie worries about the same thing. I tell her it's our job to change that on November 14th.[15]

The appeal here is to Eisenhower the father figure who will set things right just as daddy used to. (Appeal to a father figure may well be the most effective version of *appeal to authority*.) You don't have to know *how* papa fixes things, and you didn't have to know how Eisenhower was going to reduce prices. (He didn't, of course, but that's hindsight.) All you had to know was that if you voted for him, he would be on the job after the election doing something about the high cost of living.

One of the most effective TV spots was the first one used in Richard Nixon's 1968 campaign. The video portion of the spot consisted of shots from Vietnam cleverly dovetailed with Mr. Nixon's voice:

> Never has so much military, economic, and diplomatic power been used as ineffectively as in Vietnam. And if, after all of this time and all of this support, there is still no end in sight, then I say the time has come for the American people to turn to new leadership, not tied to the policies and mistakes of the past. I pledge to you: we will have an honorable end to the war in Vietnam.

(An ironic commercial, given what transpired in Vietnam after Nixon took office.) Notice, however, that the punch line, the promise to get us out of Vietnam, is extremely vague. In particular, he doesn't tell us when or how he will get us out, only that it will be honorable. Yet the tone of the commercial gives the viewer the impression that Nixon will get us out *quickly*.

I'm not an old hand at politics. But I am now seasoned enough to have learned that the hardest thing about any political campaign is how to win without proving that you are unworthy of winning.
—Adlai Stevenson, 1956

What one (losing) candidate learned from two runs at the presidency

---

[15] Quoted by David Ogilvy in *Confessions of an Advertising Man*, p. 159. Ogilvy quotes Eisenhower as moaning between television takes, "To think an old soldier should come to this." Notice again that the ploy used is to bring up a strong desire (for lower prices) and tie the product (candidate), to the satisfaction of that desire without giving a single "reason why" the product will satisfy it.

> They don't put out press releases on mistakes.
> —John Dean, commenting on how the White House manipulates the president's image
>
> ---
>
> *Like other ads, political rhetoric invites commission of the fallacy* suppressed evidence.

One of Hubert Humphrey's commercials in the 1968 campaign played on the fact that Nixon had chosen as his running mate a man who was almost unknown outside of his home state of Maryland, a man who happened to have the unusual name "Agnew." Democrats at the time often bucked up their sagging spirits by asking each other, "Spiro who?" So Humphrey's television advertising geniuses concocted a television spot consisting of almost a minute of laughter, with a voice saying, "Agnew for Vice President?" and at the end of the video reading, "This would be funny if it weren't so serious. . . ." All of which amounted to nothing other than a vicious *ad hominem* argument against Spiro Agnew.

One of Lyndon Johnson's television spots in 1964 emphasized the claim that Johnson was a peace candidate, while the Republican candidate Barry Goldwater was a violent hawk. (Lyndon Johnson as peace candidate seems foolish now, but, again, that's hindsight.) The commercial shows a cute little girl plucking the petals from a flower one by one while on the sound track we hear, "Ten, nine, eight, seven, six, five, four, three, two, one," at which point an atomic fireball flashes on the screen. (This "informative" commercial was too much even for the American viewing public, and was withdrawn after one nationwide showing.)

Thirty- and sixty-second television spots also are used as the principle device in many state and local elections. In 1972, Arch Moore ran for governor of West Virginia against Jay Rockefeller, obviously not a long-time resident of that state. Rockefeller desperately wanted to shake the image of an outsider, so that's exactly where media master[16] Robert Goodman, in charge of Moore's campaign, attacked, in a famous commercial known as the "New York spot." Several New Yorkers were asked on camera: "Excuse me, what do you think of a West Virginian running for governor of New York?"; these questions were followed by close-ups of people laughing as they dismissed this idea. They were then asked, "What do you think of a New Yorker running for governor of West Virginia?"; this was followed by the New Yorker's reply, "Ridiculous." Moore defeated "outsider" Jay Rockefeller.

Another Goodman gem, for John Tower in his 1978 race against Robert Krueger, starts out by asking, "How'd you like to have a job where you show

---

[16]See one of a series on "media masters" in *The Washington Post Magazine* (11 March 1979). The Rudy Maxa examples, which follow, are discussed in the 24 June 1979 issue.

up just 25 percent of the time and still get paid over $50,000 a year?" "Are you kidding?" replies a man in the street. "That sounds like a con game," says someone else. And then the screen copy reads, "Only one man in Texas has that job. Robert Krueger showed up 25 percent of the time but collected 100 percent of his salary." (One of those true but unfair blows because it was *deceptive*—showing up for votes isn't basically where it's at in the legislative game, as mentioned earlier.)

Another media expert, Rudy Maxa, helped Alabaman Howell Heflin defeat Representative Walter Flowers in the 1978 Democratic primary with a spot showing a baby playing with a toy airplane and a toy car on the floor (Washington skyline silhouetted in the background) as an off-camera voice stated:

Remember when you first started playing with toys? It was the beginning of learning about life. Some members of Congress have forgotten those early lessons. When Congress voted itself more money to travel by car than plane, Walter Flowers took the plane and put the difference in his pocket. But the government caught him and made him give the money back. Maybe Flowers never learned the difference between a car and a plane. Or was it right from wrong? Howell Heflin for the U.S. Senate.

Maxa also helped Bob Graham win the governorship of Florida with a series of spots showing Graham working at different everyday jobs, such as garbage collector, as part of a ploy that had Graham actually spending a day on each of these jobs. The campaign slogan tied together the bundle: "Bob Graham—working for Governor."

Perhaps the most effective television commercials of the 1976 presidential campaign were a series of twelve spots for Gerald Ford featuring Georgians rejecting Georgian candidate Jimmy Carter with remarks like "I want a Georgian for President, but not Jimmy Carter," all indicating they would vote for Ford.

Ford also used a positive approach, featuring jingles like "I'm feeling good about America," and in particular used ex-ballplayer Joe Garagiola in what became known as the "Jerry and Joe Show." One scene featured Ford speaking from Air Force One (*appeal to authority* is still great stuff in this media age—appealing to the authority of the presidency sure fire) answering Garagiola's questions: "Joe: How many leaders have you dealt with, Mr. President? Jerry: One hundred and twenty-four leaders of countries around the world, Joe." Wow!

The "Jerry and Joe Show" was interesting in that it consisted mostly of several thirty-minute-long commercials. (This was indeed different, because the thirty- or sixty-second television spot has become the mainstay of practically all big-time campaigns.) These lengthy commercials were quite effective, however; in particular the "Jerry and Joe" election-eve red-white-and-blue program, which pulled out all stops and featured the life history of Gerald Ford, even referring to his days as a football star at Michigan.

I participated in preparations for nearly forty of John F. Kennedy's [extremely effective] news conferences and can recall only two questions that had not been anticipated and discussed; neither was very important.
—Robert Manning, editor of *Atlantic* magazine, quoted in *Atlantic*, February 1977

Running for president is a long-term operation. If you're already president, the trick is to take advantage of the office in your campaign to win reelection. News conferences are scheduled primarily as an opportunity for the president to display presidential capabilities by being on top of whatever reporters are likely to ask—an easy task since what they ask is pretty much predictable, as Manning indicates. Imagery is so important in politics that a president is forced to integrate his plans for doing his job as president with his plans to get reelected. Jimmy Carter's handling of the Begin-Sadat Camp David agreement is a good example. The whole thing was planned so that the three leaders would sign on the dotted line and congratulate each other on national television programs which were watched by a very large international audience. Such exposure is free, of course, which is one reason it's so hard to beat an incumbent.

Campaigns Are Also Fought by Mail

Campaigning by mail begins the day after taking office for most elected officials, and gives an incumbent a large head start over potential opponents (one important reason why it's so hard to defeat an incumbent—and also why we're never likely to see Congress give up its franking privilege).

Of course, members of Congress aren't supposed to send out-and-out campaign literature free of charge, but they are allowed to frank letters containing questionnaires and, in particular, answers to letters from constituents. One recent *Washington Monthly* article ("Mail Fraud on Capitol Hill," by Mark Feldstein, October 1979) argues quite plausibly that at least one United States senator, Milton R. Young, North Dakota, owes his repeated reelection to his considerable ability in talking out of both sides of his mouth when answering letters from constituents. (It can't be because of accomplishments or notoriety —Milton who?—yet he has been reelected regularly since 1945, and is the senior Republican senator.)

The *Washington Monthly* article describes his and some other senators' responses to twin letters, one favoring and one opposing abortion. (Of course, no senator could possibly compose an individual reply to each letter received; every senator thus uses standard replies, classified by issue and by position taken on an issue.) Here is the main part of Young's standard reply to anti-abortion letters:

I thought you would be pleased to know that I have strongly supported the position you take. I have been a co-sponsor of a resolution in the

Senate proposing a Human Life Amendment since the Supreme Court issued its decision liberalizing abortion almost six years ago.

But here's the sort of thing you get in reply to a pro-abortion letter:

I appreciated hearing from you and receiving your views on this matter, . . . I agree with you that a woman should have a right to decide whether or not she wants an abortion.

You can make anyone say anything.
—Avram Gold, who edited Gerald Ford's television commercials in the 1976 campaign

He ought to know.

Long Campaigns Lead to Set Speeches

Presidential campaigns are grueling marathons for the contestants. Candidates have to be on public display almost continually for several months. This doesn't leave much time for thinking about what to say. So a candidate is likely to have the same set items, which are juggled to fit each particular audience. Here, for example, is Jimmy Carter in his famous *Playboy* interview (in which he admitted he lusted in his heart after other women). The question was whether he didn't feel numb delivering the same speech over and over:

Sometimes. But I generally have tried to change the order of the speech and emphasize different things. Sometimes I abbreviate and sometimes I elaborate. Of 20 different parts of a speech, I might take seven or eight and change them around. It depends on the audience—black people, Jewish people, chicanos—and that gives me the ability to make speeches that aren't boring to myself.

True. But it also gives him the chance to tell each group what it wants to hear that other groups might not want to hear.

Another Carter answer was revealing in what it said about reporters who cover presidential campaigns:

The local media are interested, all right, but the national news media have absolutely no interest in issues *at all.* . . . The traveling press have a zero interest in any issue unless it's a matter of making a mistake. What they're looking for is a 47-second argument between me and another candidate or something like that. There's nobody in the back of this [campaign] plane who would ask an issue question unless he thought he could trick me into some crazy statement.

Reporters want confrontation and controversy, because that's what gets viewer or reader attention. Carter, naïve or idealistic as he was, wanted to talk about the issues, but was rarely able to.

Speaking of issues, they, too, can be advertised successfully by the standard Madison Avenue techniques. Here is Richard E. Smith, U.S. Corps of Engineers area engineer for the Tennessee-Tombigbee Waterway boondoggle, on the Corps' "public posture on costs": "I would recommend we hold the federal cost under $1 billion. Say $975,000,000. Considering the size of the estimate, $975 million is no less accurate than $1 billion and it has less emotional impact." Does this remind you of how businesses will price an item at $49.50 instead of $50 even? (At least businesses don't jack up the price as you're about to hand over the money. In the case of government, the price —called an "estimate"—is usually raised several times.)

> The logic of campaign rhetoric is ruled by the psychologic of human nature.
> —Harold Gordon

Political image building is not restricted to candidates for office. J. Edgar Hoover, the first and for many years the only director of the FBI, was a master image builder, both for himself and for his baby, the FBI. The FBI's "Ten Most Wanted" list is one of the great image ploys of all time (no puffery here). In order to gain maximum publicity for the bureau, the list has to mirror the interests of the times. Thus, in the 1950s, it ran to bank robbers and auto thieves, leaving organized mobsters and such types alone. As the sixties wore on, left-wing radicals like Angela Davis, Bernadine Dorn, and H. Rap Brown were featured. But today, that's passé. We now have accused sex killers like Ted Bundy and alleged porno kings like Michael G. Davis, along with an occasional big-time mobster. The Ten Most Wanted list is not an important part of the bureau's crime-fighting equipment, but it is great media hype.

Political rhetoric is not much different from other rhetoric when you get right down to it. The point is to manipulate the public to buy the product. For instance, vagueness and ambiguity are used, just as elsewhere—leading Jerry Brown to remark during his 1976 gubernatorial campaign, "In this business, a little vagueness goes a long way."

This is true in particular of the vague cliché—which *is* used more frequently in political rhetoric than even in soap commercials. Mike Royko (in his column of 21 August 1976) marveled at this string of clichés from just the first paragraph of a Republican convention speech by Robert Dole: "Proud of the confidence . . . Gratified by your trust . . . Humbled by this new opportunity . . . Determined to work with all my heart. . . ." Dole then topped himself with these dazzlers: "The eyes of the world are . . . Weathered the storm of . . . The future gleamed brightly for . . . A long and noble chapter in . . . Those principles upon which America was founded are. . ."

The one thing that is in short supply in political rhetoric is humor, in particular sophisticated humor, as a distraught candidate Adlai Stevenson (the last presidential nominee with a good sense of humor) may have realized when he remarked in response to the charge that he was an "egghead": "Eggheads of the world unite. All we have to lose is our yolks."

Summary of Chapter Eight

The focus of this chapter is on the devices used in advertising to con the unwary by appealing to our emotions, weaknesses, and prejudices. The point is to better enable us to use advertising without being used:

1. *Ads don't say what's wrong with the product,* thus tempting us to commit the fallacy of *suppressed evidence.*

   Example: Ads for over-the-counter nonprescription drugs rarely tell about side effects except, as in the case of the drug nicotine (in cigarettes), when required by law.

2. *Ads play to emotions much more than to reason.*

   Example: The aid headlined "They laughed when I sat down at the piano, but when I started to play!. . . .," which appealed to our desire to become almost instant pianists without all the practice reason says is necessary.

3. *Ads often are deceptive or misleading.* In particular, they deceive or mislead in three important ways.

   a. The first is to say one thing (usually true) while implying something else (false), the device called *false implication.*

      Example: The London Fog commercials, which, by being set in London, imply but do not say the falsehood that London Fog products are made in England.

   b. The second deceptive device is the use of *ambiguity.*

      Example: The Coricidin ad, "At the first sign of a cold or flu— Coricidin." Does this imply that Coricidin will help cure a cold (false) or just that it will help alleviate attending discomfort or pain (somewhat true)?

   c. The third deceptive device is *exaggeration.*

      Example: Ads for Broadway plays, such as the one that said of a box office flop, "I haven't laughed as often or as heartily in years . . . audiences will howl with laughter."

4. *Puffery is legal* (so beware). Puffery is advertising that praises with subjective opinion, superlatives, or exaggerations, vaguely and generally, stating no specific facts. The law allows puffery on the theory (false) that it isn't deceptive even though it is often not true.

Example: The *Chicago Tribune*'s motto on the masthead of every issue, "The World's Greatest Newspaper."

5. *Ads often use meaningless jargon or deceptive humor.*

   Example: The detergent ad that says the product "gets clothes whiter than white" (jargon) or the Xerox ad that plays on the humor of a medieval monk discovering the "miracle" of Xeroxing as compared to scribbling on parchment.

6. *Ads trade on any old tendency we may have to reason fallaciously.*

   a. One way is by getting us to make a *faulty comparison.*

      Example: The paper towel ad that compares the performance of the advertised towel against others wiping up large puddles (not the main task for paper towels).

   b. Another way is by being *inconsistent.*

      Example: General Electric television set ads that tout two separate sets as the best they've ever made.

   c. Then there is the device of *appeal to authority.*

      Example: Appealing to the authority of the fact that some appealing-looking kid likes Life cereal ("Try the cereal Mikey likes").

7. *Politican candidates and programs are sold just like other products.* This means that they invite the commission of most of the standard fallacies and appeal to emotions and prejudices much more than facts.

   The chief device in recent national campaigns and some local ones is the thirty- or sixty-second spot television commercial. The trouble is that there isn't much in the way of issues and arguments that can be presented in such a short time, so as usual it's whipping up emotions and prejudices and manipulating the uninformed (most voters).

   The other important device is direct mail, in particular, replies to letters from constituents. The point is to try to convince letter writers that they have a friend in their representative. (Recall Senator Young's pro and con letters on abortion.)

Exercise I for Chapter Eight

Here are several ad snippets (usually including the main ad ploy). In each case, state: (1) whether the ad, if true, would provide a good reason for buying the product; (2) whether the ad contains questionable claims, and, if so, which claims are doubtful *and why;* (3) which, if any, of the devices employed were discussed in this (or some other) chapters (explain); and (4) which, if any, of the ads use emotive language unfairly (that is, so as to con).

*1. *Ad for Senator McGovern in 1972 presidential campaign:* Nixon has a secret plan for ending the war. He is going to vote for McGovern.

2. *Rolaids television commercial, showing a Rolaids user rejecting another brand:* Rolaids active ingredient—medically recognized safe and effective. *suppressed evidence, false implication:*

3. CHEMICAL BANK has an answer to all your borrowing needs. The answer is "Yes." ("Yes" is a chemical reaction.) *puffery "yes" meta, ambiguity*

*4. *Bloomingdale's Department Store ad, January 1975:* Our very finest sofas, now at our lowest prices in years. *questionable statement:*

5. *The Night Porter*—most controversial film of all time. *puffery*

6. *Ad for James Buckley, conservative senatorial candidate from New York:* Isn't it time *we* had a senator?

7. Take my "Hundred Dollar Knife," yours for only $4.99. *False implication*

8. The ingredient in Anacin *is* doctors' number one choice. *False implication imply not the other doctor,*

*9. Martha West's exclusive dress frames the face, and flatters the figure. *jargon*

10. There's only one King David, and there's only one King David Manor.

*11. Clorets has Actizol.

12. *British Airways ad:* "If I didn't live in Britain, I'd take these tours myself." —Robert Morley.

13. *Ad for Toronto Dominion Bank:* We have a new way to lend you money. *questionable statement,*

14. *Sign on Highland Park, Illinois, retail establishment:* 100% PRE-DRIVEN CARS. *ambiguity to pre-owner*

15. I switched from sugar to Sweet 'n Low because I care.

16. *Sign on Royal Trust Bank in Vancouver, B.C.:* Trust Royal Trust.

17. *Ad for the new Olympic Towers Apartments:* A landmark ahead of its time.

18. *Fur sale ad:* Same styles sold by prestige furriers for $495 to $6,000!

19. *Soup Starter commercial:* It's so easy, I'll feel guilty. . . . But I'll get over it.

20. *Tie-in ad in which Wright Brothers pens endorse Carefree Sugarless gum:* Two Wrights don't make it wrong.

21. *Ad for Calvert Gin:* Dry, Drier, Driest, Crisp *jargon,*

22. *Greyhound Bus ad:* Say Hello to America. Say Hello to a Good Buy.

23. RCA—TV that "thinks in color."

24. *Mail ad:* Special collector's edition. Priceless recordings. $6.98 per album.

25. *Man speaking:* My boss was right [that I should use Sinutab]. That's why she's the boss [photo of smiling woman on screen].

26. *Penthouse ad:* Statistics show 100 percent of the readers of the biggest selling men's magazine on the newsstands [*Penthouse*, of course] . . . wear clothes.

27.   *Ad depicting a rich elderly gentleman talking to another one between their palatial homes:* "I was wondering if I could possibly borrow a cup of Johnny Walker Black Label."

*28.

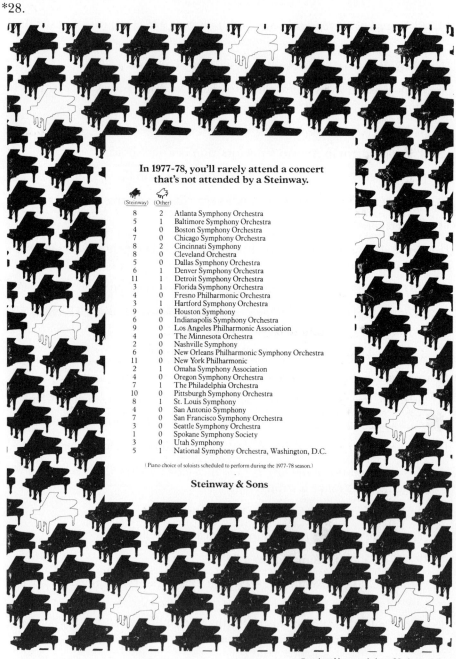

In 1977-78, you'll rarely attend a concert that's not attended by a Steinway.

(Steinway)	(Other)	
8	2	Atlanta Symphony Orchestra
5	1	Baltimore Symphony Orchestra
4	0	Boston Symphony Orchestra
7	0	Chicago Symphony Orchestra
8	2	Cincinnati Symphony
8	0	Cleveland Orchestra
5	0	Dallas Symphony Orchestra
6	1	Denver Symphony Orchestra
11	1	Detroit Symphony Orchestra
3	1	Florida Symphony Orchestra
4	0	Fresno Philharmonic Orchestra
3	1	Hartford Symphony Orchestra
9	0	Houston Symphony
6	0	Indianapolis Symphony Orchestra
9	0	Los Angeles Philharmonic Association
4	0	The Minnesota Orchestra
2	0	Nashville Symphony
6	0	New Orleans Philharmonic Symphony Orchestra
11	0	New York Philharmonic
2	1	Omaha Symphony Association
4	0	Oregon Symphony Orchestra
7	1	The Philadelphia Orchestra
10	0	Pittsburgh Symphony Orchestra
8	1	St. Louis Symphony
4	0	San Antonio Symphony
7	0	San Francisco Symphony Orchestra
3	0	Seattle Symphony Orchestra
1	0	Spokane Symphony Society
3	0	Utah Symphony
5	1	National Symphony Orchestra, Washington, D.C.

(Piano choice of soloists scheduled to perform during the 1977-78 season.)

Steinway & Sons

29. The 1978 Rabbit. It's just a wonderful car. True, we had a big advantage: we started with a wonderful car and made it even better. Over a million people all over the world have been impressed enough to buy them. What's so impressive? Easy. If you trade up to a Rabbit from a Mercedes Benz 280E, believe it or not you'll get better acceleration. If you trade up to a Rabbit from a Cadillac Seville, you'll get more trunk space. . . .

30. *Beginning of a form letter from Teachers Insurance and Annuity Association of America (TIAA):* It simply wouldn't be true to say, "Howard Kahane [alias, Alfred Hitchcock] . . . If you own a TIAA life insurance policy you'll live longer." But it is a fact, nonetheless, that persons insured by TIAA do enjoy longer lifetimes, on the average, than persons insured by commercial insurance companies that serve the general public. Lower mortality rates are an important reason why TIAA policies cost so much less.

Exercise II for Chapter Eight

This whole page was supposed to contain a Vantage cigarette ad addressing itself to the question whether there is an answer to the cigarette question. However, R. J. Reynolds Industries (which also makes Winstons, Camels, Salems, and several other brands) refused permission to reprint on the grounds that it is the policy of R. J. Reynolds not to do anything that might be construed as encouraging smoking among the young, pointing out that they do not advertise or promote on campuses, where *Logic and Contemporary Rhetoric* is primarily used. (They also refused permission to reprint from their letter of refusal.) No other advertiser has ever refused permission to reprint an ad in any of the three editions of this book, including Phillip Morris (Marlboro's) and The Tobacco Institute.

Since we don't have the original, critically evaluate the following key arguments in the Vantage ad (which appeared in many magazines in 1979—you might want to track it down and check for accuracy). The question addressed in the ad is whether people should smoke cigarettes:

Whatever the arguments, people do smoke, and will continue to. The more relevant question is thus what smokers should do. Critics could recommend that those who want to continue smoking but are worried about nicotine or tar could switch to a low-nicotine, low-tar cigarette, such as Vantage. Vantage isn't lowest in tar and nicotine, but reducing them further would very likely compromise taste. We're not going to argue about whether you should continue smoking—the fact is that you do smoke. To reduce nicotine and tar, consider Vantage Menthol cigarettes (11 mg tar, 0.7 mg nicotine per cigarette).

(You might want to critically evaluate Reynolds' reason for refusing to grant permission; was it the real reason in all likelihood?)

DOES THE GOVERNMENT SUPPORT THE TOBACCO FARMER?

NO, THE TOBACCO FARMER SUPPORTS THE GOVERNMENT.

Some people want to hear only one side of an argument.

That's not you, obviously—or you wouldn't be reading this.

You've heard the side of the anti-smokers—that the government is, in some way, "supporting" or "subsidizing" the tobacco farmer.

Here is the other side of that argument. And if you're not a tobacco farmer, you'll probably be surprised, maybe even pleased, to hear it.

Because the truth is the other way around: It's the tobacco farmer who's supporting the government.

There *is* a government program called the tobacco price support program. It began in 1933, and for the past 45 years it has been the single most successful farm program the government has ever had. It costs next to nothing, and it pays enormous dividends to all taxpayers.

The heart of it is a simple businesslike arrangement. The government offers the tobacco farmer what *he* needs: a guaranteed price for his crop. If commercial buyers do not meet this price, the farmer receives a government loan and surrenders his crop. And the government gets, in return, what the *government* needs: the farmer's agreement not to plant any more than the government tells him he can.

The government's interest, and the taxpayer's, is in preventing economic chaos. Without the weapon of the loan agreement, the government would be powerless to limit the production of tobacco. The results would be as predictable as any disaster can be: overplanting of the crop by big farmers with extra land and by

newcomers, a fall in the price of tobacco, a drop in the income of small farmers to the point where many would be squeezed off the land and onto welfare rolls, sharp decreases in tax collections in the 22 states that grow tobacco, widespread disruptions in the banking and commercial systems and, if you want to follow the scenario out to its grim conclusion, very likely a regional recession.

The value of the program to the government, and to the taxpayer, is thus very great. And the cost is unbelievably low. Over the entire 45 years of its operation, the total cost of the government guarantee has been less than $1¼ million a year, or roughly what the government spends otherwise every 79 seconds. This is because the government has been able to sell, at a profit, almost all the tobacco it has taken as loan collateral.

From the farmer's viewpoint, the tobacco support program might as easily, and more justly, be called a *government* support program, since it does more to support the government than it does to support him.

One fact above all others tells you the true story. For all his labors in planting, growing and harvesting his crop, the farmer receives $2.3 billion. And from the products of his labor, the government (federal, state and local) collects $6 billion in taxes.

It's enough to make even an anti-smoker, at least a fair-minded one, agree that, on balance, it's the tobacco farmer who's supporting the government. And doing it superbly.

THE TOBACCO INSTITUTE
1776 K St. N. W., Washington, D.C. 20006

Exercise III for Chapter Eight

Evaluate the advertisement on page 204, following the instructions given for evaluating extended passages in Chapter Seven. Also point out any ad ploys discussed in this chapter.

Exercise IV for Chapter Eight

Repeat the experiment described by Mark Feldstein in his *Washington Monthly* article, choosing a different topic than abortion. That is, write two letters to one of your senators or representatives in Washington, one letter taking a short, strong stand on some issue (energy, busing, inflation, unemployment), the other letter taking an equally strong but different stand (opposite, if possible) on the same issue. Compare the two replies you get and draw conclusions. (Send each letter from a different address or at different times.)

Exercise V for Chapter Eight

1. Watch television for two continuous hours, noting the main ploys of at least three or four commercials. Then analyze for fallacies, use of emotive language, and other advertising gimmicks discussed in this chapter.

2. Rewrite an advertisement containing highly charged emotive language and fallacies (in other words, a particularly gimmicky ad). Once you have discovered its true informational content, compare your version with the original ad, and then critically evaluate the original ad.

Drawing by Richter; © 1975 The New Yorker Magazine, Inc.

This cartoon effectively makes the point that the power of freedom of speech is relative. If you set policy for CBS news, your views will be widely heard and very influential, but if you're just one of the rest of us, you have no effective way to compete with the giants in the marketplace of ideas. You might just as well let off steam by shouting from the rooftops—or balconies.

Chapter Nine

Managing the News

*When covering the Capitol, the first thing
to remember is that every government is
run by liars.*
—I. F. Stone

*In all TV the defeat of evil is the
consequence of superior craft and power
and what becomes clear is that right is on
the side of the cleverest, the most powerful,
and the fastest gun.*
—Jules Henry

*Freedom of the press is guaranteed only to
those who own one.*
—A. J. Liebling

The headline of the Daily News *today
reads BRUNETTE STABBED TO
DEATH. Underneath in lower case letters
"6000 Killed in Iranian Earthquake"* . . .
I wonder what color hair they had.
—Abbie Hoffman

Reasoning about political and social issues requires factual knowledge. That is
why the success of a democratic form of government depends on a *well-
informed* electorate. Unfortunately, the American mass news media (newspapers, television, mass magazines, and radio) do not adequately or accurately
inform their readers or listeners. In particular, they fail to inform them of the
great gulf between the way our society is supposed to work (the ideal—the
"official story") and the way it actually works.

Yet, we all have to rely on the mass media for news. Those who understand
how and why things get reported as they do will be better able to evaluate that
reporting, better able to read between the lines, separate wheat from chaff,
and not be taken in by questionable reasoning or poor coverage. They'll also
understand why the mass media have to be supplemented by selectively
chosen nonmass media sources.

1. Television Channels, Radio Stations, Newspapers, and Magazines Are Businesses

The one overriding fact to bear in mind in trying to understand the mass
media is that CBS, the *Los Angeles Times, Newsweek* magazine, and all the rest
are *businesses*, intended to return a profit. They have two sets of "buyers"
—their audiences (readers, viewers, listeners) and their advertisers. When

they displease, annoy, or threaten either of these groups too seriously, they're likely to fail, or at least seriously reduce profits. *There is always more money in catering to both groups.*

We should expect, then, if our world view tells us large businesses are run to maximize profits,[1] that media executives will shape the news so as not to anger their buyers. And this is just about what we find to be true.

News Is Simplified for the Mass Audience

There are several standard ways in which the news is distorted to placate buyers. Perhaps the most important is *simplification*. On the whole, media audiences are not sophisticated; they cannot, or at least will not, pay attention to complicated material (we saw the result of this in political spot commercials). The trouble is that almost all social and political issues are complicated, so that simplified accounts of events or issues must in general be distorted accounts. Examples are reporting on the energy problem and the problem of pollution. (But see pages 237 and 239 for the one modestly important exception.) Take the crucial speech on the energy problem President Carter delivered in July 1979. The speech itself contained primarily a simplified account of Carter's proposals and his reasons for making them. (United States presidents are subject to the same sorts of pressures as are media moguls.) A good evaluation would require that lots of facts, figures, and theories be put together into one large theory about what the devil is going on in the energy field. But no mass media was able then to provide that service—even presenting the facts in one place would have required a good deal of work, chiefly editing and evaluating, which is too expensive and in particular would result in a product that the public will not accept.

News Selection Reflects the Interests, Opinions, and Prejudices of Its Audience

Viewer and reader interests, opinions, and prejudices must be taken into account in reporting the news. Newspaper readers and television viewers are not captive audiences (as they were, say, in Nazi Germany and Fascist Italy, where outdoor loudspeakers blared the official line to the public). They can flick the switch or turn the page. The result is *provincialism*—news reporting that tends to reflect the interests and foibles of its audience, as world travelers often are amused (or dismayed) to discover. (That was the import of the Abbie Hoffman remark quoted at the beginning of the chapter.)

The way the media played the Watergate mess is a good example. Most Americans did not want to believe the truth about Nixon, their president; so at first the media played down the story as just another campaign gimmick. Prior

---

[1] Fortunately, small circulation publications tend to be exceptions; while theoretically *in business,* they rarely make a profit or pay a dividend. People "invest" in such enterprises to champion a point of view or gain an outlet for their own opinions, not to make money.

to the November 1972 election, when it would have counted most, only one effective shot was taken against Nixon in the mass media (a CBS in-depth story). It wasn't until the spring of 1973, in Nixon's second term, that increasing evidence of Nixon's guilt gave political opponents the ammunition they needed to make Watergate the chief issue of Nixon's second administration. (The exceptional exposés of *Washington Post* reporters Bob Woodward and Carl Bernstein, revealing inside evidence obtained from "Deep Throat," a very knowledgeable informed source, helped heat up the issue.) And when the existence of a "smoking gun" (a particularly damning White House tape) became known, destroying any "plausible deniability" Nixon had left, he became fair game for everyone and was forced to resign to avoid certain conviction in Congressional impeachment proceedings. The media did become more and more willing to take on Richard Nixon, especially when other powerful factions turned on him and as more and more damning evidence became known. But when it would have counted most (before the November 1972 election), Nixon was too strong a target to attack head on—he was too popular with the American people.

By permission of Jules Feiffer. Copyright 1978. Distributed by Field Newspaper Syndicate.

Most of the U.S. media audience is white, in particular, the portion with the most money to spend. The news in most papers thus gets slanted to their interests and prejudices. Check stories in, say, the Amsterdam News *as compared to the* New York Times, *or the* Baltimore Afro-American *as compared to the* Baltimore Sun, *and the effect of reader interest on news reporting will be obvious.*

However, it isn't only in the way they handle the news that the media give away their bias in favor of their audience's biases. About 1,250 of the 1,500 or so daily newspapers remaining in the United States carry regular horoscope columns in which mostly oracular advice (extremely general and likely to "fit" almost any situation) is dished out to the faithful. Yet astrology has no scientific validity whatever, and newspapers rarely print articles that say so.

Self-censorship of socially sensitive topics extends even to advertisements. Ads for items related to homosexuality are routinely rejected by the mass media. For instance, the *Boston Globe,* relatively liberal about ads, rejected the following copy:

> Read about Father Paul Stanley, Priest to 100,000 Boston homosexuals, in the *Advocate,* newspaper to America's homosexuals.

Some newspapers reject ads for X-rated movies. Even the *Village Voice* refused to carry an ad for the movie "Tits," unless the titillating title of that flic were removed from the copy.

Comic strips are particularly sensitive, for the same reason prime times (and Saturday mornings) are sensitive—parents want to protect their kids. The recent champion victim is Gary Trudeau's *Doonesbury* strip, a typical example being strips showing Joanie Caucus in bed with boyfriend Rick Redfern. (It wouldn't have mattered much if they'd been married.)

Organized Groups Apply Effective Pressure

The power of one person is small compared to that of an organized group. All but one advertiser withdrew its support from CBS's documentary "The Guns of August," about World War I, after a letter-writing campaign organized by the National Rifle Association. Similarly, General Motors dropped out of the NBC mini-series "Jesus of Nazareth" in 1977 after criticism by Protestant church leaders. Even the PTA was powerful enough to pressure Sears Roebuck into dropping sponsorship of "Charlie's Angels" (too much sex) and "Three's Company."

In a reverse twist on the usual case where whites have their opinions pandered to at the expense of blacks, several black political groups were successful in suppressing a WNET (Channel 13, New York) Public Broadcasting System (PBS) documentary "Harlem, Voices, Faces." PBS bowed to pressure generated by producer Tony Brown, who argued that ". . . the bigoted sector of white America will have its prejudices frozen in place and reinforced, and so many black people who need positive images so desperately to overcome the despair the film so ominously reveals will be even more psychologically destitute." No one claimed that the documentary was false or misleading. Harlem residents shown the film said that "that is how it is in Harlem these days."[2]

The Safeway supermarket chain refused to sell the March 1976 issue of *Atlantic* magazine, presumably because of an article "Rip-Off at the Supermarket," which claimed supermarket chicanery. Mike Royko's book *Boss,* an excellent exposé of Mayor Richard Daley's Chicago, met with similar distribution problems in the Chicago area—few wanted to buck the wrath of a person with Daley's power.

[2] The *New York Times,* 8 June 1975.

Last year, 300,000 Americans were arrested for smoking an herb that Queen Victoria used regularly for menstrual cramps.

don r. smith

It's a fact.

The herb, of course, is *cannabis sativa*. Otherwise known as marijuana, pot, grass, hemp, boo, mary-jane, ganja—the nicknames are legion.

So are the people who smoke it.

By all reckoning, it's fast becoming the new national pastime. Twenty-six million smokers, by some accounts—lots more by others. Whatever the estimate, a staggeringly high percentage of the population become potential criminals simply by being in possession of it. And the numbers are increasing.

For years, we've been told that marijuana leads to madness, sex-crimes, hard-drug usage and even occasional warts.

Pure Victorian poppycock.

In 1894, The Indian Hemp Commission reported marijuana to be relatively harmless. A fact that has been substantiated time and again in study after study.

Including, most recently, by the President's own Commission. This report stands as an indictment of the pot laws themselves.

And that's why more and more legislators are turning on to the fact that the present marijuana laws are as archaic as dear old Victoria's code of morality. And that they must be changed. Recently, the state of Oregon did, in fact, de-criminalize marijuana. Successfully.

Other states are beginning to move in that direction. They must be encouraged.

NORML has been and is educating the legislators, working in the courts and with the lawmakers to change the laws. We're doing our best but still, we need help. Yours.

Ad censorship: *NORML marijuana ad rejected by* Time *and* Newsweek, *accepted by* Playboy. Time *and* Newsweek *readers tended to strongly oppose dope smoking.*

News Selection Reflects the Interests of Advertisers

The interests of advertisers are almost as important as viewer interests in distorting the news. It could hardly be otherwise given that most media revenue, and thus profits, come from advertisers. This is true even of newspapers, which, unlike television, charge for their product. In the late seventies, the *Washington Post,* for instance, pulled only 15 percent of its revenue from sales to readers. Most of the rest came from advertising.

New York Times columnist Tom Wicker reports, in his book *On Press* (New York: Viking Press, 1978, portions of which were reprinted in the *Washington Monthly,* January 1978), on how the power structure in Winston-Salem, North Carolina, influences local news coverage. Not surprisingly in a town named "Winston-Salem," "the cigarette-cancer connection got short shrift in [the *Winston-Salem Journal*] newsroom."

On 31 November 1977, the Williamsburgh Savings Bank (of Brooklyn, New York) contracted to purchase ads in nine editions of a local paper, the *Phoenix.* This meant $2,000 in ad revenue. But on December 1, the *Phoenix* published a list of 166 directors of the thirteen major savings institutions in Brooklyn accused of redlining (refusing to loan in certain areas, which generally results in deterioration of those areas—money deposited by people in redlined areas gets loaned out in other areas). On December 7, the Williamsburgh Bank canceled the last eight ads. (No, we don't commit the fallacy of *questionable cause* in concluding that this cancellation was probably caused by the paper's publication of those 166 names.)

Dart: to the Danbury, Connecticut, *News-Times.* The assistant copy-desk chief who ran this picture [of a disgruntled customer carrying a sign reading "Potential Customers *Beware* of Colonial Ford] in the February 18 Sunday edition was fired the next morning for "a gross lapse in judgment." The photo appeared at the end of a week in which the paper had been arranging for favorable coverage to soothe boycotting advertisers offended by its earlier used-car consumer guide. . . .

Dart: to The *Jersey Journal,* Hudson County, New Jersey, for fatuously recording in a six-column interview (with photo) on February 9 the observations of a local merchant following his return from a week's vacation in Egypt. Also carried in the same edition was a full-page ad for the man's furniture and appliance store.

These "Darts" were given by the Columbia Journalism Review, *May/June 1979, along with other darts and "Laurels," including a laurel to the* Saginaw (Michigan) News *for a front-page exposé of racial prejudice in local housing. Those outside the news business may find it hard to appreciate the guts it takes for a local paper to buck the furniture, real estate, and auto interests that provide so much ad revenue.*

We have to remember that the media themselves are very valuable business-es. The people who own them are rich. This means that we should expect them to lean toward big business and the upper crust, for the same reason that the rich in general do so (identification with those having the same problems and lifestyle as their own). Big media powers, like the three television net-works, ABC, CBS, and NBC, thus rarely take the initiative in knocking big business, although they often do transmit such knocks when they're pushed by other powerful sources.

News Selection Reflects the Power of Government

The power of government over news businesses is pretty much the same as it is over any kind of business. Government has the right and often the power to regulate business activity. It thus can harrass a news source that displeases it by being strict (as it usually isn't) about the rules it sets up and the licenses it requires.

In the case of large governments, like the federal government, officials can play favorites, leaking only to those sources that play ball in return. Since leaks are such a large source of media news, reporters have to think twice before crossing their government sources.

Henry Kissinger was famous for his use of selective leaks to keep the media in line. So was J. Edgar Hoover. Even Jack Anderson who (along with his assistants) does as much real digging for news as anyone, is alleged at one time to have agreed to write only "nice things" about J. Edgar Hoover in exchange for access to FBI files.

But then the media often lack the information that might incline them to buck the official government story. The 1976 swine flu program is a good example. There was no swine flu epidemic and little reason to think there would be. But government experts did think there would be one, or rather government officials were convinced it was prudent to think so just in case there was one (heads often roll when something like this is missed—from the bureaucratic point of view, it's better to err on the side of safety). So the media by and large played it that way—perhaps (let's be charitable) because they assumed without question that the government knew what it was talking about. It was primarily readers of nonmass circulation magazines and papers like the *Village Voice* (see, for instance, the 6 December 1976 issue) who were aware all along that the whole thing was a phony scare.

Governments also influence the media by selective exercise of their power to license. It surely was not lost on media moguls that the Pacifica Foundation, which runs left-wing "unconventional" radio stations in Los Angeles, Ber-keley, New York, and Houston failed during the six years of the Nixon administration to obtain Federal Communication Commission approval for a station in Washington, D.C.

Nor did they overlook the fact that during the same period the pro-Nixon *New York Daily News* managed to hang on to its very valuable New York television channel in the face of extremely convincing evidence that it had failed to live up to the public service rules of the FCC.[3]

Damage also is done by government to freedom of expression and the free dissemination of news when it exercises its power to censor, despite the First Amendment to the United States Constitution. Governments censor not only porno movies but newspapers and magazines also. It's true that the most common type of censorship is of alleged pornography (*Hustler* magazine's publisher, Larry Flint, got seven years for publishing material judged to be obscene—a typical example). But other cases do sometimes happen and are much more serious. The federal government lost its case when it attempted to stop publication of the Pike Report on CIA dirty doings, but in 1979 it succeeded for about two months in stopping publication of information on the basic construction of a hydrogen bomb by *The Progressive* magazine—the first case of prior restraint in United States history.[4] (In other censorship cases, the government convicted and sentenced offenders after publication—prior restraint is supposed to be contrary to the First Amendment.) And even its failure in the case of the Pike Report had a chilling effect on the media. The possibility of prosecution is bound to and does have an effect on those selecting news items.

By permission of Jules Feiffer. Copyright 1978. Distributed by Field Newspaper Syndicate.

An attempt via humor to explain the insidiousness of government power over the press.

---

[3] The politically powerful have many ways to strike back at their opponents. The U.S. military establishment regularly makes its facilities available to movie makers who present the military in a favorable light, but denies them to those whose intent is critical. For instance, the producers of the movie *Limbo,* about the wives of men missing in action in Vietnam, were denied use of a U.S. Air Force base for background shooting.

[4] Scare stories about how the information could be used by criminals, or other governments, to construct a hydrogen bomb were ridiculous, first, because they'd have to get nuclear material and, second, because they'd have to know how to (and have the materials to) build the devilishly complicated and enormously expensive equipment needed (instructions for this were not in the censored article).

News Selection Reflects the Power of Big Money

The economically powerful almost always receive better treatment than ordinary folk. An example is reporting on David Rockefeller, Nelson's brother. He and his family control the Chase Manhattan bank, the third largest bank in America, and David is the bank's chairman. Not surprisingly, the press treats the Chase and David Rockefeller with special deference.

In fact, all truly large banks get special treatment from the media. Stories with a negative bank image are played down. (For example, the U.S. Senate's 419-page report, "Disclosure of Corporate Ownership," contained a great deal of information on how huge institutions like Chase Manhattan and other super banks control most of the largest corporations in America. The *New York Times* ran only eight column inches on this report.) Stories favorable to banks or bankers are played up. (The *New York Times* ran a forty-column-inch story plus pictures on page one of the Sunday Business Section [18 February 1973] on a David Rockefeller trip to Eastern Europe, entitled "An Eastern European Diary").

The powerful also manipulate the media with the carrot as well as the stick. Media members at all levels become accustomed to their special little fringe benefits, and it *is* hard to write nasty things about someone who has just wined and dined you free of charge.

In 1972, Senator Fred Harris of Oklahoma campaigned briefly for the Democratic party's nomination for president. He gave up quickly, however, because he didn't have enough money for a media blitz and reporters just did not pay much attention to him. But suppose he had been able to give a lavish party for Henry and Nancy Kissinger, celebrating their marriage. And suppose he had been able to invite all sorts of news people like television personalities John Chancellor, Barbara Walters, and Howard K. Smith, editors Hedley Donovan *(Time)*, Osborne Elliott *(Newsweek)*, A. M. Rosenthal *(New York Times)*, James Wechsler *(New York Post)*, and Mike O'Neill *(New York Daily News)*, columnists Marquis Childs, William F. Buckley Jr., Rowland Evans, and Joseph Kraft, and publishers Jack Howard (Scripps-Howard Publications), Thomas Vail *(Cleveland Plain Dealer)*, Gardner Cowles (Cowles Communications), and Dorothy Schiff *(New York Post)*—to name just a few. It runs contrary to human nature to expect that coverage of his campaign would not have greatly improved.

Yet this is exactly the party Nelson Rockefeller threw at his immense and lavish Pocantico Hills estate in June 1974, two months before President Ford chose Rockefeller to be his vice president. It takes an extremely strong-willed person to eat and drink someone's expensive food one day and write a seriously critical article on that person the next.

News-Gathering Methods Are Designed to Save Money

If a newspaper or television station is a business, with a bottom line that determines eventual success or failure, it has to make sure that the bottom line is not written in red ink. Since it has to operate as economically as it can, just

... If you are going to dine with these people and covet their information and access, and have them to dinner, then you have to take them and their mock world of mock information and mock reality seriously and at face value.

—David Halberstam, in a letter to the editor of *Washington Monthly.* The reference is to columnist Joseph Kraft socializing with the great people he gets his information from.

Copyright 1974 G. B. Trudeau, distributed by Universal Press Syndicate.

Several papers cut this Doonesbury *strip because it showed U.S. Congressmen asleep on the job. See Mark McIntyre, "Muting Megaphone Mark," [MORE], July 1974, p. 5.*

like other businesses, the news business cannot spend more money on a story than is returned in reader or listener interest.

Most News Is Given to Reporters, Not Ferreted Out

Going out and searching for stories is very expensive. Having someone give it to us is much cheaper. The result is that the majority of news stories in the mass media are given to reporters, usually by rich and powerful interests. This is perhaps the principle reason the media reflect the opinions and interests of the rich and powerful in society much more than those of the rest of us—it is precisely the rich and powerful who can afford the expensive apparatus needed to place items into the hands of reporters. (It's hard to resist an item given to you ready to print when the alternative is to get out there and dig.)

Check the front page of almost any newspaper and you will find as often as not that the vast majority of items on that page were acquired by that newspaper (or by the wire services—AP and UPI) from someone-or-other's press release, press conference, or speech. Thus, most news stories report what someone, usually someone powerful, has said about the news, rather than what reporters have discovered for themselves. Even stories in which news is assembled usually turn out to be just a collection of statements by the powerful on some topic of interest.

Here is a front page sampling from a large metropolitan newspaper, the *Miami Herald,* considered a better than average newspaper (21 and 22 August 1974). Of their fifteen front page stories, six were taken from speeches (handouts or announcements) of federal government officials (for example, a speech by Henry Kissinger); one from a big business announcement (General Motors was going to lower auto prices); one from a speech by an expert (on the subject of nutrition and obstetrics presented before the Western Hemisphere Nutrition Conference); two from "informed sources" leaks (Dan Rather and another CBS reporter were expected to be demoted out of cushy jobs); and five from routinely covered sources (Dow Jones closing averages and bills passed by Congress).

None resulted from any serious *investigative* reporting by the *Herald,* and only the two informed source leaks resulted from investigative reporting (very mild) of wire service personnel.[5] Of course, checking two front pages, while evidence, does not constitute proof. But the proof is all around us. Check almost any edition of any newspaper—the exact figures will differ, but the general result will be the same almost every time.

It wouldn't be so bad having our daily news constructed for us out of press releases, political speeches, press conferences, and the like, if all opinions had equal access to these megaphones. But clearly they don't. It is the economically or politically powerful who can afford news conferences and publicity agents, and who tend to be invited to speak at important events and conferences. So the powerful, the establishment, have their views heard nationwide, day after day, while the voice of the rest of us is muted.[6]

The result is that the news is used for all sorts of private gain. A president of the United States who wonders how voters will respond to an impending action need only try it out in the press and assess the results. Whether he will choose to use the "informed White House source" routine, have an underling make the proposal, or risk coming out with it personally depends on particular circumstances. But in any case, he can be sure that newspapers all over the country will play up his trial balloon as news, even though nothing much of anything has happened.

Similarly, a labor leader, big business executive, or president of the Massachusetts Bar Association can sound off with personal opinions, however self-serving, confident that they will be reported as news, however much they may be designed to fog an issue. These people also can be confident that no matter how far from the truth their statements may be, they need not worry that this will be pointed out to readers. For that would constitute opinion, not objective news, no matter how correct, whereas the opinions of the powerful are news, no matter how foolish or false they may be.

News stories on the medical industry (generally referred to as the medical *profession*) illustrate all this very nicely. Most such stories are, of course, simply

---

[5] There is more investigative reporting on the inside of both these newspapers. But it tends to get buried back on page forty-nine.

[6] Business news is perhaps the worst case. Business pages probably contain more "plants" than any other section—auto items at new-model time are a notorious example.

The cover of the March 19 *U.S. News* asked, "Do Banks Make Too Much Money?" If the question persuaded you to look inside, you would have found an interview with the president of the American Bankers Association.

—Item in the *Washington Monthly*, May 1979

The answer, incidentally, was that they don't. Surprise!

rewrites of handouts either from government officials or eminent members of the industry. The result is that serious charges of malfunction in the medical industry tend to go unreported, or buried on page forty-nine.

A typical example was the charge that Blue Cross is dominated by hospital administrators and officials of the American Hospital Association.[7] The charge, more specifically, was that 42 percent of the members of the various Blue Cross boards are hospital representatives, 14 percent are physicians, and most of the rest bankers and business representatives, including many from hospital supply companies and the like.

The charge is serious because, for one thing, a government contract makes Blue Cross the intermediary in Medicare payments between hospitals and the government—the Department of Health and Human Services pays Blue Cross when a claim is made and Blue Cross then pays the hospital. But at the same time, Blue Cross has the public responsibility to see that hospital charges are reasonable, services really needed, and quality care provided. If Blue Cross boards are dominated by medical industry representatives, then the medical industry in effect has been made its own watchdog. (Another fox in the henhouse.)

Yet, most Americans have never heard these charges against Blue Cross. Nor are they likely to unless and until an important government official or medical industry expert trumpets them in a news handout or at a press conference.

2.   *Media People Are Biased, Just Like the Rest of Us*

The key to understanding any institution, from the PTA to the U.S. Department of Energy to NBC to the Soviet Politbureau, is that they are run by human beings who have the same sorts of defects and virtues as the rest of us.

---

[7] See Sylvia A. Law and the Health Law Project, University of Pennsylvania, *Blue Cross: What Went Wrong* (New Haven, Conn.: Yale University Press, 1974). The book *was* reviewed, however, in the *New York Times Book Review*, 23 June 1974.

We should remember that the people who gather the news often have *biases* or *prejudices* that distort their finished product.

In the first place, remember that a given class tends to see itself more kindly than others might. We should expect that the rich will be more understanding of the problems of the rich than of ordinary folk. And it is the rich, obviously, who own or control most of the media. From which it follows, by some valid deductive rule or other, that those who own or control the media will be more understanding of the problems of the rich than of ordinary folk. (Remember, however, that it is we ordinary folk who buy the newspapers and watch the television ads, a fact that acts as a counterforce.)

Second, the media have been managed primarily by men, who have done most of the reporting, too. The result is sex discrimination not only in hiring (recall the *Reader's Digest* and *New York Times* sex discrimination suits) but also in the way news is slanted. But times are changing. These days we rarely encounter loaded language of the kind illustrated by this *New York Daily News* headline (29 May 1974):

2 CAREER GIRLS ARE MURDERED
Librarian strangled on E. Side;
Time, Inc. Girl Shot in W'chester

By the way, imagine reading the analogous headline in your local newspaper.

2 CAREER BOYS ARE MURDERED
Librarian strangled on E. Side;
Time, Inc. Boy Shot in W'chester

But the most deep-seated media prejudice, as it has been in America as a whole, is race prejudice. Busing, for instance, became a big issue in the United States only when courts started ordering white students to be bused. The busing of blacks to inferior segregated schools received little notice prior to 1954—editors and reporters, like most white Americans, hardly gave a second thought to the education of blacks.[8]

3.   *The Media Operate According to Incorrect Theories*

As remarked in Chapter One, people don't often stand back and look at what they're doing from a wider context; they don't often theorize about their activities. Media workers on the whole theorize more than most workers. But when they do, their theories are frequently self-serving.

---

[8] Virtually all reporters, editorial employees, and owners of the major news outlets in the United States at that time were white. The vast majority still are.

The Unusual Is News, the Everyday Is Not

Theory says that news is what is *new*—the unusual, not the commonplace. Yet what happens every day is generally more important than the unusual occurrence. Prison uprisings get big play, but the poor treatment prisoners receive every day, which leads to the uprisings, goes relatively unreported. Big court cases such as the Watergate trials receive much attention, but thousands of everyday cases in which justice is flouted tend to be ignored. (A whole disgraceful area of courtroom practice, plea bargaining, was pretty much ignored in the media until Vice President Spiro Agnew "copped a plea."[9])

News Reporting Is Supposed to Be Objective, Not Subjective

Those who work on the news often say that facts are objective, conclusions or value judgments subjective, and that media workers are supposed to be objective. (Even J. Edgar Hoover subscribed to this view although he didn't practice it. His motto was that the FBI does not draw conclusions, it only reports the facts.)

But this theory of objective reporting is mistaken. Reports of facts generally depend on someone's judgment that they are facts. A reporter must conclude that they are facts. Take the following excerpts from an Associated Press story carried in the *Lawrence* (Kansas) *Daily Journal World* (30 October 1970) on an alleged riot in San Jose, California, before the November 1970 elections:

> President Nixon, the target of rocks, bricks, bottles, eggs, red flags, and other missiles hurled by antiwar demonstrators. . . .
>
> The San Jose violence was the most serious aimed at any president in this country since the assassination of President John Kennedy. . . .
>
> [Nixon's] limousine and other vehicles in the cavalcade were hit repeatedly by large rocks and other objects.

Clearly, the reporter did not actually see that the alleged attack on President Nixon was the worst attack on a president since the assassination of President Kennedy. He had to conclude to the fact—if it is a fact—by using judgment as well as eyesight.

But we usually don't notice that judgment and conclusion-drawing are required even in reporting immediate facts. Did the AP reporter—or any AP reporter—actually *see* rocks hit the president's limousine? If not, who did? Are those who think they did sure no visual distortion was at work? Did they hear a crunch as the rocks hit the car? These questions are not academic; it is well known that honest reports by onlookers frequently differ seriously about what took place. In this case, many eyewitnesses, including television and

---

[9] An exception was the excellent article by Leonard Downie, Jr., "Crime in the Courts: Assembly Line Justice." *Washington Monthly*, May 1970. Another was a *New York Times* article, 13 December 1970, p. 26.

newspaper reporters, said that nothing was thrown at the presidential limousine, although objects were thrown at the press corps bus.[10]

A great deal of reporting is of this kind. A reporter who is not an eyewitness must draw a conclusion about what happened from eyewitness accounts. Those who are not eyewitnesses need to compare different eyewitness accounts and draw conclusions as to what probably happened. For example, reporters who thought rocks were thrown at Nixon's car might have looked for rock fragments on the pavement at the correct location.[11]

The idea that reporters must stick to facts and not draw conclusions is a myth. One must *reason to the facts* just as one reasons to anything else.

Similarly, the idea that newspapers should not make value judgments is incorrect. When we read of the death of a famous movie star on page one of our morning newspaper, but read nothing of the death of an eminent philosopher, it becomes obvious that newspapers have to make value judgments to determine what is important and what is not. The same is true when a hurricane on the Gulf Coast, which kills two dozen people, gets more space than reports of the My Lai 4 massacre in Vietnam, or when the George Foreman-Muhammad Ali fight in Zaire gets more space than mass starvation in Africa.

In other words, *editing,* one of the chief tasks of any newspaper, requires value judgments about the relative importance of events. And moral value judgments are required as well as others. It should be news that thousands of children die each year in the United States from lack of proper food precisely because it is wrong and ought to be corrected.

Television reporting also requires that facts and opinions be selected. During a bomb scare break in proceedings of the House Judiciary Committee considerations of the Nixon impeachment question, most television stations filled in with interviews of members of Congress and other politicians. But WNET, Channel 13, New York, chose instead to interview a literary-political figure, Barbara Tuchman. Tuchman's comments differed greatly from those heard on other channels. (For instance, while viewers on other channels heard congressmen say it would be improper to impeach Nixon for his Cambodia activities, WNET viewers heard Tuchman state that that was precisely the most important charge to impeach him on.) Officials at WNET clearly made a value judgment that Tuchman's remarks were more important than those of others they might have interviewed. Ditto for the other channels. (Does the theory of objectivity thus function as a rule to be appealed to when it suits someone's purpose, and ignored otherwise?[12])

---

[10] See, for instance, the *Village Voice* article by Tom Devries, 5 November 1970, in which Mike Mills, a television reporter, when asked why his films of the event show no flying objects, stated, "That is because nothing was thrown." The article quoted several other reporters who supported this statement. And the San Jose police chief confirmed reporters' claims.

[11] Mr. Devries, the *Village Voice* reporter, wrote that he later checked the area for loose rocks and broken glass and found none.

[12] For what it's worth, this writer's opinion on the matter is that in everyday practice the theory of objectivity requires only that reporters stay within the social consensus when they make judgments or draw conclusions. This means that the real point of the theory of objectivity is to discourage the reporting of radical or nonestablishment, or nonconsensus views—to placate the media audience and media advertisers.

News Is Supposed to Be Separated from Analysis or In-Depth Reports

The theory of objectivity requires that facts be reported separately from conclusions or evaluations (which are thought of as "subjective").

An Associated Press photo captioned "Lawmen and Indians Fight," showing policemen apparently beating Indians, appeared on page one of the *Hartford Courant* (29 October 1970). Below the caption was a brief story about the fight between lawmen and Pit River Indian tribesmen, started, lawmen said, when the Indians tried to publicize their claim to the land by building on it "illegally." The story identified the police units and where the fight had occurred. It also stated the Indians claimed that the land was taken from them back in the Gold Rush days.

But we weren't told enough for us to deal intelligently with this news. Did the Indians resist arrest? Was police force necessary? Is there anything to the Indian land claim? Have they tried to gain redress via the courts? The picture seems to show a policeman beating someone with a long nightstick. Is he? If so, was this force necessary to subdue the person? The caption says lawmen and *Indians* fight. Did the Indians do any fighting? We aren't given the answers to any of these questions.

And yet it is impossible to form an intelligent opinion on the events described if we don't know at least some of these facts. Not that this deterred most readers. Some no doubt shrugged and muttered about drunken Indians acting up again, while others commented about more pig brutality. The story as presented justifies neither of these conclusions. In fact, it doesn't justify any conclusion at all. But it does give readers an opportunity to vent their prejudices and thus become further polarized.

What went wrong with the [*New York*] *Times*'s coverage of New York's financial agony was in part . . . a misdefinition of "investigative reporting" as the manual labor of digging out information rather than the mental process of linking fact and events not previously connected.

—Martin Mayer, *Columbia Journalism Review*, January/February 1976.

Even when they try to do investigative reporting, poor theory often keeps reporters from doing a good job. Contrast the Times's *way of "investigating" with, say, that of I. F. Stone, for many years an independent reporter who put out his own little newsletter (I. F. Stone's* Weekly). *Stone did little or no investigating of the usual sort—which he considered a waste of time. He generally used ordinary information, often from the federal government itself; his "trick" (but it wasn't a trick) was to do the obvious—add two and two and see if it added to four. When it came to adding government figures, two and two generally didn't make four, as Stone regularly pointed out.*

Inadequately reported news stories appear in the media every day, increasing misunderstanding and polarization. Reports that Georgia Governor Lester Maddox's son was sentenced to six months of weekends in jail plus a $500 fine for burglary of a service station omitted the crucial information about the same judge's normal penalty for similar crimes, as well as the sentence of another man convicted with Mr. Maddox's son for the same crime.

Yet one thing that splits this nation into factions is the question of equal treatment before the law. Millions of Americans believe that, by and large, justice in America is fair, while other millions believe it is not. At least one side must be wrong; but the matter will never be settled by appeal to the contents of daily newspapers or, for that matter, television.

The *Boston Herald Traveler* (14 November 1970) contained a story on charges by the Massachusetts Bar Association that Massachusetts' no-fault auto insurance law would result in "legal chaos" if allowed to go into effect. The story cited a paper in the *Massachusetts Law Quarterly* which stated that the law is "both inconsistent and incomprehensible." But the newspaper article failed to quote a single relevant reason *why* legal chaos would result, or in what way the law was inconsistent and incomprehensible. Instead, it quoted the claim of the president of the Massachusetts Bar Association that legal chaos would result if the law went into effect. It cited an authority's opinion on a controversial matter, but failed to provide any of his reasons, thus inviting the reader to commit the fallacy of *appeal to authority*.

To make matters worse, the newspaper article failed to point out that lawyers had a special interest in fighting this law, namely, to maintain one of their most lucrative sources of income: auto accident litigation. Instead, it quoted the charge of MBA President Donahue that the law would "result in both increasing claims and increasing rates," again without furnishing any evidence pro or con. Nowhere in the article is there any mention of the frequently cited statistic that lawyers get as large a slice of auto insurance premiums as do those suffering losses in accidents, a slice of the pie that no-fault insurance laws greatly reduce. Yet, how can anyone get any benefit from a story on the Massachusetts no-fault insurance law without at least some of these facts?

Most of the better "in-depth" or "analysis" reporting on television is done by PBS (Public Broadcasting Service). But they too often fall into the same traps as do other media workers. A documentary widely shown on PBS in 1979 attempted to get behind the façade and show us how the U.S. House of Representatives really works (a marvelous idea). But it merely followed House Majority Leader "Tip" O'Neill around for a whole (supposedly) typical day of work. The impression given was that we were getting an inside glimpse of powerful people at work; we looked over their shoulders and heard what they told each other in the halls and behind closed doors.

To no avail. The members videotaped were aware of that fact and tailored their conversations accordingly. While it seemed that we were getting the real lowdown, we got instead lots of remarks like, "We've got to move that bill by the seventh," which revealed nothing about the true behind-the-scenes wheeling and dealing (still quaintly called "logrolling" in public school textbooks, where it's described without mention of mundane things like payoffs by lobbyists, campaign contributions, betrayals, or veiled threats).

Here are excerpts from ex-*Washington Post* reporter Joseph Nocera's "Making It at *The Washington Post*" (*Washington Monthly*, January 1979). Nocera is describing one of the best newspapers in the United States, where "objective" reporting reigns.[13]

When [*Washington Post* reporter] Ron Kessler discovered three years ago that some of America's largest banks had been put on a secret list of problem banks by the Comptroller of the Currency, the *Post* had a field day running bank stories. There were a number of follow-ups by Kessler and a rising Metro reporter, Charles Babcock, who covered a series of congressional hearings on bank troubles. Then the scandal faded, as they eventually all do, and Kessler and Babcock went on to other things. The subject of banks dropped off the front page and back to the financial pages, where it was covered as it always had been—routinely. It wasn't that the subject of banks was any less newsworthy—certainly there were dozens of important stories the *Post* could have written about banks—it was just, well, the smell of scandal wasn't there anymore. Reporters lost their incentive to write about them; the subject didn't fit comfortably into the *Post's* daily news coverage; it wasn't going to get on the front page; it wasn't going to help anyone's career. . . .

. . . The news doesn't have to be dull or stale, if only the *Post* would value a different kind of story, and if its reporters were encouraged to get beyond yesterday's news. There could be a sense of mission if the *Post* wanted reporting that tried to explain why things don't work as well as they should. There is a tremendous need in journalism for a reporting that does more than break scandals and tell us what officialdom did yesterday. As government and all the other giant institutions that rule our society have become larger, more complex, and more perplexing, newspapers have not kept pace. Our papers should be helping us sort it all out—telling us which government programs work and which don't, where tax money is being spent wisely and where it is being wasted, how our institutions are helping us and how they are hurting. We need to connect what happens in Washington to what happens in places like Fairfax County and Trenton. But this kind of reporting requires a journalism that is more subjectively analytical than the traditional newspaper ethic of objectivity has allowed. It is there-

---

[13] Reprinted with permission from *The Washington Monthly.* Copyright 1979 by The Washington Monthly Co., 1611 Connecticut Ave., N.W., Washington, D.C. 20009.

fore something foreign, if not repugnant, to the *Post*'s conception of good reporting. . . .

. . . There is a deathly, almost irrational fear in journalism of analyzing and coming to conclusions. "Suppose I was assigned to analyze the HEW budget," says [ex-*Post* national editor, Richard] Harwood, "to find out where there was waste and how it could be cut. I just wouldn't feel *qualified* to do that." Although journalists at the *Post* are extremely bright people, there is that same belief that somehow they are qualified only to tell us the *what* of events and leave the *whys* to the "experts" they so dutifully quote. Thus Bradlee [*Washington Post* editor-in-chief Ben Bradlee] and Harwood, who hire all sorts of wonderfully gifted writers and reporters, insist on separating good writing from good thinking. Writers and reporters are prodded and pushed at the *Post*, but it is to get them to be more clever with their prose, or come up with front page news, or else it's in the "what-have-you-got-for-me-today" vein. There is not, at the *Post*, the kind of give and take between reporter and editor that would result in original, analytical reporting—stories full of ideas and conclusions. . . .

A few years ago, Barbara Sizemore was the Superintendent of Schools in Washington, and the Board of Education was trying to fire her. It was a story the *Post* was all over—a good political fight, with plenty of charges and countercharges, hearings, and votes —and most of the coverage made the front page. But what was happening inside the schools? Why were Washington's teachers so uniformly mediocre? What was being taught? Why weren't kids learning? Seldom could these stories be found in the *Washington Post*. . . .

The concentration on beat reporting in the suburban counties means that *Post* reporters are missing a whole range of stories that could help explain how our government works. By using Arlington and Prince George's counties as barometers, reporters could discover whether a federal program was doing all the wonderful things some spokesman in Washington was attributing to it. They could tell us about welfare in ways much more meaningful than by covering the latest from Capitol Hill and HEW. *Post* reporters could find out for themselves whether there was welfare fraud and how widespread it was, whether there were people unjustly denied benefits, whether welfare really did keep able-bodied people from working, and they could help us figure out how to make the welfare system work better. . . .

To get this kind of reporting, of course, a lot of what it takes to make it at the *Post* would have to change. . . . Above all, they would have to make judgments. Telling people what's wrong with [things] means coming to a conclusion.

The Opinions of Recognized Authorities Take Precedence

The reporters and editors who gather and assemble the news are not usually experts in the fields they cover. They couldn't be, given that they must deal with practically all the social and political questions of the day. It seems plausible, then, that they should seek out expert opinion on these matters. The trouble is that experts can be found on all sides of a really controversial issue. In everyday practice, *which* experts are consulted is determined by the other factors that influence the news.

In the first place, experts whose views are very unpopular with either the media audience, or its advertisers, or media bigwigs themselves, will tend to be passed over or played down. Take the question of the safety of nuclear power. A great many top-notch physicists (and organizations, such as the Union of Concerned Scientists) have been shouting as loudly as they can for some time now that the current state of the art makes nuclear power plants inherently unsafe. But until the serious accident at Three Mile Island, Pennsylvania, in 1979, their voices were drowned out in the media, to the point where one supposed expert, Department of Energy boss James Schlesinger (what does he know about atomic physics or how nuclear plants produce power?) received more coverage than all the protesting scientists combined. No, it was those scientists who stated that nuclear power was safe who were given the space —along with politicians like Schlesinger, of course. (When, if ever, did you first hear about the much more serious Russian nuclear disaster that occurred way back in 1957?)

Further, the fact that time is money, as they say, means that the media will often as not take the first expert it can find, which means most of the time experts in the employ of the rich or powerful, constantly being foisted on reporters via press conferences and other public relations operations.

The 23 September 1979, issue of the *Washington Post* magazine featured a cover story, *Hoover: Life with a Tyrant,* which gave lots of the nastiness, dirtiness, unfairness, and illegality of J. Edgar Hoover's long reign as FBI chief. But where was the *Post* (or any mass media outlet) when Hoover had power and was perpetrating all these crimes?

Good Citizenship Requires Self-Censorship

A *Washington Post* reporter learned that two Army intelligence officers claimed the CIA and Army Intelligence were training men in torture and assassination techniques to be used against National Liberation Front members in Vietnam.[14] But his story never appeared in the *Washington Post,* a victim of self-censorship by that newspaper.

---

[14] George Wilson, "The Fourth Estate as the Fourth Branch," *Village Voice,* 1 January 1970.

Though unusual, self-censorship is not rare. The nation's major newspapers tend to engage in self-censorship more often than other newspapers, no doubt because they have access to more sensitive information. Perhaps the most famous example of this kind occurred during the Kennedy administration, when the *New York Times* decided not to print the Bay of Pigs story.[15]

Another good example is the 1970 U.S. invasion of Cambodia. Associated Press reporters covering the invasion wrote that U.S. troops engaged in much looting during the venture.[16] But newspapers on the AP wire never received this portion of the report from Cambodia, which apparently was edited out partly because the AP wanted their men during that troubled period to report news that was "down the middle and subdues emotion," and because "in present context this report of looting can be inflammatory."

In 1970, the *New York Times* killed a story by veteran reporter Tad Szulc which stated that the United States and South Vietnam were about to invade Cambodia. According to Roger Morris, Henry Kissinger asked that the story be killed for national security reasons (for we *were* about to invade Cambodia).[17]

The problem of self-censorship is made particularly difficult by the counter tug of the right to privacy. A person in the public eye is still, after all, entitled to a private life. And yet it is difficult to know what bears on a person's public life (and thus can be exposed) and what does not (and thus ought to be censored). It was well known to newspeople, for instance, that as a Congressman and then as a Senator, John F. Kennedy was quite a lady's man (both before and after his marriage). The media, on the whole, chose not to report this feature of Kennedy's private life, and were generally applauded for their restraint (after all, stories on Kennedy's sex life would have found an eager audience).

And yet, self-censorship of similar stories concerning Kennedy's brother, Edward M. (Ted) Kennedy, may well have been a mistake, given what happened at Chappaquiddick. Knowledge of a person's sexual life *may*, after all, be relevant to his character and thus to his suitability for public office.

The shock of Dec. 7 [1941] can be well imagined. When the last Japanese plane roared off, five American battleships had been sunk and three damaged, three cruisers and three destroyers badly hit, 200 planes destroyed, and 2344 men killed. For the loss of only 29 planes, Japan had virtually crippled the U.S. Pacific Fleet at a single blow.

---

[15] President Kennedy is alleged later to have had the "chutzpah" to take the *Times* to task for this censorship on grounds that publication of the story by the *Times* might have resulted in calling off that ill-fated venture!

[16] According to a story in the September 1970 issue of the *AP Review*.

[17] Roger Morris, *Columbia Journalism Review*, May–June 1974. Also see John D. Marks, "The Story That Never Was" [*MORE*], June 1974, p. 20. (Incidentally, *New York Times* editor A. M. Rosenthal denies Szulc ever submitted the story to the *Times*.)

The American service chiefs immediately decided that news of a disaster of such magnitude would prove unacceptable to the American people, and steps were taken to ensure that they did not learn about it. So effective were these measures that the truth about Pearl Harbor was still being concealed even after the war ended. The cover-up began with an "iron curtain" of censorship that cut off the United Press office in Honolulu from San Francisco in the middle of its first excited telephone report.

So drastic was the suppression of news that nothing further, except for official communiques, came out of Pearl Harbor for another four days. These claimed that only one "old" battleship and a destroyer had been sunk and other ships damaged, and that heavy casualties had been inflicted on the Japanese. It cannot be argued that these lies were necessary to conceal from the Japanese the extent of the disaster they had inflicted on the U.S. Pacific Fleet. The Japanese knew exactly how much damage they had done, and reports in Tokyo newspapers accurately stating the American losses meant that the Americans knew that the Japanese knew. The American censorship was to prevent the American public from learning the gravity of the blow.

After flying to Hawaii on a tour of inspection, the Secretary of the Navy, Colonel Frank Knox, held a press conference in New York at which, with President Roosevelt's approval, he gave the impression he was revealing the full extent of the American losses at Pearl Harbor. Colonel Knox told correspondents that one United States battleship, the Arizona, had been lost and the battleship Oklahoma had capsized but could be righted.

This must have made strange reading for anyone actually at Pearl Harbor, who had only to lift his eye from his newspaper to see five United States battleships—the Arizona, the Oklahoma, the California, the Nevada, and the West Virginia—resting on the bottom.[18]

In wartime, truth is the first casualty, censorship the first expedient.

4.   *The Media Use Standard Devices to Slant the News*

So far we have been considering *why* the media slant the news, and how that effects the selection of stories. Now let's look at the devices used to slant stories (primarily in newspapers and magazines).

---

[18] From *The First Casualty*, copyright © 1975 by Phillip Knightley. Reprinted by permission of Harcourt Brace Jovanovich, Inc.

Stories Can Be Played Up or Down

Within limits, you can bury a story, if you don't like it, or give it page one space if you do. The *Canton* (Ohio) *Repository* may have set some sort of record on this in its 28 July 1974 issue. Under the front-page headline "Wowee. . . . What a Weekend," the *Repository* devoted most of its front page to an account of the first National Football League exhibition game of the season, plus a description of ceremonies surrounding the induction of four new members into Canton's Football Hall of Fame. Relegated to a bottom corner of page one was the decision of the House Judiciary Committee to recommend impeachment of President Nixon, a key event in one of the biggest ongoing news stories in American history.

A *New York Daily News* headline during the 1976 primary campaigns had it this way, in large type: "REAGAN BEATS FORD IN NEB.," below which they tell us in much smaller type: "But President Wins in W. Va." Had they been for Ford, they could have reversed that quite easily.

Another night on the South Side [of Chicago] this guy went berserk and shot his wife and kids and himself—a quadruple murder and suicide. I was very excited. I went and reported the story, and there I was dictating it to a rewrite man [the common practice]. . . . All of a sudden the old editor at the news service . . . got on my wire and said to me, "My good, dear, energetic Mr. Hersh, do the poor, unfortunate, alas, victims of this crime happen to be of the American Negro persuasion?" I said they did. And he just said, "Well cheap it out," and hung up. Of course, to "cheap it out" meant that it would get only one paragraph for this whole murder and multiple suicide. Since then, I've had no illusions about the newspaper business. The experience gave me a cynical approach to what the news is, and what the news isn't.

—Seymour Hersh, at that time *New York Times* reporter, whose earlier exposé of the My Lai massacre and subsequent Pulitzer prize lifted him to fame (quoted in [*More*] September 1976)

Misleading or Unfair Headlines Can Be Used

Many more people read the headline on a story than read the story itself. So even if a story is accurate, a misleading headline distorts the news for many readers. Here are a few examples:

New York Daily News:

Secret Bar Study Pounds Five Judges

New York Times headline (same general story):

> ## Bar Report Clears 3 on State Bench
> ## of Accusations Leveled in Magazine

Hartford Times (21 May 1972):

> ## North Viets Repelled in Attack

Hartford Courant (same day, same general story):

> ## S. Vietnam Repulsed in Push Toward
> ## Beleaguered An Loc

Boston Globe (same day, same general story):

> ## Battle See-Saws at An Loc

Hartford Times (18 September 1970):

> ## $500 Million U.S. Aid to Israel

But below, in the AP story, we learned that:

> *President Nixon* reportedly *was preparing today to promise Israel Premier Golda Meir* . . . officials say no final decision on exactly what the package will contain has been made.

The *Washington Post* (7 March 1979, headline for story on page D7):

> ## Recession Only Inflation Cure, Economist Says

Same newspaper (same date, headline for story on page D10):

> ## NAM Asserts Inflation Only Cure for Recession

(This item is from the *Columbia Journalism Review's* regular back-page feature, *"The Lower Case,"* May/June 1979, which also contained this headline from the *New York Post:* "Bishop defrocks gay priest.")

Information Can be Buried Well into a Story

In playing a story one way or another, the headline obviously is most important (next to its location), since it is read by many who never read further. But the first few paragraphs are more important than what follows, for the same reason—readership drops off after that point.

For instance, a television debate between three Connecticut candidates for the U.S. Senate was played quite differently by the *Hartford Courant* and the *New York Times* (28 October 1970). The *Courant* started their story with three paragraphs on Senator Thomas J. Dodd's performance, while the *Times* went five paragraphs before mentioning any participant other than Lowell P. Weiker, Jr.

Nonnews Features Can Be Slanted

Editorials, of course, are expected to be slanted, except that it is called editorializing and is not contrary to the rules of objective reporting (as are most of the devices discussed so far). Similar remarks apply to the custom of selecting political columnists and cartoonists who espouse the "right" point of view.

But any nonnews feature of a newspaper or magazine can be, and often is, used to intrude political bias. Even photos are so used—papers run more and better photos of candidates they support than they do of their opponents.

During the Watergate period, with the Nixon presidency collapsing, the *Boston Globe*, anti-Nixon all the way, ran an *extremely* unflattering photo of Nixon on a story headlined, "Nixon felt besieged by bureaucrats." Under the photo we read (the quote is from the Nixon tapes):

"Fire, demote him or send him to the Guam regional office. There's a way. Get him the hell out."—President Nixon (AP photo from files).

Few will notice that small print (AP photo from files); most readers must have believed the photo was of Nixon saying the very words quoted, instead of, as a matter of fact, having been taken at another time during a political address.

Newspapers start when the owners are poor and take the side of the people, and so they build up a large circulation, and presently, as a result, advertising. That makes them rich, and they begin most naturally to associate with other rich men—they play golf with one and drink whiskey with another, and their son marries the daughter of a third. They forget about the people.

—Joseph Medill Patterson

The late newspaper mogul was in a position to know.

Follow-up Stories Can Be Omitted

When the Office of Economic Opportunity (OEO) was established to help the poor, it was played up as big news, showing that America does indeed provide opportunity for all. But when the Nixon administration effectively throttled OEO, this news was buried in small print on back pages.

Similarly, the Attica prison uprising and massacre (notice that emotive word) were big news, including a promise by Attica Commissioner Oswald to implement prisoners' demands for twenty-eight improvements, which Oswald agreed were "reasonable and desirable." But later reports that none of the twenty-eight improvements were made received hardly any play at all.

The media covered Richard Nixon's political campaigns from 1946 through 1972. Stacked away in their files, their "morgues," were mountains of items on Nixon campaign rhetoric and performance, showing that Nixon's performance bore little relation to his campaign promises. Worse, it showed Nixon's attacks on his opponents *always* consisted primarily of *false dilemma, straw man,* and *ad hominen* arguments. Yet it was rare for a news outlet to follow through on the news and point out this great disparity between his words and subsequent actions or between his portrayal of opponents' positions and their actual positions.

Follow-up stories rarely make headlines, primarily for two reasons. The first is that they are relatively difficult to obtain. It takes much less time and effort to report a prison uprising than to investigate day-to-day prison conditions. The second is that the public (and media) conception of "news" is what is *new,* and therefore different. Follow-up is reporting on "old news," which isn't really news. But isn't it news if, say, a president of the United States fails to keep his word, or a bill passed by Congress fails to get implemented?

I think human beings are unpleasant and they should be shown as such. In my view we live in a banana-peel society, where people who are having a rotten, miserable life—as 99.9 percent of the world is—can only gain enjoyment by seeing the decline and fall of others. They only enjoy people's sordidness, their divorces, whether their wives have relieved them of $5 million, how their children turned round and beat the crap out of them. Then they suddenly realize that everything is well in the state of Denmark, that everyone else is leading a miserable, filthy life which—but for me and other journalists around—they would not know about. They see that those who obtain riches or fame or high position are no happier than they are. It helps them get along, and frankly that is what I give them.

—British gossip columnist Nigel Dempster (*New York* magazine, 3 May 1976), justifying having gossip columns in newspapers

---

Emotive Language Can Be Used

Since we've devoted most of a chapter to the emotive side of language, let's just give one illustration at this point from the media. The *Vancouver Sun* (15 July 1975) headlined its story about American and Soviet spacemen "Astronauts *Chase* Cosmonauts Into Space" (italics added). This had a much better ring than the more accurate "American Astronauts *Follow* Soviet Cosmonauts Into Space."

Ignorance Can Be Cloaked in a False Aura of Authority

Way back in the 1920s and 1930s, *Time* magazine developed a "you are *there*" style of news reporting, which became an essential part of the "*Time*style" that all newsmagazines have copied at one time or another. In their 2 November 1970 issue, *Time* ran a story whose main point was to emphasize how much of our air effort in Vietnam had been turned over to the South Vietnamese. *Time* reported that:

> "The target today is a suspected enemy location near the gully behind that clump of trees," says the American Forward Air Controller (FAC) from a tiny spotter plane just above the treetops some 30 miles northwest of Saigon.

Obviously, if *Time* reporters are so knowledgeable that they can quote word for word the remark of a FAC man in action, they surely must have been correct about the main point of their article—which happened to be quite controversial.

Has any reader ever found perfect accuracy in the newspaper account of any event of which he himself had inside knowledge?
—Edward Verrall Lucas

The same issue of *Time* contained an article on Charles Reich's book, *The Greening of America,* which started out:

> Sociology has spawned more games than Parker Brothers. But all the *divertissements* rest upon a single process—the breakup of phenomena into categories. It has been so ever since Auguste Comte invented the "science" and divided human progress into three stages, theological, metaphysical and positive.

Forgetting the question whether any one person invented sociology, does the *Time* writer really understand the complex philosophy of Comte to which he so blithely refers?

Whatever the answer may be in that particular case, it seems true that experts in various fields frequently find errors when *Time* and *Newsweek* report on their own areas of knowledge. This fact casts serious doubt on the general competence of newsmagazine writers who talk so flippantly of technical matters. Here is a particularly revealing flub, which occurred in *Time*'s 14 April 1967 review of the autobiography of the philosopher Bertrand Russell. Wrote the *Time* reviewer:[19]

---

[19] Pointed out by a *knowledgeable* layman, C. W. Griffin, Denville, New Jersey.

> [*Russell's*] historic collaboration with Alfred North Whitehead . . . that resulted, after ten years' labor, in the publication of *Principia Mathematica,* named after Newton's great work, *which in many respects it superseded.*

The writer didn't mention in which respects Russell's work superseded Newton's *Principia,* since there aren't any. Newton's *Principia* formed the foundation of mechanics, a topic on which Russell's *Principia* has nothing to say.

Few foreign correspondents know the language or customs of the countries to which they are sent. (The same is true to a lesser extent of our diplomats.) The result is that correspondents tend to stay in big cities, in particular capital cities, where they're fed handouts by government agents and others who speak English. You can't interrogate people whose language you don't understand. The results of this cultural incompetence of reporters is well known in the case of Vietnam, but the same thing happens in most foreign countries.

As We See It

It's getting so that almost every time a fire is reported on the local news, some obnoxious character on the minicam team can be expected to corner the hapless squire of the blazing house, thrust a microphone in his face, and demand: "Do you feel bad about this?"

Or: "Were you surprised when you smelled the smoke?"

We have reconciled ourselves to news shows' unswerving preoccupation with flames (they all photograph the same way, orangy-red), but we cannot get used to the thoughtless or callous (read "stupid") questions that are so often hurled at the victims of catastrophe by callow reporters.

—*TV Guide,* railing against low quality reporting

---

5. Television: Tail Wags Dog

Although still a relative baby, television, the newest of the mass media, is by far the most important. Television gives us the closest thing we have to a way to bring a whole nation together. It's the town meeting, town crier, certifier, authenticator, grapevine of modern industrial life. That's why political campaigns are fought on it, the news is broadcast on it, and (more and more) a nation's mood and tone are set on it.

The medium of television has so taken over the country that it has become our *only* mass medium. The number of people who read a best-selling book, the subscribers to the most successful magazines, the listeners to even the most powerful radio stations, and the readers of the most popular newspapers, the pre-TV film crowds, are all statistical gnats when compared to the viewers of a network series canceled for lack of an audience.

—Jeffrey Schrank, *Snap, Crackle, and Popular Taste* (New York: Delacorte Press, 1977)

TV Entertainment Gives a Juvenile Impression of Life

How then does television compare with the other media? The answer is complex. In the first place, in terms of overall world view, television is a minus. Most television programs are fictionalized adventure stories or comedies, which give us a hopelessly juvenile impression of human nature and human society. Hollywood endings are the almost universal rule—the good guys win in the end, or the foolish misunderstandings that sustained half an hour of comedy are cleared up, and everyone is happy (except for a few villains).

Even "All in the Family," praised widely for its exposure of bigotry, in particular racial bigotry, bears little resemblance to the genuine article. It's hard to imagine Archie Bunker killing anyone, even indirectly. He talks against blacks, but never *ever* raises his fist against them, or anyone else. He's a friendly bumbler. Real life bigots are another matter. They frequently do things that *kill*, as did U.S. State Department bigots during the Nazi period who refused entry into the United States to thousands of Jews trying to escape from Hitler's horror.[20]

Television is chewing gum for the eyes.
—Frank Lloyd Wright

But then, how many viewers ever heard of Frank Lloyd Wright?

Here is Ron Nessen, President Ford's press secretary, lamenting the inaccurate portrayal of life on television (quoted in *TV Guide*, 2 December 1978):

Nessen: I learned that there are no ugly people on local television [news programs], no baldheaded men, no stringy-haired women, no one with a big nose or pimples. The glossy-lip-and-powdered-cheek school of

---

[20] Arthur D. Morse, *While Six Million Died* (New York: Random House, 1969), has the grisly details.

broadcast journalism has taken over. Everywhere I went, I saw anchor-persons—men and women—devoting the crucial 30 minutes immediately before air time not to gathering and writing the news, but to applying makeup to their faces and spraying their hair into immobility.

In his book, *The View from Sunset Boulevard* (New York: Basic Books, 1979, quoted in *TV Guide*), Benjamin Stein discusses the "cleaned-up" world of television entertainment programs:[21]

Today's television is purer, in terms of backdrop and story endings, than the lines of a Mercedes convertible. Every day's shows bring fresh examples. A while ago, I saw an episode of "Charlie's Angels" about massage parlors that were really houses of prostitution. The three beautiful "angels" of the show were compelled to pretend they worked at massage parlors in seamy areas. Anyone who has ever passed by a massage parlor knows that they are invariably dirty, shabby places, with pitiful and degraded denizens. On "Charlie's Angels," the Paradise Massage Parlor compared favorably in terms of cleanliness with the surgical theater at Massachusetts General Hospital. The girls were immaculate and well-groomed, soft of speech and clear of eye and skin.

On "The Waltons," we are supposed to believe that we are in a Depression-era farming town in backwoods Virginia. Anyone who has been to a backwoods farming town in the South knows that, whatever else may be said about them, they are invariably dirty and bedraggled. On "The Waltons," even the barnyard is immaculate. Marie Antoinette could not have asked for more agreeable play-farm quarters.

Beyond the physical and visual cleanliness on television is an attitude appealing far beyond most of what real life has to offer. On television, everything ends happily, which might be a way of summarizing the TV climate. There is far more, however. Every problem that comes up on television is cured before the show is over. No one suffers from existential terrors. They are not even hinted at.

The distortion of life's realities on television results from the same forces as it does in the other portions of the media: viewer preferences, advertiser interests, media worker biases, and political pressure. To give just one example here, ABC's series "Soap" received so much criticism even before it was first shown that ABC programming chief Fred Silverman was moved to guarantee that ". . . no character in "Soap" is ever rewarded for immoral behavior. There will always be retribution." Unfortunately, real life doesn't work that way.

TV entertainment is propaganda for the status quo.
—Erik Barnouw

---

[21] © 1979 by Basic Books. Reprinted by permission.

But Television Tends to Break Down Ethnic Prejudices

Still, the television picture isn't all that dark. Television has helped to reduce prejudice against blacks, women, and other groups, one of the great improvements in life that has been taking place in post–World War II America.

The record-breaking docudrama "Roots" let Americans know how hard and unfair everyday life has been for blacks through most of our history by showing relatively simple things, like the difficulties Alex Haley and his family had in finding a motel room, and also more serious things, like the humiliating treatment blacks received in the segregated (until after World War II) United States Army. Many white Americans learned about the extent of these lapses from the American ideal of equality and freedom for the first time —they did not read about them in their school textbooks. (Not that television docudramas are all that accurate. Historians railed against the inaccuracies and distortions of "Roots"—forgetting how accurate it was compared to what most people are generally exposed to. For more on the negative side of the docudrama drama, see "Docudramas Unmasked," *TV Guide,* 4 March 1979.)

Television news reporting, it should be added, also helped to break down these prejudices. It was an important event when the first woman, Barbara Walters, and the first black person, Max Robinson, read the eventing news to us on national TV. But TV shapes our ideas in more subtle ways also. Take the way several scenes were handled on a Colombo late movie. Trying to solve a murder case, Colombo has to wait in a long line at a government office to find out the answer to a question that takes just a minute or two. Then he's instructed to go down the hall to wait in another line. Then he goes back to the first office with the document in hand, but the clerk is now out to lunch and Colombo has to wait. The point was obvious, and made much better than by just saying it: bureaucracies are a pain in the neck and aren't run for *our* convenience. Very true, and very important.

News Is Presented More Effectively on TV Than in Newspapers

What about television news programs? How do they compare with other news sources? While there is no consensus on news quality, even within political groups on the right, center, or left, the opinion of this writer on the matter is that the network evening news shows are in some ways the best mass source of news in the United States today. This doesn't mean they're doing a good job, just a better one than you'll find on the radio, in newspapers, or in the mass circulation magazines.

Television does a better job than the others in assembling stories and in making the news meaningful, helping average viewers to better understand what is happening. A good example is the network coverage of the 1979 gasoline shortage. For whatever reason, perhaps because they sensed public outrage at having to wait hours in long lines, the networks finally "told it like it is"—just a little bit. The best of this (temporarily) good lot was CBS's explana-

Reprinted by permission of Edward Sorel.

Theodore White Working on New Nixon Portrait

NEW YORK, Sept. 25—Atheneum in conjunction with Readers Digest Press has paid Theodore White an advance of $150,000 to write "The Nixon Story." The forthcoming book will be about "the abuse of power" and will, presumably, be quite different from his "The Making of the President 1972," in which Mr. Nixon was depicted as wise, commanding and judicious. Questioned about that book and his flattering portrait of the former President, Mr. White defended himself: "I was lied to."

Theodore White has made a fortune by writing a series of "Making of the President" books. Yet White, for all his "inside" information, was completely wrong on Nixon (a fact that did not seriously hamper his writing career).

tion of windfall profits to Exxon, Atlantic Richfield, Standard of Ohio, and others, resulting from the fact that Alaskan oil prices are pegged by law to world market prices, so that owners of Alaskan fields profit every time OPEC raises prices. Getting large numbers of people to understand economic facts like that is difficult; CBS did it.

CBS also did a great job on the 1972 Russian wheat deal. They used Madison Avenue techniques to explain the all-important economic details that most Americans find either boring or too difficult to bother with. They showed *graphically* how small U.S. farmers profited the least on the deal, large grain corporations the most. They also showed how the Russians not only solved their own wheat shortage, but purchased at a price that was almost immediately below the very rapidly expanding world market price. CBS named the U.S. companies that made the largest profits, and explained how unfair inside information enabled these large corporations to make much larger profits than did small farmers.

Of course, newspapers did carry most of this material on the Russian wheat deal, but they either could not or did not present the material in a way that made it sufficiently easy for the average American to understand.

But Most News Is Given to TV Outlets, Not Ferreted Out

The most important reason why television news coverage leaves much to be desired is that, as in the case of newspapers, *television is given most of its news;* it does not regularly go out and seek it by true investigative reporting. In fact, because television channels must fill a television *screen* as well as sound track, they rely on handouts, news conferences, political speeches, and the like even more than do newspapers. It's very expensive to put on a network half-hour evening news program and extremely hard to meet daily film deadlines. If you rely on government and big business handouts, you have a secure source of supply.

Let's look at the box score for two CBS Evening News programs (19 September and 1 October 1974) chosen at random. (The reader may want to compare this with the box scores for the *Miami Herald* given on page 217.)

There were, altogether, thirty-two separate news stories (excluding two Eric Sevareid editorials).[22] Fourteen were taken primarily from speeches, statements, handouts, or press conferences of federal government officials or candidates for federal office (for example, a Pentagon report on increased weapons costs); one from local government officials (a banker was kidnapped); one from a foreign government official (Venezuela raised the taxes of foreign oil companies operating in their country); one from a big business

---

[22] The Sevareid editorials illustrate another serious defect in television news reporting, that is, lack of editorial opinion and political "columnists." Most good newspapers carry at least three or four political columnists voicing their personal opinions and several editorials expressing the newspaper's opinions.

conference to which reporters were invited (industrialists assembled in Detroit to discuss economic problems); and nine from routinely covered sources (Dow Jones closing figures; a Senate vote to cut off economic aid to Turkey). Of the remaining five stories, three resulted from mild investigative reporting, all on inflation (a check of supermarkets in several large cities showed prices up); and two from serious investigative reporting, including one with a few in-formed-source statements (South Vietnam President Thieu would seek reelec-tion with chances not as good as before, according to the CBS investigation). So twenty-seven of the thirty-two stories resulted from the handouts, state-ments, or press conferences of the politically or economically powerful, a record comparable to that of most daily newspapers.

I'm not an unimpeachable authority on anything.
—Walter Cronkite

Perhaps the best story was a true "backgrounder," informing viewers of an extremely serious and ongoing trend, namely, the flow of wealth to the Arab oil countries and its reinvestment in Western industry and real estate. CBS even managed to score with the powerful by interviewing a big business giant (David Rockefeller) by way of balancing out "expert" (that is, interested party) opinion on both sides of the issue. This was true in-depth reporting on prime time of an ongoing event of the type often overlooked or relegated to back pages by newspapers because there is no particular day on which anything spectacularly different happens (Arabs were buying into the West every day —what else is new?). Indeed it was fairly outstanding for any of the mass media.[23]

Looking backward, it is easy to see now that while "CBS News" excelled at big set-piece journalism of the 60s and 70s—space, the political con-ventions, the Kennedy assassinations, the civil rights march on Washing-ton—the news organization floundered when it came to enterprise or investigative reporting. The Pentagon papers, My Lai, the Tonkin Gulf fakery, Michigan State University's CIA connection, auto safety, the perils of DDT, and Watergate itself were all stories that we who worked at CBS in those years were frustrated to find had shown up first in such

---

[23] Not that it could compare with newspaper investigative reporting of the Watergate type (extremely rare), where reporters uncover important dirty linen others suspect but cannot prove. CBS's story simply made available to a mass audience what the knowledgeable already knew.

magazines and newspapers as *The Nation, Ramparts, The New Yorker, I. F. Stone's Weekly, The New York Times* or *The Washington Post.*

—Desmond Smith, veteran ABC and CBS news reporter, quoted in *The Nation,* 16 September 1978

TV Documentaries Are a Mixed Bag

A careful television viewer can get a remarkable amount of accurate background from TV documentaries, as well as from programs like CBS's sometimes excellent "60 Minutes" (the only news or information program that has ever topped the Nielsen ratings).

On the other hand, some of the documentaries on network television are absolutely awful, pandering to the worst irrationalities of their audience. Some recent ones were on the Bermuda Triangle (trying to make a case for the silly idea that something funny is going on down there in the Atlantic Ocean), and on Eric von Daniken's even sillier ideas about astronauts having visited the Earth in ancient times, being responsible for humans having had the knowledge to build the Maya pyramids and move the Easter Island stone figures. (In fairness, the networks also have run occasional rebuttals, shredding this nonsense with scientific evidence and accurate facts—after protests from the scientific community.)

Even when they try to present a true picture, they sometimes fail. (The job *isn't* easy.) An ABC Close-Up, "State of Washington vs. Jack Jones," presented an actual court case videotaped while in progress; viewers even got to listen in on ordinarily confidential conversations between Jones and his lawyers. The trouble was that the case, supposedly typical, wasn't. All those involved, even the judge and prosecuting attorney, were scrupulously fair, and acted in accord with standard theory of good courtroom procedure. Even the Seattle cops behaved themselves. Since that isn't at all what happens 99 percent of the time, this totally accurate portrayal of a court case was extremely misleading. (Recall the discussion in the advertising chapter about the requirement that ads not be *deceptive.*)

The brightest spot on television is PBS, the Public Broadcasting Service. In a typical week (the first week of July 1979), one PBS station (Channel 22, Annapolis, Maryland), had about (depending on who's counting) ten informative and interesting evening documentaries.

One of their best series is "NOVA." "NOVA" programs are well organized and easy to watch; they're also pretty accurate, according to the best expert opinion available.

An example is the "NOVA" cosmology documentary that explained the big bang theory of the universe and the discovery of low-frequency background radiation that confirmed it. Another superb "NOVA" feature, "Key to Paradise," explained the latest exciting developments concerning the morphine-like chemicals in the brain which control pain, mood, and other features of human consciousness.

In contrast, NBC's documentary "Reading, Writing, and Reefer," on marijuana (recall the angry analogy on a scene from this "documentary" presented in Chapter Three) was so bad, so prejudiced, so false, that Henry Lewis's

From *Penthouse*. Reprinted by permission of Edward Sorel.

Truth at the movies. Motion pictures have an important influence on cultural standards and world views (although not as important as before television). This Sorel cartoon makes the point that their portrayal of the FBI hasn't been exactly accurate (nor has TV's—think of the series "The FBI"), and suggests that fat-cat movie moguls know there's more money in going along with public opinion and power than in bucking it.

characterization of it (in the *Libertarian Review,* February 1979) as "ignorance, innuendo, and intolerance" erred only in being too mild. (Stoned potheads found NBC's effort hilarious.)

But only a relative handful of people watch "NOVA," or much of anything on PBS. (Most people think it's a bore, which it is a lot of the time.) By way of contrast, NBC's schlock was one of the most popular documentaries they've ever aired (unfortunately, several times). *Moral:* You can't even lead a mass audience to television quality, much less make them drink. But smart viewers do tune in (very selectively), and their reward is substantial.

Well, perhaps that's the note on which to end this chapter. The situation is not dismal. Because of TV, the average person has a better idea of what's going on than ever before in our history, even if it isn't all that accurate. And those who want something better can find more to their taste now than ever before.[24] Which sounds like progress.

Summary of Chapter Nine

1. The news media are businesses. They have to satisfy their audience, their advertisers, and the government.

   They cater to their audience in two ways that distort the news: (1) they simplify the news to make it more understandable; and (2) they slant coverage to reflect audience convictions, especially of members of organized groups (such as the NRA and various religious groups).

   They cater to their advertisers primarily by suppressing news that reflects badly on advertisers (suppressing cancer-cigarette connection items in Winston-Salem). And, to a lesser extent, they cater to the government, first in return for favors (for instance, leaks), and second to avoid harrassment (for instance, over licenses). The government, for its part, puts pressure on the media by its legal power to censor.

   News-gathering methods are designed to save money whenever possible. That's one reason most news items are given to reporters, not sought out by them. The result is that news tends to get distorted in favor of those most able to hand it out—government agencies and the rich and powerful.

2. Media workers are biased, just like the rest of us. Individual media outlets are owned by the relatively rich, whose sympathies naturally lie more with their own economic class than with the poor. And they have been managed primarily by men, with resulting sex discrimination. And they have been managed primarily by whites, with resulting racial discrimination.

3. The media theorizers tend to draw wrong conclusions about what makes for good journalism. They tend to conclude that the usual is not news, because it is not *new,* thus missing many of the everyday events that ultimately add up to the difference. They're supposed to be "objective" and

---

[24]Of course, we don't want to go overboard on television. The nonmass magazines are a much better source of background news and information than television can ever be, precisely because they survive on a small readership. (The best magazine on politics and how our society works, in the opinion of this writer, is the *Washington Monthly,* whose circulation is about 25,000.)

not mix news reporting with opinion, conclusions, or evaluations, forgetting that *editing* requires evaluation and also forgetting that reporters draw conclusions all the time, because they have to (since facts don't stare reporters in the face—take the Nixon rock-throwing example).

It is also theorized that in-depth items should be separated from the straight news, which is a mistake because we need those in-depth items most exactly when we're reading the news, so we can make sense of it.

Theory in addition says that recognized authorities should be consulted first, which sounds fine, but in practice means that choice of expert is determined mostly by economic and political factors, so that those who can afford to hold press conferences have their experts consulted first (and sometimes also last).

Theory says further that good citizenship requires self-censorship in some cases. Which means in practice things like cover-up (Bay of Pigs).

4. Newspapers (and magazines, to a lesser extent) have several standard devices they can use to slant the news. For one thing they can play items either up, say, on page one, or down, on page forty-nine. For another, they can fool around with headlines, which are read by more people than the stories themselves and so are crucial. They can also bury unwelcome news back towards the end of a story where fewer people are likely to read it.

They also can slant the news by their choice of "nonnews" features such as political columnists and cartoonists. Or by omitting follow-ups. They can use charged or misleading language. And they can cloak their ignorance, when they are ignorant, in a false aura of authority (say, while proclaiming that Russell's *Principia* somehow superseded Newton's).

5. Television, the newcomer on the scene, dominates the mass audience. On the whole, television entertainment features tend to distort world views, in particular about human nature, other people's lives, and the certainty of the triumph of good over evil.

But television does tend to break down prejudices, racial, sexual, and otherwise. And it presents the news in a way that most people find more understandable than do newspapers (CBS coverage of the Alaskan oil windfall).

Further, some documentaries provide excellent background information ("NOVA," "60 Minutes"). Others are godawful ("Reading, Writing, and Reefers").

Which means that on the whole a person can learn quite a bit while being entertained to boot by *selective* viewing of what's on the tube.

Exercises for Chapter Nine

1. Evaluate the coverage of a particular event or issue of national importance covered in your local newspaper with respect to: (a) objectivity; (b) original vs. second-hand reporting of the news; (c) use of headlines; (d) "establishment" viewpoint; and (e) other matters discussed in this chapter.

2. Do the same for a recent issue of *Time* or *Newsweek,* including their use (if any) of *Time*style.

3. Do the same for an ABC, NBC, or CBS evening news program.

4. Listen to several episodes of some television series and determine what world view is illustrated (for example, "Marcus Welby, M.D." presented a world in which doctors are conscientious, professional, and successful in treating patients, a world in which all who need medical attention get it).

5. Dig through back issues of some mass media publication (for instance, *Time, Newsweek, U.S. News and World Report)* and evaluate their coverage of some important long-term national issue (such as nuclear energy, inflation, or unemployment).

Community Up In Arms
Over School Textbooks

BY MANNIX PORTERFIELD

CHARLESTON, W. Va. (UPI) — "Edith is the 'saved' broad who can't marry out of her religion . . . or do anything else out of her religion for that matter, especially what I wanted her to do.

"A bogus religion, man!

"So dig, for the last couple weeks, I been quoting the Good Book and all that stuff to her, telling her I am now saved myself, you dig."

When Charleston school bells rang this month, such passages from a new series of textbooks set off a controversy that spread from this capital city to the nearby coal camps and farmlands of Appalachia.

The furor generated closed schools and mines and inspired shootings, beatings and other violence.

Hundreds of outraged parents poured into the streets, chanting "burn the books." Book advocates within the education system saw shades of fascism, not unlike the fever that swept through Nazi Germany.

The school superintendent moved his family into hiding, fearful of the anonymous death threats he received. Police forces were strained beyond their capacity, dashing from one hot spot to another to quell disturbances.

"It's mob rule," one official said at the height of the protest.

Kanawha County School Board member Alice Moore, a minister's wife, was the first to say the books, for all grades from kindergarten through senior high school in Language Arts classes, were unfit for classrooms. They quickly became the reading material most in demand. Many parents became incensed by what they found.

A poem in one text reads:

"Probably you were a bastard

"Dreaming of running men down in a Cadillac,

"And tearing blouses off women . . ."

One book compares Daniel and the lion's den from the Bible with a fable. Another likens the Genesis account of creation to a myth. Another tale is concerned with a young boy's thoughts on suicide.

Parents feel other passages instill contempt for American leaders and encourage the use of marijuana.

Parental unrest, however, runs deeper than the pages of the texts.

Beneath the protest beats another and louder drum — one that fundamentalist Christians have been sounding in the hills and hollows since their ancestors arrived on the Atlantic Coast to escape religious persecution.

Fearing a new surge of religious intolerance, the fundmentalists thus have engaged in another confrontation — another clash between Christians who believe the Bible in its entirety as the literal truth of God, and those inclined to a liberal interpretation of the scriptures.

Such forces have collided before in West Virginia. They fought in the 1950s when fundamentalist preachers successfully waged war on liquor-by-the-drink and again during the next decade over Sunday closing laws.

The textbook row began weeks before schools opened Sept. 3.

Parents organized a boycott against a store where one of the school board members who supported the texts had connections. When that failed to bring a reversal of the board's 3-2 decision to adopt the books, parents elected to keep their children home,

fearing they would be exposed to antibiblical and un-American teachings.

Fundamentalist preachers led the protest. On the first day of school, nearly one-fourth of the students stayed home.

Armed with picket signs, parents roamed the county in search of support. They found it at coal mines and some industrial plants. Public buses became targets of pickets and 11,000 daily commuters were deprived of transportation.

Thousands of miners, traditionally reluctant to step across picket lines, refused to work. When the protest crusade showed signs of sagging, the miners shored it up.

In the center of the turmoil was Indiana-born Kenneth Underwood, the county schools superintendent.

"It's like a nightmare," he told UPI. "I wonder, when people tell me to burn books, whether we live in Nazi Germany. But I have faith in the democratic process. It will work out."

But at one point, fearing a new outbreak of violence, Underwood closed all county schools for two days. He reopened them after Gov. Arch Moore agreed to use 200 more state troopers in roving patrols to guard bus garages and school property.

Supporters of the books view them as harmless, they defend the off-color language and passages from revolutionaries as chronicles of contemporary America.

Disgruntled parents view things differently.

"Anti-Christian, un-American, filthy and rotten," declared protest leaders, such as Rev. Marvin Horan.

By the end of the first week of the boycott, the protest had escalated from minor pranks to shootings incidents and beatings. Philip Cochran, 30, a United Parcel Service truck driver who was not involved in the protest, was wounded seriously at Rand, near Charleston, by a protester shooting at random. A picket received superficial wounds when shot by a janitor whose path to work was blocked by demonstrators.

Underwood and Horan then announced that they had reached a compromise in which the board agreed to a 30-day moratorium on the books.

Horan's followers, however, refused to bend, and the minister backed out of the agreement. He said the board would not put its promise in writing.

Two days later, the board consented to a signed offer, and Horan relented.

Not all clergymen and not all parents sided with dissidents.

Rev. James Lewis, one of 10 Episcopal clergymen who publicly deplored the violence, chided Gov. Moore for his initial reluctance to beef up sheriff patrols with state troopers.

Lewis said he read some of the books and saw nothing objectionable, but rather found the material "conducive to the kind of freedom our country was based on."

"The material opens up all kinds of human concern and godly concern," he said. "There is a lot of potential in it."

During the third week of the controversy, nearly 1,000 parents, waving American flags, demonstrated on the Capitol lawn and shouted down the 30-day moratorium. They demanded books be stricken on a permanent basis, without benefit of a review.

Two parents decided to set wheels in motion for a legal settlement and filed suit in U. S. District Court.

Reprinted by permission of United Press International.

Chapter Ten

Textbooks: Managing World Views

The easiest way to change history is to become a historian.

—Anonymous

Probably all education is but two things: first, parrying of the ignorant child's impetuous assault on the truth; and second, gentle, imperceptible initiation of the humiliated children into the lie.

—Franz Kafka

The less people know about how sausages and laws are made, the better they'll sleep at night.

—Bismark

1. Societies Need to Indoctrinate (Educate) Their Young

Every society tries to educate its youth to be *good citizens,* and tries to look the best it can in the eyes of its youth. Every society tries to play up its bright spots in history, culture, and tradition and play down its dark spots. Raw human nature is roughly the same throughout the world, as is the survival advantage in having loyal citizens.

Let's now take a look at public school textbooks, important in shaping the beliefs most of us have about our country and its institutions.

2. Textbooks Are a Commodity

The first thing to dredge up from our world views is the fact that textbooks are a commodity, manufactured to sell, and thus to make money. As in any relatively open market, sellers tailor their products to suit prospective buyers' tastes. (Of course, sellers leave their imprint on the finished product, but to have an effect on students that product has to be purchased by someone.) In America, public school textbooks are selected either by local school boards alone, or else by school boards in conjunction with state book-certifying boards. (Teachers and principals also have a say, but the final authority rests with local or state school agencies.)

The next thing to remember is that school boards and (indirectly) state certifying agencies get their authority by winning local (or statewide) elections. They thus reflect local grassroots power, or at least organized local power. So before we crack a single public school textbook, our world views should tell us

> ... The first requirement of any society is that its adult membership should realize and represent the fact that it is they who constitute its life and being. And the first function of the rites of puberty, accordingly, must be to establish in the individual a system of sentiments that will be appropriate to the society in which he is to live and on which that society itself must depend for its existence.
>
> —Joseph Campbell, in *Myths Men Live By*

> Throughout history, . . . people have had to be taught to be stupid. For to permit the mind to expand to its outermost capabilities results in a challenge to traditional ways. . . . A certain amount of intellectual sabotage must be introduced into all educational systems. Hence all educational systems must train people to be unintelligent within the limits of the culture's ability to survive.
>
> —Jules Henry, in *On Sham, Vulnerability, and Other Forms of Self-Destruction*

that the primary shapers of public school textbooks will be local school boards and state agencies, which on the whole reflect organized local power. In other words, we should expect public school texts to distort reality so as to conform to the ideas and wishes of organized local citizens. And that, in fact, is pretty much what we find when actual textbooks are examined. (For what happens on occasion when local boards fail to reflect local opinion in their choices of books, take a good look at the United Press International item that starts this chapter.)

3.   *Ethnic Groups Have Become More Visible*

Since World War II, a social revolution of major proportions has taken place in the United States, resulting in much greater political power and recognition for minority groups such as blacks, chicanos, homosexuals, and Jews, and also for women. Starting in the early 1960s, public school textbooks began to take more notice of these groups, to deal more fairly with them, in order to catch up with public opinion, and thus satisfy local school boards and sell books.

American Indians also became visible, and the fact that white Americans took the continent away from them by force, killing Indians all along the way, was finally recognized in better texts by an occasional reference to a notorious slaughter, or perhaps to the "Trail of Tears" march of the Cherokee Indians from Georgia to Oklahoma. While these references tend to get lost in a text that runs to 500–800 pages, at least they are now often there for the thinking student to ponder.

In earlier editions of this book, we showed how new editions of popular textbooks were brought out in the 1960s precisely in order to get in step with public opinion or at least political power in their treatment of ethnic groups, in particular blacks. For instance, we showed cases where the only significant differences between old and new editions were in photos—replacing pictures of whites with those of blacks—and in mentioning more blacks—Frederick Douglass, Harriet Tubman, W. E. B. DuBois—than just the standard or token blacks, the Uncle Toms like Booker T. Washington who had always been mentioned. This change in public school texts is now very well documented (see, for instance, the three-part series by Frances FitzGerald in the *New Yorker*, 26 February, 5 March, and 12 March 1979). But let's look at one particularly obvious, some would say hilarious, example, from earlier editions which typifies the cleansing process established texts underwent during that period, and thus indirectly the way in which local political power translates into changes in textbooks. The civics text *Building Citizenship* had the following snippet on President Theodore Roosevelt in its 1961 edition:

> Some people found fault with Theodore Roosevelt because they said he acted as if he had discovered the Ten Commandments. Quite likely, however, many more people become interested in applying the Ten Commandments to present-day life because they admired something in "T.R."

This is changed in the 1966 edition (same page, same exact spot on the page)[1] to read:

> Some people find fault with [brace yourself] Martin Luther King because he acts as if he had discovered the Ten Commandments. Quite likely, however, many more people have become interested in applying the Ten Commandments to present day life because they admire Dr. King's fight against racial discrimination.

This was one of very few changes introduced in the 1966 edition. Most were changes in photos to include some blacks who were heretofore invisible, or in tiny paragraphs like the one in question. In this context, the purpose of the T.R. to M.L.K. switch becomes obvious—say something about a black leader that will fit a particular spot so the new edition can be published as quickly and cheaply as possible.

---

[1] This text was in use for a long time. The original author was Ray Osgood Hughes (Boston: Allyn and Bacon, 1921); it has been revised by C. H. W. Pullen and by James H. McCrocklin, the latter being responsible for both of the versions considered here.

'Drums' Removed from Book List

Manchester, Tenn. (UPI)—The Coffee County School Board has voted to remove "Drums Along the Mohawk" from the assigned reading list because it contains the words "hell" and "damn." School Superintendent James G. Jarrell said Thursday the Board's action was unanimous endorsement of a motion by Board member Jesse Garner, a Baptist minister, who labeled the 1936 book by Walter D. Edmunds "obscene."

---

4.   Textbooks Are Sometimes Slanted to Conform to Religious Views

It isn't only minority groups like blacks who exert grassroots pressure on publishers. Religious groups can and sometimes do exert such pressure. Places where a majority of citizens (or a minority of *active* citizens) share certain religious beliefs often censor opposing opinions in their local schools.

Take the censoring of texts on evolution by the state of Texas, particularly important, because Texas (along with California) exerts the most powerful censoring influence on textbooks in the United States. Texas law requires local schools to adopt only those textbooks that have been approved by the Texas State Textbook Committee. Publishers thus either tailor their textbooks to satisfy this screening committee or risk loss of the enormous Texas market. The result is that textbooks used in Ohio, Oregon, or Oklahoma—in fact, anywhere in the United States—in effect have been censored by a commission of the state of Texas.

An example is the Houghton Mifflin textbook *Biological Science: Molecules to Man*, which was revised in subtle but important ways to satisfy the Texas screening committee.[2] The changes are designed to convey the impression that the theory of evolution is just a theory, an assumption that reasonable men might doubt, rather than an established scientific principle or set of laws. Students thus are protected from the challenge of an accepted scientific doctrine which may run counter to their religious beliefs.

Here are a few of the changes required by the Texas textbook committee:

Original: Evolution is not a faith, but a scientific theory. The theory has been developed to account for a body of facts.

Revision: Evolution is not a *belief,* nor an *observational fact*—it is a scientific *theory.*

---

[2] For details on this and many other cases of textbook censorship, see Hillel Black, *The American Schoolbook* (New York: William Morrow, 1967) and Jack Nelson and Gene Roberts, Jr., *The Censors and the Schools* (Boston: Little, Brown, 1963).

The point of this change is to convey the false idea that the theory of evolution is a mere theory, in the weak sense of proposal or suggestion, rather than an established, well-confirmed, scientific explanation of many different observational facts.

The House of Representatives of the State of Texas, in a 1961 Resolution, desires ". . . that the American history courses in the public schools emphasize in the textbooks our glowing and throbbing history of hearts and souls inspired by wonderful American principles and traditions."
—From *The Censors and the Schools*, p. 134

Original: Like all scientific theories, the theory of evolution has been both *strengthened* and revised as research discloses more and more facts.

Revision: Like all scientific theories, the theory of evolution has been both *modified* and revised as research discloses more and more facts.

This change is important for antievolutionists, because they want students to get the idea that the basic theory itself has been changed to take account of conflicting evidence, and thus may still prove altogether false in future. Yet the truth, conveyed accurately by the original passage, is that new evidence has continually strengthened the theory. No biological discovery has ever weakened it or led to rejection of any single major idea in it.

Original: Biologists are *convinced* that the human species evolved from nonhuman forms.

Revision: Many biologists *assume* that the human species evolved from nonhuman forms.

If there is any biological principle that biologists may be said to *know*, then surely they *know* that the human species evolved from nonhuman forms. Yet the revision intends to, and does, cast doubt on this idea *as knowledge*, relegating it to the role of an assumption. Further, it isn't even pictured as an assumption of all or even most biologists ("many biologists" could be less than half), yet *all* reputable biologists believe that the human species evolved from nonhuman forms.

Finally, Houghton Mifflin was forced to delete the following explicit, accurate, and important statement:

To biologists there is no longer any reasonable doubt that evolution occurs.

Texas censors wanted this sentence removed above all, because it runs counter to the religious beliefs of many Texans, including in particular the almost million Texas members of the Church of Christ (who campaigned against textbooks teaching evolution). In this case, "the truth" about the origin of the human race was determined primarily by the power of a religious group acting as a political unit.

Such censoring does serious damage to the atmosphere of the book publishing business. Publishers are in business. However altruistic or patriotic they may be, they need to make money to stay in business. The two censored texts lost sales in Texas and throughout the country simply because they were challenged by the Texas screening committee, even though their censored versions were approved by that committee. Prudent publishers from then on tailored their textbooks to avoid the notoriety of a challenge by the state of Texas.

The number of books and magazines censored out of public school classrooms and libraries runs into the thousands every year. Here are a few examples:[3]

Huckleberry Finn (Samuel Clemens)
The Merchant of Venice (William Shakespeare)
The Sun Also Rises (Ernest Hemingway)
The Catcher in the Rye (J. D. Salinger)
The Grapes of Wrath (John Steinbeck)
Andersonville (McKinley Kantor)
Look Homeward Angel (Thomas Wolfe)
1984 (George Orwell)
Brave New World (Aldous Huxley)
The Invisible Man (Ralph Ellison)
Native Son (Richard Wright)
Slaughterhouse Five (Kurt Vonnegut, Jr.)
Majorie Morningstar (Herman Wouk)
Ms magazine
The Naked Ape (Desmond Morris)
The American Heritage Dictionary (banned because it included "gutter words" like "ball," "nut," and "tail")

If you were wondering why you read books like, say, Sir Walter Scott's Ivanhoe *in high school, or Charles and Mary Lamb's cleansed versions of Shakespeare, maybe the answer is that they were the only ones left.*

---

[3] The American Library Association's *Newsletter on Intellectual Freedom* contains a list each issue of "Titles Now Troublesome," which means books somebody or other is censoring.

School History Books, Striving to Please All, Are Criticized as Bland[4]

"America! America!" isn't a traditional history book. In its pages are black cowboys, woman pirates, Haight-Ashbury hippies, an Indian boy, a Chicano grandmother and a middle-aged Oriental.

There's something for everybody in this two-year-old American history textbook for eighth-graders, and that's by design.

"We don't want to get complaints from anybody," says Landon Risteen, editorial vice president at Scott, Foresman & Co., the book's publisher. "No matter where you come from, you're going to find yourself in this book."

His concern is understandable. Scott Foresman shelled out $500,000 and four years of effort to put out "America! America!" With 20 other eighth-grade history texts battling for shares of the $7 million-a-year business, the competition is fierce. Moreover, the competition is fierce throughout the $700 million elementary and high-school textbook market. . . .

Publishers feel they are being forced to please the parents, religious groups, political organizations, and state and local authorities that are wielding increasing influence over textbook selections. If a book should offend any group—veterans or war protesters, smokers or non-smokers—its chances of being a big winner are narrowed. So publishers carefully consider their presentation of minorities, treatment of Vietnam and pictures of tobacco fields, aiming to mollify as many of these groups as possible.

"There are all those people out there who will go through our books, so we have to judge what the market will accept," says Ralph Sterling, director of marketing at Houghton Mifflin Co. in Boston. "We can't afford to have a book sit on the shelf.". . .

[But many critics claim that the result is an] uninspiring blandness of American history textbooks. The problem, they say, is that by trying to please everyone, publishers take the edge off history, eliminating the exciting stuff that the past is made of.

"Textbooks minimize the real conflicts in history, like pretending the Civil War solved the problem of race relations in this country," says Douglas Price, a former high-school history teacher and current manager of Jocundry's bookstore in East Lansing, Mich. "If the real regional and racial tensions were written about," he adds, "the textbooks wouldn't sell to all the markets."

Justin Kestenbaum, a professor of history at Michigan State University, agrees. He says, for instance, that while textbooks describe the reform movement of the 19th Century, they ignore "its ugly overtones, like the

---

[4] Lawrence Rout, *Wall Street Journal,* 5 September 1979. Reprinted by permission of the Wall Street Journal. © Dow Jones & Company, Inc. 1979. All rights reserved.

anti-Catholicism. They don't want anybody to appear in an unfavorable light."

Balking at Blandness

In Stanford, Calif., historian Thomas Bailey refuses to write for the high-school and junior-high markets because of publishers' attitudes. "If you want to sell a maximum number of books, you have to make them so bland that you don't get into the tougher issues," he says. "But you also don't tell the truth."

Mr. Bailey grouses that efforts to include women and minorities make the books more ideological than intellectual. He admits that he grudgingly included 1972 presidential candidate Shirley Chisholm in one of his college books, even though "she was so unimportant that I wouldn't have normally put her in. When you write history, you should write about the main actors in the show."

Publishers argue that it isn't their place to take stands on controversial issues. Besides, they say, just presenting ideas is, for some readers, tanta- 'mount to condoning them. "Authors may want to tell it like it is, but with the constraints on us, we really can't do it that way," says Dorothy Collins, an executive editor at Allyn & Bacon Inc. in Boston. . . .

The emphasis on [minority] groups is also said to have dispelled many of the stereotypes that filled history books just a few years ago. Dorothy Davidson, an associate commissioner for general education in the Texas Education Agency, recalls a book that quoted a letter written by Abigail Adams to her husband, President John Adams. "Abigail says things like, 'I hope to get the drapes up,'" Miss Davidson says. "You know she must have had some thoughts on the administration, but the publisher instead chose to show her as a housewife at the White House, waiting for the furniture to move in."

"America! America!," with its black cowboys and female pirates, reflects concerns that were uppermost in Mr. Risteen's mind when work on the project began in the early 1970s. Scott Foresman's market research had shown that the public was looking for a book with "more variety exemplifying the pluralism of America," Mr. Risteen says, and "we were determined to have that in there."

A Group Project

The idea was to come up with three or four historians and school administrators who could work with the editors on the book. "The day of the single author is past" in history textbooks, says Gordon Hjalmarson, president of Scott Foresman. "We feel a group authorship brings various strengths."

These strengths include more than the author's field of interest or his or her familiarity with American history programs. Authors are also considered for their regional popularity. A professor from Texas, for instance, may help sell the book in that big market, and a Hispanic teacher could make a book more marketable in New York City.

In the case of "America! America!," four authors were finally selected: two male university history professors, a male school administrator and a woman who had worked as a consultant to schools in curriculum development. A professor from Texas who was originally part of the group dropped out, Mr. Risteen says, because he wasn't "willing to let us run the show."

Influence of States

The influence of the large states goes beyond the selection of authors; they also have a major effect on a book's content. "We are very sensitive to the big markets, particularly Texas and California," Mr. Risteen says. "It wouldn't make sense to publish a book and leave out the history related to those states." He says, for instance, "We made sure we didn't underplay the Texas independence."

The power of these two states is magnified by the fact that they are two of about 26 states that have state-wide "adoption committees." These committees select a certain number of books from which local school boards can choose and still receive state funds. While "adoption" doesn't guarantee that the book will sell in the state, exclusion of the book guarantees that it won't. . . .

Publishers admit to spending a lot of time gearing their books to meet the guidelines of states. The Texas rules call for textbooks to "promote citizenship and understanding of the free-enterprise system." One editor says of these rules, "They hang over our heads all the time. We try to give the books as nationalistic a feel as possible."

In California, "a book is almost automatically thrown out if it doesn't have ethnic balance," says James Eckman, a high-school teacher who was on the textbook committee that evaluated "America! America!" two years ago. Not surprisingly, "America! America!" is the biggest seller for eighth-graders in the state today.

A book is also dumped in any state if its reading level is too high. Authors typically have trouble "writing down" to a young audience, and editors must often rework manuscripts.

Scott Foresman tests its books by counting the number of words in a sample section that aren't on a list of "appropriate" words and by counting the number of words in sentences. The editors then can come up with a number indicating the book's reading level. Mr. Risteen's staff took 70 samples of 100 words each to ensure that "America! America!" would be acceptable among eighth-grade teachers.

That approach, which is taken by practically all publishers, is assailed by many critics. "The publishers write to such a formula that they lose sight of conveying facts in an interesting manner," says Barry Fetterolf, an editor at Random House Inc., which publishes primarily college books. "If a kid who reads on a ninth-grade level finds his parents' sex book which is on a 15th-grade level, he will read it and understand it," Mr. Fetterolf says. "But they can't read a history text on a seventh-grade level because it's so boring." Still, he concedes, "you have to look at it, since that's what the market asks for."

Big Seller

Indeed Scott Foresman has been giving the market what it wants. "America! America!" is one of the biggest sellers on the eighth-grade market today. The book, selling at about $10 each, came out in September 1977 and sold 67,000 copies that year, Scott Foresman says. The company estimates that it sold 160,000 copies last year. Competitors say the 1978 figure seems a bit high, but they agree that "America! America!" is doing well. . . .

The book, meantime, has received its share of complaints. The first edition of "America! America!" had a special section on countercultures, but it was criticized for "glorifying hippies," Mr. Risteen says. So in a new edition, out this year, that section was changed to one on people discovering their roots.

Primarily, though, users say the book's faults are much the same as those of all textbooks. "While it isn't as much of an absolute history of the perfecting of America as are some books," it still suffers from some of that, says Henry Hicks, a director of social studies for the Needham, Mass., public schools. . . .

Significantly, one of Mr. Hicks's reasons for liking the book—its limited listing of facts—may work against it over the next few years. The "fads in American history textbooks change quickly, and publishers currently are seeing a swing back toward the more-traditional approaches that dominated until the late 1960s.

Mr. Risteen expects to undertake a major revision of "America! America!" in about two years, and the inclusion of more hard facts may be part of that revision. "I hope we don't get to the point where we think to be good a book has to be big and grim," says Mr. Risteen. "But I see some signs that we might be."

5.   *United States History Is Sanitized*

We said before that every society tries to make itself look good in the eyes of its youth. If that is true, then we should expect public school history texts to slant the history and culture of the United States so as to cover up as much as possible of the sordid in our past and to shine the spotlight on our better moments, so as to enhance the appearance of our own country in the eyes of its youth.

We should expect, for instance, that our leaders will be portrayed as better people than they are, or were, all dressed up and minus warts. Take the way in which President Theodore Roosevelt, affectionately called *Teddy* in many texts (the teddy bear was named after him), is spruced up for textbook readers. In textbooks, Roosevelt is pictured as energetic, hard driving, exuberant, brave, a trustbuster, conservationist, big-game hunter, reformer, progressive, against big business, for the workers, although (in some very recent texts) a bit of an imperialist who made the Panama Canal possible as an American enterprise —a great man well deserving of his place on Mt. Rushmore.

And perhaps he is. But no textbooks say much about another side of good old T.R. They don't describe him as a bloodthirsty bigot who, though unusually brave, reveled in the slaughter he personally dealt out and witnessed during the Spanish-American War, a man who expressed pleasure that thirty men had been shot to death in the Civil War draft riots—"an admirable object lesson to the remainder," a person who justified slaughtering Indians on the grounds that their lives were only ". . . a few degrees less meaningful, squalid, and ferocious than that of the wild beasts" and said that "no triumph of peace is quite so great as the supreme triumph of war." Not exactly a Teddy bear, this Teddy Roosevelt.

Drawing by David Levine. Copyright © 1969 NYREV, Inc. Reprinted by permission from *The New York Review of Books*.

Hamburger Hill: *David Levine's drawing of Hamburger Hill (a hill in Vietnam on which many soldiers lost their lives) pictures two American presidents as jolly mass murderers. Would the Texas State Textbook Committee give its approval to a book containing this caricature?*

6.   *America's Role in History Is Puffed Up*

Cleaning up the past is by no means the only way in which texts distort American history. They also distort, for instance, by puffing up American achievements and America's role in history at the expense of other nations. The portrayal of World War II in public school texts is a good example.

Although reliable statistics on World War II are sometimes difficult to find, common estimates place the total killed in that war at between 30 and 40 million, and the Soviet Union's dead at 15 to 20 million, roughly half of the total. The United States lost 322,000 soldiers (almost no civilians), about 88 percent of them in the European theater of war. The Germans were defeated by a combination of British, American, and Soviet military action, but the Russian effort was incomparably greater than that of Britain and America combined. From the period June 1941, when Germany invaded Russia, to the end of the war in Europe, the largest and most powerful element of the Germany Army fought on the Russian front against the Soviet Army. The overwhelming majority of German military losses, in equipment and men, were inflicted on them by Russian forces on the Eastern front, not by British and American forces in Africa or Western Europe. There were several times more Russian *civilian* deaths than all the American deaths in all the wars in our history.

But public school textbooks don't play it that way. They emphasize our role in Europe in World War II and play down the Soviet role. One reason for this is to make our own country look better than other countries. Another is to prejudice readers against communism, communist governments and countries, and in particular the Soviet Union. The Cold War had to be fought in textbooks as well as elsewhere, and it was. It still is.

Here is how a reasonably typical junior high school text, *The Free and the Brave* (Skokie, Ill.: Rand McNally, 1977), portrays the Russian effort in World War II. The text allots about thirteen pages to World War II, including thirteen photos, drawings, and maps. And here is every word in this text about the fighting between Germany and Russia:

> *Hitler's turnabout.* Then in June 1941, Hitler made a surprise move. He turned his army against the Soviet Union, which had been his ally. He was sure that his troops could defeat the Soviets quickly. He was wrong. And his mistake gave Britain a chance to build up its defenses. Also, it brought the Soviet Union into the war on the *Allied* side. . . . [Several pages later] In March, 1945, the Americans took the city of Cologne . . . on the Rhine River. At the same time, Soviet armies were pushing into Germany from the east. As the Allies rushed toward the capital city of Berlin, Hitler committed suicide. The Soviets took Berlin while Eisenhower sent his soldiers across central Germany . . .

That's not much attention out of thirteen pages on the war. In fact, more space is given to the internment of Japanese-Americans in camps during World War II (satisying another ethnic group?). This paucity of information on the

Soviet effort in World War II is not due to the fact that this is a *United States* history text—the British war effort, miniscule in comparison with that of the Russians, received several times more attention, including more space on the Atlantic Charter signing between Churchill and Roosevelt than is devoted to the entire Russian war effort. (Anyway, world history texts, while better, also grossly distort Russia's part in the war.)

The box score for another text, *Let Freedom Ring* (Morristown, N.J.: Silver Burdett, 1977), is similar. This text devotes about ten pages to World War II. Here is every word in this text about the fighting between Germany and Russia:

> In the early summer of 1941, Germany turned east and attacked the Soviet Union. Blitzkrieg carried the Germans nearly to Moscow, the Soviet capital, before they were stopped. The United States offered lend-lease materials to the Soviet Union and these were accepted. Why was the defense of the Soviet Union at that time essential to the United States? . . . [Two pages later] Congress then declared war. . . . In this way, the United States, Great Britain, and the Soviet Union lined up in World War II against Germany, Italy, and Japan.

It should be noted that textbook distortion is greater in lower level texts than higher. Students thus are exposed to the worst account when just starting out. Here is the entire account of World War II provided in the fifth grade United States history text *Windows on the World: The United States* (Boston: Houghton Mifflin, 1976) minus five photos with captions (all of Americans), an almost page-long letter home from a pilot in England, and a paragraph on the atomic bomb:

> In the 1930's, three nations set out to conquer as much of the world as they could. Japan, run by a group of military officers, wanted an empire in Asia. Italy, ruled by a dictator, hoped to prove national glory through war. And Germany, led by Adolf Hitler, set out to conquer all of Europe.
>
> Once again, the United States tried to remain neutral. But by 1940, Hitler had conquered most of Europe. And Japan controlled much of northern China. Led by President Franklin Roosevelt, the United States sent aid and supplies to England. Great Britain seemed to be the last fortress of freedom against the military powers.
>
> Then, on December 7, 1941, the Japanese attacked the United States naval base at Pearl Harbor in Hawaii. The United States immediately declared war on Japan and then on Germany.
>
> The war lasted until 1945. The United States produced great amounts of war materials—guns, ships, planes, bombs, supplies. American technology and armed forces played a big part in the outcome of the war. . . .
>
> With help from the fighting forces of the British, the Russians, and others, the United States defeated Germany and Italy. Then, in the summer of 1945, a United States plane dropped two atomic bombs on Japan. One destroyed the city of Hiroshima, and the other wiped out

Nagasaki. No one knows how many died from these two bombs. Probably it was at least 200,000. But it ended the war with Japan.

Every fifth grader who reads this text is bound to get the impression that the United States did the principal fighting and winning against both Germany and Japan in World War II, with just a little help from our friends Britain and Russia. (Most textbooks overemphasize the fighting in the Pacific at the expense of that in Europe; perhaps one reason is that the United States did do most of the fighting and winning against the Japanese, so that less distortion is called for.)

7. *The Gulf Between Ideals and Practice Is Minimized*

Even the best texts shield students from knowledge about some of the most important facts they could learn about their society—the ways in which actual everyday practice fails to live up to American ideals. It's important for us to know our chances of getting justice when arrested, or when going to court, and of knowing the chances that our elected representatives will represent *us* as well as they do large election campaign contributors (such as the oil industry—how can students come to a sound conclusion about the energy problem if they have no idea, for instance, that oil companies routinely contribute several million dollars every year to members of Congress?)[5]

But even when these topics are mentioned, punches are usually pulled. For instance, here is how one secondary school text, *The Young American Citizen* (New York: Saddlier-Oxford, 1978), mentioned the problem of big money buying the votes of elected officials:

> Organizations, groups, or corporations that take a great interest in a bill can spend large sums of money trying to persuade Senators and Representatives to vote for or against it. This is called *lobbying*. While citizens have the right to lobby Congress, few individuals can afford the great amount of money that some *pressure groups* can. Because members of Congress do not have time to get the opinion of everyone on a particular bill, they often rely heavily on the arguments of lobbyists. This is helpful when the pressure group represents a large number of citizens. Sometimes, however, lobbyists representing only a small number of powerful people can have laws shaped to further their interests.

This makes it sound as though the problem results from the pressure of time, and that lobbyists influence legislation chiefly by providing timely information, not by taking advantage of the human tendency to line one's own pockets

---

[5] Students also need to know the persuasive power of such "contributions," how hard it would be for almost anyone to remain unbribed in the face of, say, a $50,000 campaign contribution. But we can't expect public school social studies texts to provide that kind of information.

at the expense of the general public. (The word *bribe* is not mentioned in this context in any text this writer has seen.)

Another secondary school text, *Free Enterprise in America* (New York: Harcourt Brace Jovanovich, 1977), describes supply and demand in terms that would have delighted Adam Smith (and set someone like John Kenneth Galbraith to howling) describing how a small onion crop resulted in higher prices, while a high tomato yield resulted in lower prices for tomatoes—supply and demand in the classic sense. The implication was that this is the way all markets operate—supply and demand. No mention here about international conglomerates or OPEC creating artificially controlled prices for major items like oil and gas; nothing here about collusion to fix prices (*a la* the 1960s electrical conspiracy) or how price competition is such a negligible factor in marketing retail items like cigarettes, cosmetics, and beer, whose supply is generally greater than demand (for instance, they fail to point out the common interests of, say, beer manufacturers in keeping retail beer prices high).

Even the best texts fall down in reporting on actual practice. The relatively excellent secondary school text *Foundations of Our Government* (New York: Scholastic Book Service, 1977), which does mention some of the evils and problems of our court system, our system of justice, does so while at the same time stressing the good in everyday practice. It lets readers know about the problems poor people have in getting decent legal help by way of introduction to the Supreme Court *Gideon* decision, which states that an accused person has a right to a lawyer, court appointed if necessary, in order to assure equal protection of the law. Similarly, it lets its reader know about police tactics designed to worm or force "confessions" out of innocent suspects while introducing students to the Supreme Court *Escobedo* decision, which declared such confessions illegal. (No, they didn't tell students how often both of these Supreme Court decisions are flouted, especially when a defendant is poor or powerless, and they didn't say anything about the quality of court-appointed lawyers as compared to, say, the lawyers a member of Congress hires when charged with a crime.)

The point of all this is not just to knock American public school texts. Check the textbooks of other countries and you'll find similar—in fact, usually worse —distortions. Read a British text on the Revolutionary War, or a Russian or Hungarian text on the 1956 Hungarian Revolution (which they call "the events of 1956"). The point is that a nation's textbooks are going to be slanted in favor of that nation. All have the same goal: to make their youth into good citizens. That may or may not be best for a nation as a whole, but it does make it more difficult for students who would like to know the true history of their countries or the way their countries really function. Public school textbooks are not going to tell them right out. But perceptive, selective readers can learn a great deal from slanted texts—in particular, naked facts, like dates—so that all is not lost by any means. A careful reader can get a good deal of information even from Russian textbooks, compared to which our texts are treasure troves of information.

The test of true education is *understanding,* and the best test of understanding is the ability to foresee events, or at least not be unduly surprised at their occurrence. If American public school textbooks helped students to true understanding of their own system and how it really works, would the Watergate scandal have been such a shock to them? Would they have accepted our government's denial that we had interfered in the internal affairs of Chile and then later accepted the clearly untrue explanation of *why* we had in fact interfered? Would they have been so surprised by the overthrow of the Shah of Iran and the odiousness of this regime of one of our "allies"?

Of course, indoctrinating textbooks are only one reason so many Americans were taken in by their leaders on these issues. It is, however, an important reason, and one about which something could be done, since citizens at a local level do exercise primary control over public schools.

But textbooks are only a part of the public school educational setting. Students are not taught how to think *critically*. On the contrary, they are taught to accept what "authorities" tell them, even in areas in which experts disagree.

This text was written in a completely different spirit. A student who accepts its contents uncritically has missed its main point, which is that in controversial social and political matters free men and women must be their own experts, or at least must be able to judge for themselves the opinions of those who call themselves experts. A free society does, after all, depend on a *correctly informed and thinking* electorate, not an indoctrinated one.

Postscript on College Texts

The question naturally arises about college textbooks. Do they distort American history and practice, as do public school texts? If the forces at work are the same in both cases, we should expect the results will be roughly the same (taking into account the greater maturity of college students). If they aren't, we should expect the finished products to be different. What do our world views tell us about this question?

The first thing to notice is that the sellers of college texts have exactly the same motives as those who sell public school texts. In fact, many publishers in one field also publish in the other. The second key point is that most college texts are adopted (bought) by the teachers who will use them in their own classes (or, in the case of large classes with several sections, by group faculty decisions, not by school boards or state agencies).

The reason for this important difference is the history (and current funding) of higher education in America as compared to primary and secondary education. Primary and secondary school traditions are largely home grown, intended for a mass audience. Public school teachers have always had their rights to academic freedom infringed by local school boards, or, more accurately, have never had such rights. But American colleges and universities evolved on the model of their European counterparts (chiefly in Germany and Britain), which were intended for an elite clientele. Professors, at least, were granted a great deal of academic freedom. Transferred to this, the freest Western society, the result has been academic freedom for almost all college faculty members, so that, by tradition, college teachers themselves select the texts they and their students will use. It follows, then, as night follows day, that college textbook publishers will try to publish books that please college faculty members, their potential buyers.

And that's the main reason why college texts, wherever they may rest on an absolute scale, are unlike their public school counterparts. College teachers want widely differing things from their textbooks, creating a split market in which all sorts of views (and to a lesser extent qualities) find a constituency. College texts even tend to be less dull than lower level counterparts, a happy note on which to end this particular college textbook.

Summary of Chapter Ten

1. Every society needs to indoctrinate its young. Public school textbooks are just one device used in this educational process.

2. But textbooks are a commodity. So in the United States they are tailored by publishers to reflect buyer preferences, which means the preferences of local school boards and state agencies responding to local citizens (in particular, organized citizens). We should expect, then, that texts will reflect the views of local citizens. And they do.

3. In recent years this has meant increased visibility for ethnic minorities in America (in particular, for blacks), because these minorities have gained a great deal of social and political power since World War II (as also have women).

4. Organized religious groups on the state and local level often force the censoring of books in their area, which sometimes results in nationwide censoring. An example is the censoring of biology texts to water down the theory of evolution to allow room for fundamentalist Christian creationist principles.

5. American history texts present a cleaned-up version of our history, covering up dirt as much as they can, shining bright lights on our better moments. They thus tend to portray our leaders as one sided "goody goody" types, omitting or playing down their nastiness. An example is the treatment of Teddy Roosevelt, who is not pictured as the bloodthirsty bigot he in fact was.

6. United States history texts also distort our history by playing up our role in history and playing down that of other nations. An example is the way we play down the role of Russia in World War II while playing up our own role (which also fits in with our desire to fight the Cold War in textbooks as elsewhere).

7. Social science (civics) texts tend to shield students from knowledge of the size of the gap between theory (ideals) and practice in American life. For

example, they fail to prepare us for the "justice" most of us can expect to receive in our court systems.

But college texts are different. *(Vive la différence.)*

Exercise for Chapter Ten

In college, the subject matter dealt with in high school civics classes becomes the province of political science and (to some extent) other social science courses. Along with this change in title, there is a broadening of subject matter and a change in motive. Indoctrination with the "American way" surely is not attempted in the typical social science course or text. But some social science texts still display a few of the defects we have been discussing, including an "objectivism" that hides a controversial point of view, distortion of the difference between theory and practice (often by ignoring practice that doesn't conform to theory) and an unconscious bias against certain groups (for example, women). College history texts also often display these defects.

Examine one of your history, political science, or other relevant social science texts (or get one from the library) for evidence of bias, distortion, suppressed evidence, or "textbook objectivity," and write a page or two on your findings. Be sure to *argue* (present evidence) for your conclusions, trying, of course, to avoid fallacious argument.

Exercise for the Entire Text

This text, as all others, has presuppositions (only some of them made explicit), and no doubt contains fallacious reasoning in spite of the author's best efforts to reason cogently. So, as the final exercise, write a brief critique of this textbook with respect to: (1) its major presuppositions (that is, the world view of the author as exhibited in the text), and (2) possible fallacious arguments. (Be sure to *argue* for your findings.) And then, as part three of your paper, evaluate the presuppositions you discovered, and if you find them faulty, explain what (if anything) you would put in their place.

Bibliography

1. Good Reasoning (Chapter One)

Aronson, Eliot. "The Rationalizing Animal," *Psychology Today*, May 1973.
Baum, Robert. *Logic*. New York: Holt, Rinehart and Winston, 1975.
Copi, Irving. *Introduction to Logic*, 5th ed. New York: Macmillan, 1978.
*Henry, Jules. *On Sham, Vulnerability and Other Forms of Self-Destruction*. New York: Vintage Books, 1973.
*Kahane, Howard. *Logic and Philosophy*, 3d ed. Belmont, Calif.: Wadsworth, 1978.
Purtill, Richard L. *Logic: Argument, Refutation, and Proof*. New York: Harper & Row, 1979.
Salmon, Wesley C. *Logic*, 2d ed. Englewood Cliffs, N.J.: Prentice-Hall, 1973.
Skyrms, Brian. *Choice and Chance*, 2d ed. Belmont, Calif.: Dickenson, 1975.
Weinland, James D. *How to Think Straight*. Totowa, N.J.: Littlefield, Adams, 1963.

2. Fallacies (Chapters Two–Five)

Chase, Stuart. *Guide to Straight Thinking*. New York: Harper & Row, 1962.
Fearnside, W. Ward, and William B. Holter. *Fallacy, the Counterfeit of Argument*. Englewood Cliffs, N.J.: Prentice-Hall, 1959.
Gardner, Martin. *Fads and Fallacies in the Name of Science*. New York: Dover, 1957.
Hamblin, C. L. *Fallacies*. London: Methuen & Co., 1970.
Huff, Darrell. *How to Lie with Statistics*. New York: W. W. Norton, 1954.
Kahane, Howard. "The Nature and Classification of Fallacies." Paper delivered at Conference on Informal Logic, Windsor, Canada, 1978.
Michalos, Alex C. *Improving Your Reasoning*. Englewood Cliffs, N.J.: Prentice-Hall, 1970.
*Morgenstern, Oscar. "Qui Numerare Incipit Errare Incipit," *Fortune*, October 1963.
Thouless, Robert H. *Straight and Crooked Thinking*. New York: Simon & Schuster, 1932.

3. Language (Chapter Six)

Gambino, Richard. "Watergate Lingo: A Language of Non-Responsibility," *Freedom at Issue*, November/December 1973.
*"Guidelines for Equal Treatment of the Sexes in McGraw-Hill Book Company Publications." In-house eleven-page statement of policy, generally adopted in the publishing business.
*Orwell, George. "Politics and the English Language," in *The Collected Works of George Orwell*.
Rank, Hugh, ed. *Language and Public Policy*. Urbana, Ill.: National Council of Teachers of English, 1974.
Safire, William. *Safire's Political Dictionary*. New York: Random House, 1978.

4. Advertising: Selling the Product (Chapter Eight)

Atwan, Robert; McQuade, Donald; and Wright, John W. *Edsels, Luckies, & Frigidaires: Advertising the American Way*. New York: Delta, 1979.
*Baker, Samm Sinclair. *The Permissible Lie*. Cleveland: World Publishing Co., 1968.
*Feldstein, Mark. "Mail Fraud on Capitol Hill," *Washington Monthly*, October 1979.

---

*Asterisks indicate items referred to in the text.

Gibson, Walker. *Sweet Talk: The Rhetoric of Advertising.* Bloomington: Indiana University Press, 1966.

Goffman, Erving. *Gender Advertisements.* New York: Harper & Row, 1976.

Gunther, Max. "Commercials," *TV Guide,* 2 December 1978.

*Glatzer, Robert. *The New Advertising: The Great Campaigns from Avis to Volkswagen.* New York: Citadel Press, 1970.

*Hopkins, Claude. *Scientific Advertising.* New York: Crown Publishing, 1966.

*McGinniss, Joe. *The Selling of the President 1968.* New York: Trident Press, 1969.

Napolitan, Joseph. *The Election Game and How to Win It.* Garden City, N.Y.: Doubleday, 1972.

*Ogilvie, David. *Confessions of an Advertising Man.* New York: Atheneum, 1963.

*Preston, Ivan L. *The Great American Blow-up: Puffery in Advertising and Selling.* Madison: University of Wisconsin Press, 1975.

Price, Jon. *The Best Thing on TV: Commercials.* New York: Viking Press, 1978.

*Rowsome, Frank, Jr. *They Laughed When I Sat Down.* New York: Bonanza Books, 1959.

Schrank, Jeffrey. *Snap, Crackle, and Popular Taste.* New York: Delacourte Press, 1978.

Whiteside, Thomas. *Selling Death: Cigarette Advertising and Public Health.* New York: Liveright, 1971.

Zwerdling, Daniel. "Non-Prescription Drugs—The Ultimate Confidence Game," *New Times,* August 1976.

5.   *Managing the News (Chapter Nine)*

Comstock, George; Chaffee, Steven; Katzman, Natan; McCombs, Maxwell; and Donald Roberts. *Television and Human Behavior.* Irvington, N.Y.: Columbia University Press, 1978.

"Docudramas Unmasked," *TV Guide,* 4 March 1979.

Fallows, James. "The President and the Press," *Washington Monthly,* October 1979.

Gans, Herbert J. *Deciding What's News.* New York: Pantheon, 1978.

Hentoff, Nat. "Fair Play on the Printed Page," [*MORE*], January 1972, p. 9.

*Hersh, Seymour M. *My Lai 4: A Report on the Massacre and Its Aftermath.* New York: Random House, 1970.

Kempton, Murray. "The Right People and the Wrong Times," *New York Review of Books,* 8 April 1971.

*Knightley, Phillip. *The First Casualty.* New York: Harcourt Brace Jovanovich, 1975.

*McIntyre, Mark. "Muting Megaphone Mark," [*MORE*], July 1974, p. 5.

Nelson, Madeline, "Money Makes the Press Go 'Round," [*MORE*], March 1974, p. 1.

*Nocera, Joseph. "Making It at The Washington Post," *Washington Monthly,* January 1979.

Perry, James B. *Us and Them: How the Press Covered the 1972 Election.* New York: Potter, 1973.

Powers, Ron. *The Newscasters.* New York: St. Martin's Press, 1977.

Rowse, A. E. *Slanted News: A Case Study of the Nixon and Stevenson Fund Stories.* Boston: Beacon Press, 1957.

Smith, Robert M. "Why So Few Investigative Reporters?" [*MORE*], November 1973, p. 7.

*Stein, Benjamin. *The View from Sunset Boulevard.* New York: Basic Books, 1979.

Sterling, Christopher H. and Timothy R. Haight. *The Mass Media.* New York: Praeger, 1979.

von Hoffman, Nicholas. "Where Not to Find Your New Car," [*MORE*], November 1973, p. 7.

Wheeler, Michael. *Lies, Damn Lies, and Statistics: The Manipulation of Public Opinion in America.* New York: Dell, 1976.

6. Textbooks: Managing World Views

*American Indian Historical Society. *Textbooks and the American Indian*. San Francisco: Indian Historian Press, 1970.

*Black, Hillel. *The American Schoolbook*. New York: William Morrow, 1967.

*Elson, Ruth M. *Guardians of Tradition: American Schoolbooks of the 19th Century*. Lincoln: University of Nebraska Press, 1964.

FitzGerald, Frances. "History Textbooks," *New Yorker*, 26 February, 5 and 12 March 1979.

Harrison, Barbara G. *Unlearning the Lie: Sexism in School*. New York: William Morrow, 1974.

Hentoff, Nat. "The Right to Read," *Inquiry*, 11 December 1978.

*Nelson, Jack, and Roberts, Gene. *The Censors and the Schools*. Boston: Little, Brown, 1963.

Popovitch, Luke. "Realerpolitic: The Texts Are Getting Better," *Washington Monthly*, March 1973.

*Rout, Lawrence. "School History Books, Striving to Please All, Are Criticized as Bland," *Wall Street Journal*, 5 September 1979.

Non—Mass Media Periodicals

One of the themes of this book is that good reasoning requires good information sources. Here is a selected list of (primarily) non-mass media periodicals, with one person's brief comments on them:

Atlantic Monthly. Modestly good; middle to left wing.

Columbia Journalism Review. Now that [*MORE*] is no more, the best journalism rag.

Consumer Reports. Publication of Consumers Union, an unbiased, nonprofit organization.

Harper's. Center to left of center; editor Lewis Lapham's column worth price alone.

Inquiry. Left wing; occasionally excellent.

Commentary. Neoconservative, formerly left wing; overrated, too establishmenty for some tastes.

Libertarian Review. Libertarian; will appear conservative to some, because of free enterprise, anti—big government view. Sometimes has excellent articles, with ideas most magazines never air.

Mother Jones. Successor to *Ramparts;* radical left publication.

The Nation. One of the oldest political journals in existence, and again one of the best.

National Review. Bill Buckley's conservative magazine, occasionally interesting.

Ms. Magazine of the women's movement; sometimes good, sometimes too doctrinaire.

New Yorker. The main long article in each issue sometimes stunningly good, although usually written in dull *New Yorker* low-keyed style.

New York Review of Books. Left-wing intellectual publication; one of the three or four best periodicals on the social/political scene.

The Progressive. Interesting left-wing publication.

Psychology Today. Very poorly edited, but with the demise of *Human Nature*, there is no high quality psychology magazine—unless you want to wade through the professional journals.

Science News. Weekly on what's new in science; useful.

Scientific American. The best science journal; the trick for a lay reader is to learn how to glean knowledge from articles over one's head.

Skeptical Inquirer. Excellent debunking of pseudo-science.

Soviet Life. Interesting to read this slick, picture-filled propaganda product to see how wonderful schlock (the current Soviet system) can be made to appear.

TV Guide. Perhaps the only valuable, informative, mass publication; ironically, the largest selling magazine in the United States.

The Village Voice. Left wing; more on New York than national scene, but filled with exposés by such as Jack Newfield, plus Feiffer cartoons.

Washington Spectator and Between The Lines. Attempt to continue tradition started by *I. F. Stone's Weekly.* Four-page, basically one-man operation.

The Washington Monthly. The best magazine, in this writer's opinion, on how our system works—a must.

Wall Street Journal. The best of the business publications; chock full of interesting facts, figures, and ideas.

Answers to
Starred Exercise Items

These answers certainly are not presented as revealed truth. They represent one person's thoughts on the matter, which it is hoped will prove useful to the reader.

Chapter Two, Exercise I

1. *Popularity*. On this planet, all sort of things, some quite monstrous, have become popular. *Example*. Daughter to mother (Berlin, Germany, 1932): "Naziism is the coming thing."

4. *Traditional Wisdom*. But for some, given their world views, it isn't fallacious. Suppose Smith believes that God transmits his wishes by means of long-term traditions. Then, the fact that long Catholic tradition excludes women from certain roles would be a good reason for continuing to do so, since the tradition would be a sign of God's will. The point is that for most of us, including most Catholics, accepting this argument is fallacious.

5. *Two Wrongs*, or *Common Practice*. This certainly is not a case of needing to fight fire with fire.

13. *Ambiguity*. Roche meant political repression—for instance, of limiting freedom of speech or movement. Freud was talking about psychological repression—for instance, of the desire to sleep with one's mother.

18. The previous edition of this book says this is an example of *slippery slope*. And it certainly would be, if it read ". . . an ignorance which leads inexorably to total contempt for free speech." But in fact it has the word "contempt" placed differently, to read ". . . inexorably to contempt for total free speech," so that perhaps there is no *slippery slope* here.

31. *Irrelevant Reason*. Suppose the police mistakenly charge you with murder. In defending yourself, you don't have to prove that someone else, Smith, did it; you just have to prove *you* didn't do it—say, by providing an air-tight alibi. Why, then, should Warren Commission critics have to prove who did murder John Kennedy, if they can show Lee Harvey Oswald couldn't have done it alone?

Chapter Three, Exercise I

3. *Questionable Analogy*. Depending on the kind of accident, knowing how to drive *is* a help, as every driver knows, even though not absolutely essential (say, in judging a case of alleged negligent driving). The line also suppresses a bit of evidence —namely, that judges who drive are easily obtained to try auto accident cases, but judges who have been raped (or mugged, or murdered) are in very short supply.

6. *Ad hominem Argument*. She argues that we shouldn't pay attention to these people because they're in effect paid to say that health advocates are quacks. But she neglects to mention that not all who shout "quack" are so paid, nor does she respond to opponents' specific arguments concerning research alleged to prove her points about health foods. Some of those who shout quack do explain why they are not convinced by her arguments.

13. *Questionable Classification*. Homosexuals burned the books. But so did males, human beings, people between the ages of 16 and 60, and so on. The *relevant* classification of those against whom Ms. Bryant has brought evidence is *Bible burners*,

since most homosexuals would no more burn Bibles than anyone else. (There's also a bit of *suppressed evidence*, a fallacy to be discussed in the next chapter.)

15. Whether you should conclude that the fallacy of *questionable analogy* has been committed depends on what else you believe, in particular about marijuana. The angry people who wrote in believe marijuana is a terribly harmful, addictive drug that destroys people's lives, while Henry Louis obviously believes (along with medical texts and this writer) that coffee is more harmful and more addictive than pot. Assuming the best current medical opinion is correct, those angry writers were guilty of some other fallacy (for example, *suppressed evidence*—Edwin Newman could pick up a book on pharmacopoeia without too much trouble), but not *questionable analogy*.

18. *Questionable Cause.* This question is a preview of the next chapter. It's plausible for a candidate to campaign harder where support is weak rather than where it is strong. The relevant figures to prove he should have stayed at home would have to show, say, that his popularity dropped in a given area after Taft campaigned there—figures not provided, one suspects, because they don't exist.

19. *Questionable Analogy.* The relevant differences are, first, Nixon did not ever consult the House and Senate on this—it wasn't just a matter of rush rush. And, second, contrary to his claim, there was no emergency where even a day or two to consult Congress would have made it too late (it's generally agreed the invasion was a mistake anyway), while in the Cuban Missile Crisis even a few hours might have ruined EVERYTHING.

Chapter Four, Exercise I

1. *Questionable Premise.* How did Evans and Novak get information on the North Vietnam government's private fears? Was he on their mailing list?

4. *Begged Question.* The questioner asked why McG's rise, why the momentum, and was told because McG was on the rise and had momentum.

5. *Inconsistency.* The only way we had to stop a Communist takeover was to defeat them in battle. Taking out troops, then, was not consistent with our being unable to "afford to let the Communists take over in Vietnam," since it made such a takeover just that much more inevitable.

9. *Suppressed Evidence.* Stare knew, as did others who were informed, that (1) it's mainly the milk, not the cereal, that makes, say, a Wheaties and milk breakfast in the same league with bacon and eggs as a source of protein and (to a lesser extent) of minerals and vitamins; (2) while some vitamins and minerals are now commonly added to such cereals, even more nutrients (for example, most of the protein) are usually taken out in processing the grain; (3) most of these cereals contain gobs of unhealthy refined sugar; and (4) no expert would think of spinach (much over-rated as a food anyway) as a complete breakfast—spinach is recommended for roughage and some vitamins and minerals (it has next to no protein), so that Stare's comparison of cold cereal and milk with spinach was faulty.

11. No fallacy; certainly not *inconsistency*. Aristotle intended to point out to his friends that in this harsh world, friendship, alas, has its limits—that even good friends can be counted on only so far. This sour view has its exceptions, but on the whole is true.

16. *Straw Man* and *Ad Hominem Argument.* Meany started out discussing the idea that we should *listen* to the younger generation, but then he switched to the straw idea that we should entrust the government to them. His argument against young people was *ad hominem* because it attacked their habits (pot smoking and Woodstock get-togethers), not their views, and it was their views that "these people constantly" suggested we listen to. (What would Meany have thought about the argument that we shouldn't listen to the older generation, since they drink more alcohol than the younger?)

23. *Suppressed Evidence.* This is one of those cases where at least a small idea of what's been going on lately is required. The postwar period 1946–1962 was on the whole one of rapid expansion. Few large corporations seeking Ogilvy's services were likely to suffer sales losses no matter who did their advertising (as Ogilvy himself admitted).

24. *Inconsistency* (between words and actions). While allowing a 15 minute tape to be shown wasn't *exactly* crossing a picket line, it's in the same spirit. The point of Hope's not crossing a picket line was to show solidarity with ordinary laborers—in this case, by depriving those inside of the benefit of Hope's entertainment. (People who sneak out of obligations this way are derisively called "legalists.")

Chapter Five, Exercise I

4. *Questionable Cause.* An even greater percentage of heroin addicts first drank milk, coffee, tea, and booze, and smoked cigarettes. (And, as the greeting card noted, they all are habitual breathers). To support a causal connection, we need evidence showing that all or most pot smokers go on to heroin, but in fact we have all sorts of statistics proving that the vast majority who smoke dope never even try, much less get hooked on, heroin.

6. *Suppressed Evidence* and *Faulty Comparison.* As Hoover and Kilpatrick knew very well, practically all uses of certain drugs (marijuana, LSD, heroin, cocaine) are illegal in the United States today, while almost all alcohol consumption is perfectly legal. (What if Hoover had compared 1920s drug and alcohol arrests, when alcohol was illegal while pot was legal?)

11. *Faulty Comparison.* Three percent is insignificant as the total support a candidate receives, but quite significant as the difference between one candidate and another in an election, since even a one-vote margin wins an election, while a 3 percent total vote wins only a booby prize.

15. *Faulty Comparison.* Britain is wealthier than it ever was. It is, however, poorer relative to other northern European countries. (Their economies have been growing much faster.) The comparison relevant to whether Britain can still afford to be preoccupied with distribution is between the wealth she had then (when she could afford that preoccupation) and now, not between what she has now and what other nations have, since the latter is irrelevant to the consumption of goods in Britain.

17. *Hasty Conclusion.* The statistic quoted certainly is evidence for the conclusion. But it isn't sufficient. It still could be that similar family environment is the principal reason why alcoholism tends to run in families (example: the higher incidence of alcoholism among present-generation Jews in America as compared with the incidence among their genetically similar grandparents).

21. *Questionable Cause* and *Suppressed Evidence.* This is one of those cases where background information and world views are crucial. Each of these presidents died under different circumstances—Kennedy was shot, Roosevelt had a stroke after twelve health-destroying years in office. Further, we have vast amounts of higher-level evidence and theories to the effect that mere passage of time cannot cause anything so complicated as the death of an incumbent president.

Chapter Six, Exercises

4. (Simplifying translation): We shall use the expression "social problem solving" to refer to cases where an actual or expected result will (possibly) solve a problem. (Put that way, it doesn't sound like much.)

Chapter Seven

2. Here is a summary of the arguments given by Jeffrey St. John in his column (margin notes have been omitted) in support of his conclusion that the Equal Rights Amendment (ERA) to the Constitution should not be passed:
   a. Legal scholars believe that the legal position of women cannot be stated in a simple formula. The reason Justice Frankfurter gives—that a woman's life cannot be expressed in a simple relation—comes close to just saying the same thing (*appeal to authority*—because their reasons are not provided, and other experts disagree).
   b. Senator Sam Ervin and legal scholars argue that the amendment will have no effect on discrimination (*appeal to authority*).
   c. And would nullify all existing (possible or future) laws that made distinctions between men and women (*appeal to authority*).
   d. Passage of the ERA would create a great court backlog of cases leading to legal and social anarchy (*questionable premise*).
   e. Which is the aim of a minority of women's liberationists, who intend to exploit this result to achieve political power (very *questionable premise*. Also a bit of *straw*, uh . . . *person*, because not true of the great majority of those favoring ERA).
   f. The effect of ERA, desired by Women's Liberationists, would be to do away with marriage contracts, the home, and children, and push us into a lifestyle like that in hippie communes (extremely *questionable premise*. St. John apparently believes marriage contracts would be illegal because entered into between *men* and *women!*)[1]
   g. Women's liberationists desire this in order to bring down the whole of society (another extremely *questionable premise*).
   h. The women's liberationist campaign is false, misleading, and dangerous (*questionable evaluation*).
   i. The discrimination it is against is based not in law but in custom and in social attitudes, especially concerning careers and employment. [see below]
   j. Women's lib wants to use the power of the state to forbid individual discrimination (as opposed to discrimination forced by law). [see below]
   k. A distinction not made by those who favor ERA (*questionable premise*—in fact just plain false).
   l. The same chaos will follow passage of the ERA that followed the 1964 Civil Rights Act. (*Begged question: Did* chaos result from the 1964 Civil Rights Act? *Questionable analogy:* Even if it did, why compare that to the ERA?).
   m. Legal scholars argue that the "due process" and "equal protection of the law" clauses of the Fifth and Fourteenth amendments are sufficient for the reforms demanded by Women's Libbers (i.e., ERA is not necessary). (*appeal to authority* —other experts have challenged this—and *irrelevant reason*—If true it shows ERA to be superfluous, not wrong.)
   (Most of the persuasive emotively charged words—"*militant* minority of women"; " *legal avalanche* would be *unleashed*"—have been omitted from this summary along with the low blow analogy comparing political feminists with Lenin.)
   Item (c) is the crux of St. John's argument against ERA. Is it true that passage of ERA would make laws that distinguish between men and women illegal? Since many believe it would, we should not say dogmatically that it would not. Yet, there are simple arguments (none mentioned by St. John —*suppressed evidence?*) indicating it would not, which must be refuted or at least

---

[1] However, it is *possible* that courts would hold marriages between homosexuals legal. Why he thinks this would be a threat to heterosexual unions only St. John can say.

examined, before (c) can be accepted. For ERA only provides women what one would have supposed they, as do men, already have, namely equal protection, or equal rights, before the law.

Rational discrimination always has been thought to be legal. Lenders and borrowers, for instance, have equal rights under the law, as do adults and children. This means that they cannot be discriminated against (or for!) *without a relevant reason*. A child cannot be treated differently from others except for good reason; for instance, lack of experience or developed intelligence may lead to laws instructing courts to provide legal guardians to protect the economic or legal rights of children (exactly as it does for senile adults). But no one would suppose this automatically violates a child's or adult's right to equal protection of the law. Similarly, it would seem plausible to suppose that laws distinguishing between the child-raising duties of a husband and wife based on the wife's special ability to provide mother's milk, or laws providing separate rest rooms for men and women on grounds of social custom, or laws forbidding women the right to engage in professional boxing on grounds of anatomical differences, would *not* violate women's rights to equality before the law. In short, it seems plausible to hold that equality before the law does not rule out *relevant* or *reasonable* discrimination, whether towards women, children, bankers, or thieves, but only irrelevant or irrational discrimination, again whether directed against women, children, bankers, or thieves.

The interesting aspect of (i) and (j) is that they muddle the issue, (i) because most but not all of the relevant discrimination is individual as opposed to forced by law, and (j) because women's liberationists want ERA to help fight against both kinds of discrimination. Moreover, it is curious to be against rectifying individual discrimination by law since that is the way most harms done by individuals are rectified. Rape, for instance, is not a harm required by law—it is an unfair harm done by one individual against another—which is the main reason why there are laws against it. Of course, it does not follow that we should try to rectify all unfair harms by law. For one thing, a danger of greater harms may result; for another, it depends on one's overall political and moral theories. But surely the reverse does not hold either, and that is what Jeffrey St. John has to claim.

Chapter Eight, Exercise I

1. *Deceptive Humor.*
4. *Questionable Statement.* With prices going up and up, their very finest almost certainly cost more, not less.
9. *Jargon.* What does it mean to "frame the face"? *Puffery.* Or that such a dress "flatters the figure"?
11. *Meaningless Jargon.* "Actizol" is just one of those phony names, like "Platformate," for a widely used ordinary ingredient.
28. Definitely not a fallacious appeal to authority. Concert pianists tend to be extremely fussy about pianos, and while the sheer availability of Steinways tends to increase their use, there can be no doubt that concert pianists prefer Steinway overwhelmingly *and* are more likely to know piano quality than thee and me.

Exercise For the Entire Text

I'll never tell.

Indexes

Index of Topics

Index of Publications

Index of Names